SECOND EDITION

Friends Always

The Y-Indian Guide Programs Participant's Manual

YMCA of the USA

Cover designer: Jack Davis
Cover and interior illustrator: Roberto Sabas

Printed in the United States of America

10 9 8 7 6 5 4 3 2 1

Copies of this book may be purchased from the YMCA Program Store, P.O. Box 5076, Champaign, IL 61825-5075, (800) 747-0089

The YMCA of the USA does not operate any parent-child programs.

Contents

Preface

"Friends Always" captures the essence of Y-Indian Guide Programs—the opportunity to strengthen parent-child relationships through activities that are challenging and fun! Y-Indian Guide Programs are aimed at both parents and their three- to nine-year-old children. Parent-child pairs meet in small groups called "tribes," which get together regularly for planned events and outings. Activities are often based on an American Indian theme, a theme that stimulates creative projects and activities through which relationships are enhanced for a lifetime. This theme should always be used with great respect and dignity.

In these and in all other YMCA programs there are common goals for individuals and families, such as personal growth, appreciation of diversity in thought and traditions, and development of leadership skills. Such programs provide opportunities for accomplishing these essential goals.

This handbook offers a wealth of information on Y-Indian Guide Programs to enhance the experience for you and your child. The beginning section, Program Framework, provides an introduction to the programs and an explanation of what you can expect when you join a tribe. This is followed by the Indian Theme section, in which the Indian culture and its relationship to the programs is described. The Invitations section contains ideas for Y-Indian Guide Program meeting invitations, while the Tribal Property section consists of directions on how to create gear and costuming for tribal use. Next is the new Ceremonies section, which includes several different kinds of ceremonies that your tribe can use. The large Crafts section is full of activity ideas for meetings. Other fun tribal meeting activities are covered in the sections on Games, Stories, Songs, and Family Activities. The new Alternative Parent-Child Programs section describes the Y-Voyager, Y-Guides, Y-Westerners, Y-African Guides, and Y-Family Guides programs. Addresses for further resources can be found in the Appendix.

The contents of this manual can get your tribe off to a good start. Add your enthusiasm and active participation to help build a relationship that will make you and your child "Friends Always."

Acknowledgments

This manual was developed for use by all Y-Indian Guide parents and participants. It contains information and ideas from many sources, including a number of local Ys too numerous to mention by name here.

Development of the first edition of this manual was coordinated by George Leinard, past National Y-Indian Guide Chief, with help from members of the National Program Council, who provided feedback and advice. The final manuscript was written by Sue Baugh; developmental editing was done by Patricia Sammann. Thanks go to Buena Washburn for carefully reviewing the Crafts section.

A special thanks to the YMCAs of Los Angeles, St. Paul, and Minneapolis for their permission to use text and art collected or developed by the Y-Indian Guide and alternative programs. For the logos and information on alternative programs that appears in this second edition, we wish to thank the following YMCAs:

- Y-African Guides
  YMCA of Cincinnati
- Y-Guides
  YMCA of St. Paul
- Y-Voyagers
  YMCA of Minneapolis
- Y-Westerners
  Mid-Peninsula YMCA (Palo Alto, CA)
- Y-Family Guides
  YMCA of Central Florida (Orlando, FL)

List of Invitations

List of Tribal Property

List of Ceremonies

List of Crafts

List of Games

List of Stories

List of Songs

List of Family Activities

Program Framework

WHAT IS THE YMCA?

*Y*ou are the YMCA. The Young Men's Christian Association is not a building or a gym or a swimming pool, but is a fellowship of people who gather together in the name of the "Y" for the purpose of achieving YMCA goals. The stated purpose of the YMCA is as follows: "The Young Men's Christian Association is a worldwide fellowship united by a common loyalty to Jesus Christ for the purpose of building Christian personality and a Christian society." The mission of the YMCA is to put Christian principles into practice through programs that build healthy spirit, mind, and body for all.

There are over 2,200 YMCAs in the United States, serving more than 15 million people. In addition to family programs like Y-Indian Guides, YMCAs also provide aquatic, camping, child care, health and fitness, sports, and teen programs. Contact your sponsoring YMCA for information on membership and programs.

The Y-Indian Guide Programs have a long history of providing children between the ages of five and nine and their parents with opportunities for good times, learning, and mutual understanding. In this program you and your child will meet with other parent-child teams in a small group, called a tribe, to hold tribal meetings or participate in fun and educational outside activities. This Program Framework section contains a review of the basic ideas behind the Y-Indian Guide Programs, a description of how the programs work, and an explanation of how a typical Y-Indian Guides Programs tribal meeting is conducted. It also includes tips for beginning a new tribe and guidelines for program evaluation.

WHAT ARE THE Y-INDIAN GUIDE PROGRAMS?

From small beginnings, the Y-Indian Guide Programs have grown to serve many thousands of people. This section starts with a discussion of the programs' origins and Indian theme. A short description of each of the four program branches is followed by the overall program objectives and a review of the characteristics of children in the Y-Indian Guide Programs age group.

How YMCA Indian Guide Programs Began

The first Y-Indian Guide Program was developed to support parents' vital role as teachers, counselors, and friends to their children. Harold S. Keltner, St. Louis YMCA Director, initiated the program as an integral part of Association work. In 1926, he organized the first tribe in Richmond Heights, Missouri, with the help of his good friend, Joe Friday, an Ojibway Indian, and William H. Hefelfinger, chief of the first Y-Indian Guide tribe. Inspired by his experiences with Joe Friday, who was his guide on fishing and hunting trips into Canada, Harold Keltner established a program of parent-child experiences that now involves over 200,000 children and adults annually in the YMCA.

Joe Friday planted the seed for this program during a hunting trip he and Mr. Keltner took to Canada. One evening, the Ojibway said to his white colleague as they sat around a blazing campfire: "The Indian father raises his son. He teaches his son to hunt, to track, to fish, to walk softly and silently in the forest, to know the meaning and purpose of life and all he must know, while the white man allows the mother to raise his son." These comments struck home, and Harold Keltner arranged for Joe Friday to work with him at the St. Louis YMCA.

The Ojibway Indian spoke before groups of YMCA boys and their fathers in St. Louis, and Mr. Keltner discovered that fathers, as well as boys, had a keen interest in the traditions and ways of the American Indian. At the same time, Harold Keltner, being greatly influenced by the work of Ernest Thompson Seton, great lover of the out-of-doors, conceived the idea of a father-and-son program based upon the strong qualities of American Indian culture and life—dignity, patience, endurance, spirituality, harmony with nature, and concern for the family. Thus the first Y-Indian Guide program was born more than half a century ago.

The rise of the family YMCA following World War II, the genuine need for supporting little girls in their personal growth, and the demonstrated success of the father-son program nurtured the development of YMCA parent-daughter groups. The mother-daughter program, now called Y-Indian Maidens, was established in South Bend, Indiana, in 1951. Three years later, father-daughter groups, now known as Y-Indian Princesses, emerged in the Fresno, California YMCA. In 1980, the National Longhouse recognized the Y-Indian Braves Program for mothers and sons, thus completing the four programs and combinations in Y-Indian Guide Programs.

Although some Y-Indian Guide groups had extended their father-son experiences beyond the first three school grades from the beginning, it was not until 1969 that Y-Trail Blazers was recognized by the National Longhouse Executive Committee for nine- to eleven-year-old boys and their fathers. Trail Maidens, Trail Mates, and Coed Trail Blazers also have been developed and recognized in YMCAs across the country.

The Y-Papoose Program, a program for a preschool child and his or her parent, is another logical extension of the Y-Indian Guides Program, and it was sparked by a real-life need. A Y staff member in Orlando, Florida, had an older daughter in a Y-Indian Princess tribe. Each week, when he and his older daughter went to tribal meetings, the younger daughter—a preschooler—began to cry. She couldn't understand why there wasn't a special time for her. In asking around, the Y staff member found that other families had the same problem. It was easy for him to find enough parents to put together the first Y-Papoose tribe.

Some YMCAs have created parent-child programs similar to those listed above but have oriented the program around a non-Indian theme. Examples are included in the Alternative Parent-Child Programs section of this handbook.

The American Indian Theme

The Y-Indian Guide Programs can present parent-child teams—as well as families—with opportunities for new insights into the significant contributions Native American people have made to our nation's history and heritage. The past and present cultures of the American Indians can challenge a father or mother to be aware of his or her role as parent, guide, friend, and example for a son or daughter and help develop the child's natural curiosity and enthusiasm.

The teaching of values, attitudes, fitness and health, knowledge, and ethics to children is an integral part of the Indian way of life. At the same time, the Native American people feel a profound responsibility for the well-being of all family members. The sharing of food and clothing with all is a natural response for them whenever the need arises.

The American Indian culture gives the non-Indian parent a common interest and learning experience in working with his or her child. The genuine concern among Indian people for parent responsibility in teaching and guiding children to adulthood is a fine standard for all parents and children to live by today.

The American Indians have exceptional poise, dignity, and pride. Honesty and the given word have been inviolate in their way of life. Indians place a high priority on things of the spirit as opposed to a strictly material existence. Their deep appreciation for the Creator is apparent throughout their religion, traditions, and way of life. In addition, their understanding of the interdependence of the forces of nature is highly significant. All parents and children can recognize the great value of conserving resources and eliminating waste in our urban-centered world.

Through the purposeful parent-child experience of Y-Indian Guide Programs, the YMCA can be instrumental in upgrading the image of American Indians by supporting their self-pride, aiding the struggle to preserve their history, and recognizing their meaningful contribution to society.

The Five Branches of Y-Indian Guides

There are now five Y-Indian Guide Programs: Y-Papoose for a preschool child and a parent; Y-Indian Guides for fathers and sons; Y-Indian Princesses for fathers and daughters; Y-Indian Maidens for mothers and daughters; and Y-Indian Braves for mothers and sons. On the following pages the purpose, slogan, aims, and headband for each branch are described.

Y-Papoose Program

Purpose

The purpose of the Y-Papoose Program is to get an early start on fostering understanding and companionship between parent and child.

Motto

"Friends Forever"

Aims

1. To keep my thoughts happy.
2. To be friends forever with my father or mother.
3. To love my family.
4. To listen while others speak.
5. To be kind to my neighbors.
6. To keep the world around us clean and beautiful.

Pledge

"We, parent and child, promise to be friendly, helpful, and loving to each other, our family, and our community as we seek a world pleasing to the eye of the Great Spirit."

Y-Indian Guide Program

Purpose

The purpose of the Y-Indian Guide Program is to foster understanding and companionship between father and son.

Slogan

"Pals Forever"

The slogan, "Pals Forever," does not mean that father and son relate to each other as equals, such as two boys who are pals. Rather, it means that father and son have a close, enduring relationship in which there is communication, understanding, and companionship. The Y-Indian Guide Program encourages such a relationship by providing a means for father and son to share enjoyable experiences, to observe and learn about one another, and to develop mutual respect.

Aims

1. To be clean in body and pure in heart.
2. To be pals forever with my father/son.
3. To love the sacred circle of my family.
4. To listen while others speak.
5. To love my neighbor as myself.
6. To seek and preserve the beauty of the Great Spirit's work in forest, field, and stream.

Pledge

"We, father and son, through friendly service to each other, to our family, to this tribe, to our community, seek a world pleasing to the eye of the Great Spirit."

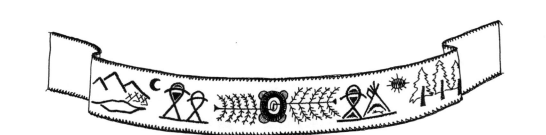

Headband

The central theme of the headband is the eye of the Great Spirit surrounded by the four winds of heaven. The feathered arrow designs that extend right and left from the central symbol represent the useful services of father and son. Among the American Indians, whenever someone achieved an outstanding feat, its significance was recognized by the Indian tribe, often in the form of feathers. The fact that the father-and-son achievements are united in the center of the design is interpreted to mean that fathers and sons together, under the eye of the Great Spirit, are seeking to help each other in the services they render.

On the right side of the headband are the symbols of the mother and the home. A line connects the mother symbol to home, which is symbolized by the fire in the tepee. On the left are symbols of father and son. Their relationship is represented by the line that joins the two symbols. These symbols add to the richness of the central theme, for it is in service to mother and home that many of the more significant achievements of father and son will take place.

Far to the right are symbols of day and forest. Far to the left are symbols of mountain, lake, field, and stream, with the moon for night. These symbols enrich the central theme, giving broader scope to services by centering the efforts of father and son on village and community life, and, as the aim states, "in forest, field, and stream."

Y-Indian Princess Program

Purpose

The purpose of the Y-Indian Princess Program is to foster understanding and companionship between father and daughter.

Slogan

"Friends Always"

Aims

1. To be clean in body and pure in heart.
2. To be friends always with my father/daughter.
3. To love the sacred circle of my family.
4. To listen while others speak.
5. To love my neighbor as myself.
6. To seek and preserve the beauty of the Great Spirit's work in forest, field, and stream.

Pledge

"We, father and daughter, through friendly service to each other, to our family, to this tribe, to our community, seek a world pleasing to the eye of the Great Spirit."

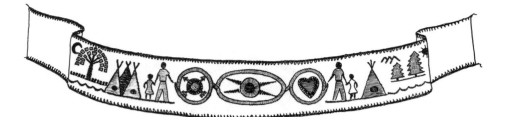

Headband

The central theme of the headband is the sign of the eye of the Great Spirit with the crossed arrows of friendship on the left side and the circled heart of love on the right side. The symbols for father and daughter are next to the grouped tepees, which indicate happy work in the community, and the single tepee, which denotes happy work in the home. The trees, water, and grass exhort the wearer to see and preserve the Great Spirit's beauty in forest, field, and stream.

Y-Indian Maiden Program

Purpose

The purpose of the Y-Indian Maiden Program is to foster understanding and companionship between mother and daughter.

Slogan

"Friends Always"

Aims

1. To be clean in body and pure in heart.
2. To be friends always with my mother/daughter.
3. To love the sacred circle of my family.
4. To listen while others speak.
5. To love my neighbor as myself.
6. To seek and preserve the beauty of the Great Spirit's work in forest, field, and stream.

Pledge

"We, mother and daughter, through friendly service to each other, to our family, to this tribe, to our community, seek a world pleasing to the eye of the Great Spirit."

Headband

The central theme of the headband is the sign of the eye of the Great Spirit with the crossed arrows of friendship on one side and the circled heart of love on the other. The symbols of mother and daughter are next to the grouped tepees, which indicate happy work in the community, and the single tepee, which denotes happy work in the home. The trees, water, and grass exhort the wearer to see and preserve the Great Spirit's beauty in forest, field, and stream.

Y-Indian Brave Program

Purpose

The purpose of the Y-Indian Brave Program is to foster understanding and companionship between mother and son.

Slogan

"Friends Always"

Aims

1. To be clean in body and pure in heart.
2. To be friends always with my mother/son.
3. To love the sacred circle of my family.
4. To listen while others speak.
5. To love my neighbor as myself.
6. To seek and preserve the beauty of the Great Spirit's work in forest, field, and stream.

Pledge

"We, mother and son, through friendly service to each other, to our family, to this tribe, to our community, seek a world pleasing to the eye of the Great Spirit."

Headband

The central theme of the headband is the sign of the eye of the Great Spirit surrounded by the four winds of heaven. The feathered-arrow design on each side represents the useful service of mother and son. Mother and son stand to the left next to the single te-pee, symbolizing mutual support in a happy home. To the right is a group of tepees symbolizing happy work in the community. The water, trees, mountains, and sky exhort the wearer to preserve the Great Spirit's beauty in forest, field, and stream.

Objectives of YMCA Indian Guide Programs

The YMCA locally, nationally, and internationally is dedicated to providing good opportunities for people to achieve their greatest and most satisfying potential as honest, caring, respectful, and responsible human beings. Y-Indian Guide Programs help fulfill this mission when they provide the following benefits to parents and children:

- Foster companionship and understanding and set a foundation for positive, lifelong relationships between parent and child.
- Build a sense of self-esteem and personal worth.
- Expand awareness of body, mind, and spirit.
- Provide the framework to meet a mutual need of spending enjoyable, constructive, and quality time together.
- Enhance the quality of family time.
- Emphasize the vital role that parents play in the growth and development of their children.
- Offer an important and unique opportunity to develop and enjoy volunteer leadership skills.

The Three- to Nine-Year-Old

Although all three- to nine-year-olds are not the same, they do share some general characteristics in their development. Considering these suggestions can help you understand your child and, along with other parents in your tribe, plan activities that are appropriate to the ages of your children.

Developmental Tasks

The YMCA program goals for three- to nine-year-olds are based on the developmental tasks of helping children to

- develop a growing confidence that they are liked and accepted by adults close to them;
- feel secure in their parents' love and be able to share some of this love with others;

- develop a sense of personal worth within the family, feeling responsible for tasks and for others;
- find increasing satisfaction in playing with others their own age and in sharing their possessions;
- develop identification with their fathers/mothers and a growing pride in being male/female;
- derive increasing satisfaction from physical skill development and active play;
- become useful in their homes and share in household tasks;
- find something they can do well and on their own;
- develop a growing appreciation of the need for rules and the ability to take direction; and
- accept and value each person for himself or herself.

Family Relationships

Positive relationships within the family provide a pattern for relationships with others outside the home. Y-Indian Guide Programs are designed to strengthen families by improving ties between parent and child. It is important, however, to consider the entire family as you make plans for the tribe. The following hints may be helpful:

- Provide opportunities for the rest of the family to be involved (you could design several events for the families).
- Do craft projects in tribal meetings to give to other family members.
- Occasionally include family happenings as a part of scouting reports.
- Consider the rest of the family when scheduling tribal outings/events. For example, avoid scheduling a trip for parent and child on Mom's/Dad's birthday.
- Occasionally schedule activities for Mom and Dad away from the children, such as a dinner for tribal parents and their spouses.
- Use communication games in tribal meetings and encourage members to repeat the games at home with the rest of the family.

You'll find many additional activities to strengthen family relationships in the Family Activities section of this book and in other YMCA family resources.

Spiritual Development

Parents and family are the primary source of children's spiritual development. Three- to nine-year-olds are often curious about spiritual concerns, and parents can do much to help children's questioning minds by offering clear and honest explanations. Children of this age group observe and imitate their parents, who serve as models in developing a positive attitude toward people of different backgrounds and in gaining a sense of appreciation and reverence for God as Creator and source of comfort, strength, and power.

PROGRAM DESCRIPTION

If you are new to the Y-Indian Guide Programs, you will want to read the beginning of this section, where the overall organizational structure is explained. This section also provides information on tribal activities and both parents' and children's responsibilities within the programs.

Program Structure

Every participant in a Y-Indian Guide Program is also a part of the YMCA movement, which is active throughout the United States and in 130 countries around the world. Each Y-Indian Guide Program is organized through a local Y, and the YMCA director remains in contact with each tribe. Several levels of organization exist, beginning with the primary unit, the tribe—although flexibility is encouraged at the local level to more accurately reflect the terms and traditions of local Native Americans. For example, in some Indian Nations, lodges may be a more appropriate term than tribes. Do some research to find out what terms and structure work best for the families in your community.

Tribes

All Y-Indian Guide members participate in small neighborhood groups called *tribes*. A tribe usually consists of seven to ten parent-child teams. They meet at each others' homes regularly throughout the school year for program activities. Tribes elect a Chief and other officers, plan their own events, and conduct projects. The parents meet several times a year to develop plans and address problems.

Nations

Tribes may be affiliated with other tribes as part of a Y-Indian Guide *Nation*. A Nation may be any number of tribes grouped by YMCA branch, participant age, neighborhood, or other criteria. The tribal chiefs and Nation representatives (one parent from each tribe) usually meet each month to plan events in which all tribes may participate, such as a camp-out. Ideas are exchanged on tribal activities, stories, games, and the like, which helps promote tribal morale and strength.

Federations

Some YMCAs organize *Federations*, which are groups of several Nations. The term *Federation* also may refer to all Y-Indian Guide participants in a single YMCA.

Longhouses

Longhouse is a term used in this manual meaning "meeting" or "conference." A *Nation Longhouse* is a gathering of all participants in a particular Y-Indian Guide Nation. A *Federation Longhouse* is for all participants in that Federation. Some YMCAs organize *Longhouses* that include the heads of tribes or Nations in program planning. They may refer to these longhouses as *Chief's* or *Nation Longhouses*.

The National Y-Indian Guide Longhouse

The National Advisory Committee of Y-Indian Guide Programs is a committee of the Program Development Division of the YMCA of the USA. The committee is made up of local YMCA volunteers and staff. Its purpose is to follow trends, provide support to local programs when requested, facilitate training for volunteers and staff at cluster and regional levels, assist with the development of program resources, and select the host and site for a national convention.

Y-Indian Guide Programs Tribal Activities

Each tribe has two or more tribal activities a month, at least one of which is a tribal meeting. The others may be either meetings or outside activities. Several times a year large intertribal events are held also.

The Tribal Meeting

Meetings are held in the homes of members on a rotating basis. A typical tribal meeting includes the following:

- Ceremonies such as opening and closing rituals (see "Tribal Rituals" section on pages 26-28).
- Activities such as crafts, stories, Indian lore, games, songs, and service projects.
- Refreshments provided by the host family.

Tribal meetings start and end on time and generally do not last longer than 90 minutes. Business and planning activities are kept to a minimum, as these can be taken care of during parents' meetings (described later).

The following are some sample activities for tribal meetings:

Cooking projects	Health/fitness education
Safety/first aid education	Treasure hunts
Ecology projects	Craft projects
Communication exercises	Gift making
Service projects	Backyard carnivals
Values discussions	

You should plan activities that are easy for both children and parents to understand. Parent-child pairs should work as a team whenever possible. Try to use discussion activities and experiences, as well as crafts, as part of your tribal meetings.

Refreshments are served prior to the closing ritual or prayer, which is the official ending of the meeting. Parents and children sit together during refreshments as well as during the rest of the meeting to avoid breaking the tribe up into separate groups of parents and children.

Outside Activities

A key to the success of a tribe is the planning of varied outside activities, some examples of which are included in the following lists. Many of the outings are also appropriate for Nation events. Consult your YMCA Director for additional information and assistance.

TRIBAL EVENTS

Scavenger hunt	Rain gutter boat races
Christmas caroling	Kite flying
Evening with a Native American	Potluck dinner
	Nature walks
Dinosaur egg hunt	Tent camping
Swim night at the Y	

TRIBAL OUTINGS

Visit an Indian reservation

Agriculture

Flower gardens	Farm or stables
Cattle or horse ranch	Apiary (beekeeping)
Chicken hatchery	Dairy farm
4-H Center—fair or stock show	Fruit orchard
Arboretum or conservatory	

Civic

Fire station	Library
Police station or jail	Power and light station
City hall	Telephone company
U.S. customs	Health department
Water treatment station	U.S. mint
College campus	Courthouse
Post office	State capitol or legislature

Commercial

Fast food restaurant	Shopping mall
Pizzeria	Auto repair shop
Shoe repair shop	Bakery
Supermarket	Pet show
Plant nursery or greenhouse	

Historical

Early churches or missions	State or national parks
Monuments	American Indian centers

Birthplaces

U.S., state, or local landmarks

Geographical oddities

Archeological sites

Rodeo

Arcade

Haunted house

Batting cages

Industrial

Auto assembly plant

Snack foods plant

Dairy

Newspaper office or printer

Tire plant

Toy makers

Candy factory

Cannery

Military installation

Plastic factory

Bottling company

Paper mill

Transportation

Airport (control tower, terminal, cockpit)

Airplane factory

Railroad yards

Shipyards

Harbor tour

Riverboat trip

Truck terminal

Train ride

Bus trip

Subway ride

Bicycling

Balloon ride

TRIBAL PROJECTS

Costumes/tribal property

Tribal plaque

Scrapbook

Family involvement

Photo album

Museums

Natural history

Doll

Railroad or transportation

Science

Marine or seaport

American Indian

Sports

Art gallery

Wax

Air and space

Community Service Projects

Planting trees in the town park

Cleaning the park of trash

Keeping a section of highway free of trash

Cleaning up a vacant lot in the community

Painting over graffiti on a building

Sponsoring a child through the mail

Visiting a senior citizens' center or nursing home around the holidays

Building a float for a local parade

Volunteering for a work weekend at the YMCA camp

Working a booth at a town activity (fair or carnival)

Trick or treating for food for a food bank

Holding a Thanksgiving dinner at the Y for adults who have no place to go

Collecting clothing for families for the winter

Nature and Science

Bird sanctuary

Wildlife refuge

Fish hatchery

Caves

Nature trails or centers

Forest ranger station

Zoo

Observatory

Weather station

Planetarium

Aquarium

Aviary

Beach

Radio, Television, or Theater

Radio station

Television station

Theater (film or live)

Youth symphony

Photography studio

Puppet show

Dance studio

Fashion show

Artist's studio

High school band concert

Recording studio

OTHER YMCA PROGRAMS

Call your YMCA for information on any of the following:

Y-Trail Blazers, Mates, Maidens, and Coed Trail Blazers (for older children)

Swimming lessons

Gymnastics

Day and resident camping

Saturday gym and swim

Fitness programs for adults, children, and families

Special interest classes

Service groups

YMCA Family Time events

Family support programs

Family volunteer opportunities

Sports and Recreation

Archery

Miniature golf

Riflery

Swimming

Sledding

Sleigh ride

Amusement or water park

Ice show

Dog or cat show

Fishing

Tribal softball or football game

Bowling alley

Ice- or roller-skating

Horseback riding

Boating or canoeing

Hayride

Snow shoeing

Cross-country skiing

Circus

Camping (tent or cabin)

Professional sporting events

Snorkeling

Intertribal and Family Activities

The Longhouse or Nation usually will sponsor large intertribal events several times during the year. The following are some possible activities:

Y-Indian Guide induction ceremony

Arts and crafts fairs

Picnics

Sporting events

Amusement parks

Swim or gym at the Y

Sleep over at the Y

Camp-out

Slo-pitch softball

Bowling

Sledding

Beach party

Square dancing

Scavenger hunt

Treasure hunt

Snow sculptures

Dinosaur egg hunt (with watermelons)

Easter egg hunt

Potluck dinner

Pinewood derby races

Canoe or sailboat races in the pool

Pig roast cookout

Kite flying

Parent-child banquet

Pancake breakfast

Christmas party

Such activities also lend themselves to including families as well as the parents and children involved in the program. Although the primary purpose of the Y-Indian Guide Programs is to provide opportunities to strengthen and foster individual parent-child relationships, the parent and child are often part of a larger family group. You can involve other family members in tribal, Nation, or Federation activities in the following ways:

- Create and deliver tribal meeting invitations as a family project.
- Include all family members on outings such as hayrides or picnics.
- Hold a potluck supper to end the year.
- Sponsor a Family Day at a sports event.
- Have the child in the program teach or adapt a program activity to the rest of the family.
- Invite one other family in the tribe to be a part of special occasions such as holidays and celebrations.
- Discuss values learned in the program at the family table.
- Participate in fund-raisers, like a pancake breakfast or a carnival. Or, sell items like candy, nuts, paper, or popcorn.

Parents' Responsibilities

Parents' foremost responsibility in the Y-Indian Guide Programs is attending meetings with their children. Y-Indian Guide Programs are not children's programs but rather parent-child programs. Their purpose is to foster the companionship of parents with their children.

Parents also are expected to attend parents' meetings for long-range planning of tribal activities, to hold offices in the tribe, and to help with the crafting of tribal property.

Parents' Meetings

Most of the common shortcomings of tribes can be eliminated by meeting without the children several times during the year. The main purpose of these meetings is to iron out tiresome business details and avoid boring the children during tribal meetings. Any business that takes more than five minutes in a tribal meeting should be referred to the parents' meeting. Planning for trips, special events, and so forth goes much smoother when parents meet alone.

Advance planning can be done for a month or semester at a time at a parents' meeting. Also, the parents with logical excuses for not doing a certain task can explain their reasons without having the children present. Special events or surprises can be discussed without exciting the children too far ahead of time. For example, a weekend camping trip two months away can be planned by the parents without making the children wait too long.

Parents' meetings also offer excellent opportunities for learning. Tribal meetings can be evaluated, improvements suggested, and weak points discussed objectively by the parents alone. This is the most appropriate time for your Y Director or your organizer to listen to your problems and help you solve them.

Your time in the parents' meeting is best spent trying to understand your own child better, learning how to be a closer pal and friend to your son or daughter, or trying to learn to cope with behavior problems. Although the Y is ready to help in this regard, often considerable understanding can be gained by a frank discussion of issues and problems among parents.

At these parents' meetings, you will have a chance to review the program manuals or books and magazine articles that will help you to be a better parent and program participant. You can share ideas on improving invitations, games, or stories. Y staff is always available to help your tribe develop good parents' meetings.

The following agenda and checklist should help you organize your parents' meetings.

TYPICAL PARENTS' MEETING AGENDA

8:00 p.m.	Devotional thought
8:10 p.m.	Review of agenda for this meeting
8:15 p.m.	Consideration of items you desire to coordinate and plan (upcoming tribal meetings, special events, trips, etc.)
8:30 p.m.	Special training and/or discussion of tribal problems
8:50 p.m.	Any unfinished business
9:00 p.m.	Scheduling of the next meeting and adjournment

CHECKLIST FOR MEETING

❑ Call parents the night before to ensure attendance.
❑ Start on time.
❑ Give everyone a chance to contribute.
❑ Reach agreements on items.
❑ Make specific assignments.
❑ Set a date for the next parents' meeting.
❑ Serve refreshments during the meeting.
❑ Close on time.
❑ Distribute minutes of the meeting to all members.

To assist you in long-range planning, a group planning chart is included on the next two pages. An activity planning guide and a Nation event planning checklist are also included on pages 40 and 41 to help you plan. The parent-child roster on page 42 can be copied for use by the YMCA and each parent-child pair. The program rotation sheet on page 43 will help organize your activities and ensure that all families are equally involved in your program.

Suggested Parents' Leadership Roles

Offices held within each tribe provide shared leadership opportunities for personal development of both parents and children. Training opportunities for tribal chiefs are essential for effective tribal functioning. The roles found in many tribes include the Chief, Assistant Chief, Wampum Bearer, Tallykeeper, and Sachem.

- *Chief (Elder* or *Leader* may be a more appropriate term for some tribes). One of the parents is selected to see that there is continuity in meetings, conduct portions of the meetings, and act as the leader of the group. He or she presides at parents' meetings, delegates assignments, and checks to see that tasks are being done. He or she is the tribal contact person for the YMCA and represents the tribe at the monthly or semi-monthly Longhouse/Nation meetings. (Some tribes change Chiefs every six months, but tribes should recognize the need for continuity and ongoing contact with the YMCA Director.)

- *Assistant Chief.* He or she assumes the duties of the Chief when the Chief is not able to attend meetings. He or she may accompany the Chief to Longhouse/Nation meetings and may be in training for the Chief's job.

- *Wampum Bearer,* or money collector. (Wampum is a term used by some New England Indians.) This parent is responsible for the collection and safekeeping of the tribal wampum (dues) and has responsibility for collecting and forwarding to the YMCA monies for membership, camp-outs, and so forth.

- *Tallykeeper.* This parent takes care of attendance and minutes at tribal meetings. He or she might also be responsible for sending information on tribal activities to the YMCA and birthday cards to the tribal Braves/Princesses/Maidens on their birthdays.

- *Elder, Sachem, or Advisor* (depending on the tribe you select). The wise parent of the tribe—usually a former Chief—assumes this role. He or she reminds all members of the aims of the program, leads the tribe in many service projects, and helps to establish new tribes.

A tribe is free to create new or additional offices, and all parents should hold some office; however, offices should have specific tasks assigned to them. One word of caution: **Avoid**

Group Planning Chart

Name of group or tribe _____

Number of adults _____ Number of children_____

What are our fixed activities for the year (e.g., meeting dates as planned at the fall parents' meeting, YMCA camp-outs, Pinewood Derby)?

_____   _____

_____   _____

_____   _____

_____   _____

_____   _____

What activities would we like to include (e.g., additional camp-outs, group outings)?

_____

_____

_____

_____

_____

_____

_____

_____

_____

_____

_____

_____

Month	First Meeting	Second Meeting	Camp-Outs	Other Activities	Special Outings/ Camp-Outs
September					
October					
November					
December					
January					
February					
March					
April					
May					
June					
July					
August					

using names that have a religious meaning (Medicine Man or Woman) or demeaning implications among American Indian people. And if you're not sure, ask. Office titles such as Craft Maker, Sign Maker, Council Judge, and the like are acceptable and have been adopted by some groups.

Y-Indian Guide Programs Tribal Property

Every tribe should make its own set of tribal property, which may include the following items (to be genuine to a specific tribe you should research it first to determine if the property is authentic):

- *Tribal drum.* The tribal drum is used to open and close each tribal meeting and represents the unity of the tribe.
- *Property box.* This box holds most of the tribal property, but should be small enough to be handled easily.
- *Totem pole.* One of the most important tribal properties, the pole is constructed of different sections made by each parent-child team. The totem pole has a strong religious connotation to some Indian tribes and should be used respectfully and sparingly.
- *Talking sticks or rocks.* During tribal meetings, the person holding the talking stick or rock is granted the right to speak. Talking sticks and rocks can be decorated with paint, feathers, beads, leather, or any other materials.
- *Council fire.* A "fire" made by nailing or screwing six to ten sticks together in the shape of a tepee, log cabin, or combination of both mounted on a plywood board, and placing a light bulb in the center to simulate a fire.
- *Coup stick.* These large decorated sticks are displayed outside the home to welcome tribal members. Each parent-child team can insert a feather when they arrive and remove it when they leave.
- *Tallykeeper's book.* A book constructed for the purpose of holding records of meetings and events. It may be decorated with various Indian designs.

- *Wampum* or *money pouch.* A leather container for holding tribal funds, often decorated with beads and feathers.

Tribal property belongs to the tribe and is made by tribal members. All materials should be purchased with tribal funds. The tribal properties are kept in the property box, which is taken by the next host after each meeting. Thus all property is kept intact and is readily available at the site of each successive meeting.

Each parent and child should share responsibility for making some of the tribal property. Perhaps two families can work together to make the larger items. The important point is to make all properties as quickly as possible by including all parent-child teams in the fun and responsibility. Successful tribes complete these projects early, an achievement that helps knit the tribal members closely together. Moreover, the equipment adds color and meaning to meetings, increasing the satisfaction of all members.

Children's Responsibilities

Like parents, children have specific responsibilities in conducting the tribal meetings and maintaining the strength of the tribe. These responsibilities are paying dues, presenting scouting reports, and assuming some leadership functions.

Dues

In addition to the program fee charged by the YMCA, each tribe may collect tribal dues (wampum money) from the children for its own tribal use. The amount is set by the tribe and handled by the Wampum Bearer. Tribes use the money to pay for special treats, craft costs, gasoline on trips, and other items and events.

Each child should be prepared to tell other tribe members what he or she did to earn the wampum. This approach helps children learn the value of money and encourages them to do things for others.

Scouting Reports

The scouting report is an assignment given to the little Braves/Princesses/Maidens by the Chief to be completed between meetings. By making a short report to the tribe, children develop poise and speaking ability, exercise their inquisitive and thoughtful natures, and practice responsible behavior. Scouting reports could include bringing in magazine pictures of certain scenes, activities, or cultures; making a list of insects found in the backyard; and the like. It's a good idea to recognize the children for their efforts in giving scouting reports.

Suggested Children's Leadership Roles

Children can learn leadership qualities by filling one or more of the suggested leadership roles in tribal meetings. These roles include the following:

- *Young Chief.* Usually the Chief's son or daughter assumes this role. He or she helps keep the children attentive, assists in the ceremonies, and reports tribal activities to the Nation or Longhouse news editor.
- *Drum Beater.* Usually the host child assumes this role. He or she is in charge of the tribal drum, calls everyone to council, and assists in ceremonies.
- *Runner.* He or she keeps all headbands and tribal property in the property box and runs errands for the Chief.
- *Wampum* or *Dues Collector.* Usually the son or daughter of the Wampum Bearer assumes this role. He or she helps the Wampum Bearer to collect tribal dues and asks the young Braves/Princesses/Maidens whether they earned their money by service to family or community. In addition, this child finds out what activities parents took part in with their children in the past weeks.
- *Roll Taker.* The son or daughter of the Tallykeeper calls the roll using the tribal members' Indian names.

CONDUCTING TRIBAL MEETINGS

The outline shown here is a suggested guide for conducting a typical Y-Indian Guide Programs tribal meeting. It is followed by more detailed information on different parts of the

meeting: tribal rituals, collection of wampum, scouting reports, Chief's talks, and the Tallykeeper's reports. The final section offers some hints for running interesting meetings.

7:00 p.m.	Chief calls meeting to order by asking one of the children to beat on the tribal drum once for each parent-child team present. Talking should stop. Chief leads prayer or opening ceremony and flag salute (if flag is available).
7:10 p.m.	Tallykeeper takes roll (and may also read minutes of last meeting). Wampum Bearer collects tribal dues; each little Brave/Princess/Maiden explains how he or she obtained wampum. Wampum bag is passed around.
7:15 p.m.	Chief asks for scouting reports. Use of the talking stick is recommended as each child presents a scouting report. (Chief's talk may follow.)
7:25 p.m.	Chief announces any upcoming intertribal events, YMCA news, and so forth. Plans are reviewed for next meeting, using the "Group Planning Chart" on page 23 of this manual.
7:35 p.m.	Tribe makes a craft or plays a game.
7:50 p.m.	Host serves light refreshments.
8:00 p.m.	Tribal member tells a story and/or tribe sings songs.
8:20 p.m.	Chief leads closing ritual and/or prayer.
8:25 p.m.	Tribe heads for home.

Tribal Rituals

Opening and closing rituals add a great deal to your meetings. Rituals are exciting to children of this age. They should be simple, brief, and dignified. You can vary procedures and content if the additions make the ceremony more meaningful to your tribe. In the first few meetings, the parts of the rituals can be read, but they should be memorized as soon as possible.

Do not underestimate the importance of rituals. A tribal ceremony should be used at every tribal meeting, and it should be performed consistently from meeting to meeting.

Opening Rituals

All meetings begin on time with the beating of the drum. A drum should be one of the first tribal craft projects, as it adds a great deal to the meetings. Parents and children form a double circle, with the children standing in the inner circle in front of their own parents. When all are quiet, the ceremony is conducted with dignity and meaning. The beginning of each meeting can follow a ritual format as shown in the following outlines. Where multiple choices are offered (such as Braves/Princesses/Maidens), use only the one appropriate for your group.

OUTLINE 1

Drum Beater (the host child) gives the drum twelve beats (or one for each parent-child team present).

CHIEF: (*Raising hands and eyes to the Great Spirit*) Great Spirit, as we gather around this council fire, dwell among us and guide us. Give us wisdom and understanding. We are grateful for _____ (*something simple that the children will understand: the beautiful weather; the large attendance; the beautiful outing we just had*), O Great Spirit, hear our words.

OR

CHIEF: Let us give thanks for our loved ones, for the beauty of the Earth, and for the Creator's blessings.

OR

CHIEF: O God, as we gather for this council, be with us and guide us. Grant us wisdom and understanding, that we may do those things that are pleasing to you. We thank you for _____.

Drum Beater beats drum twice.

CHIEF: What is the slogan of Y-Indian Guides/Princesses/Maidens/Braves?

ALL: The slogan is "Pals Forever"/"Friends Always."

CHIEF: Drum Beater, what is a Y-Indian Brave/Princess/Maiden?

DRUM BEATER: A boy/girl with a dad/mom like mine.

CHIEF: And your office, what does it mean?

DRUM BEATER: The beating of the drum calls the tribe together and tells its members to come to order.

CHIEF: Runner, what are the duties and meaning of your office?

RUNNER: I stand guard over the tribal property.

CHIEF: What is the pledge of all Y-Indian Braves/Princesses/Maidens?

ALL: Our daily pledge is "We, father/mother and son/daughter, through friendly service to each other, to our family, to this tribe, to our community, seek a world pleasing to the eye of the Great Spirit."

CHIEF: This council is now open. Sit. (*Each parent takes a seat on the floor, with the child in front.*)

CHIEF: Tallykeeper, read the Birch Bark Scroll.

TALLYKEEPER: (*Reads the minutes of the last meeting.*)

CHIEF: Tallykeeper, will you take the roll while the Wampum Bearer collects the dues and calls for scouting reports?

(*The children pay their dues, tell how they obtained the money, and report on any special thing that occurred during the time between meetings. Each child should have a turn to speak and should be encouraged to participate.*)

TALLYKEEPER: Chief, the roll has been called.

WAMPUM BEARER: Chief, the dues are collected and the scouting reports received.

OUTLINE 2

CHIEF: Drum Beater, beat the drum to call the tribe to order.

(Drum Beater strikes twelve beats on the drum slowly.)

CHIEF: All stand for the Pledge of Allegiance.

ALL: (*Say the Pledge of Allegiance.*)

CHIEF: Young Braves/Princesses/Maidens, what is a Y-Indian Brave/Princess/Maiden?

CHILDREN: A boy/girl with a dad/mom like mine.

CHIEF: What is the purpose of the Y-Indian Guides/Princesses/Maidens/Braves?

ALL: To foster the understanding and companionship between father and son/father and daughter/mother and daughter/mother and son.

CHIEF: What is the slogan of the Y-Indian Guides/Princesses/Maidens/Braves?

ALL: "Pals Forever"/"Friends Always." (*Chief then leads all in repeating aims of their program.*)

CHIEF: Drum Beater, what are the duties of your office?

DRUM BEATER: The duties of the Drum Beater are to beat the drum to call the meeting to order.

CHIEF: Runner what are the duties of your office?

RUNNER: My duties are to answer all calls and run errands for the tribe.

CHIEF: Tallykeeper, what are the duties of your office?

TALLYKEEPER: The duties of the Tallykeeper shall be to record all events of each meeting of the tribe and give a copy of the record to the Chief at the following meeting.

CHIEF: Tallykeeper, read the record from the last meeting.

TALLYKEEPER: *(Reads the minutes of the last meeting.)*

CHIEF: Wampum Bearer, what are the duties of your office?

WAMPUM BEARER: The duties of the Wampum Bearer are to collect the dues and handle the finances of our tribe.

CHIEF: Tallykeeper, call the roll while the Wampum Bearer collects the dues.

(The Tallykeeper now calls the children one at a time by their Y-Indian Guide program names. As the child's name is called, he or she stands up and goes to the Wampum Bearer. The Wampum Bearer asks the child how the money was obtained. The child replies.)

TALLYKEEPER: Chief, the roll is called.

WAMPUM BEARER: Chief, the dues have been collected.

Closing Rituals

Each meeting should close with a short, simple ritual. This joins the tribe together once more before leaving and provides a suitable ending to the meeting. The following are some examples.

And now *(index finger pointing to the ground)*, may the Great Spirit *(all fingers circling up, imitating smoke)* of all good spirits *(arms outstretched)* be with *(arms coming in close)* you *(index finger pointing across circle)*, now *(all fingers pointing down)* and forever more *(action of shooting bow and arrow)*.

May the Great Spirit *(sign of "V" with right hand up and forward from shoulder)* look down upon us *(the "V" fingers bent forward and down and wrist bent forward, so that the V fingers "look down")* while we are absent *(two index fingers held before body, about a foot apart, then drawn together)* for a little while *(index fingers drawn apart, the left forward, the right backwards, for about a six-inch space)*.

During each of the following prayers, raise your arms above your head at the beginning of the prayer and slowly lower them during the prayer:

Great Spirit of the Universe, guide us until we meet again.

O Great Spirit, watch over us during the passing moon, hear our voices and guide our thoughts.

O Chief of Gods, aid us in our tribe, watch over our tepees, and protect our Braves/Princesses/Maidens.

Great Spirit, hear our voices asking for guidance and direction from the winds; we will watch the setting sun as a sign of your power.

One by one, the children remove their own and their parents' council feathers from the tribal coup stick to indicate that the tribal council is over and that the members are leaving.

Other Ceremonies

Certain special ceremonies should be a part of your program as well: the induction of new members and tribes, the induction of new officers, and the passing of the headdress from the old Chief to the new one. Suggested formats for some of these ceremonies are included in the Ceremonies section of this manual. Make these ceremonies impressive and see how they add spark to your program.

Collection of Wampum

The collection of wampum can be one of the most effective portions of the tribal meeting for both children and parents. It gives the children a chance to learn about the value of money, to gain confidence in speaking before the group, to be inspired to do things for others, and to listen while other children report. It presents parents with an opportunity to observe their own children's poise and thinking processes as they speak and to learn how all of the children obtain the money for dues.

There should be a definite ceremonial flavor to this procedure. The Wampum Bearer should rise and display the contents of the wampum bag for all to see while proudly announcing how much is in the bag. The Wampum Collector then stands before each child and receives his or her wampum and the story of how it was obtained.

The Council Judge stands erect near the Chief. When all wampum is collected and all reports are in, that person says, "O Chief, I have heard the Braves/Princesses/Maidens of the mighty *(tribal name)* Y-Indian Guides/Princesses/Maidens/Braves tribe report the ways they have received their wampum, and I find those ways helpful to all."

The Chief then asks the Wampum Collector to deliver the wampum to the Wampum Bearer, who ceremoniously puts it into the tribal wampum bag.

A variation would be to have one of the parents tell how he or she earns wampum at work each day. Parents could bring examples and/or pictures of their work.

The Wampum Bearer and Wampum Collector will want to make a wampum pouch or bag. It can be made inexpensively from rawhide or leather or calfskin (with hair still on) in a number of simple ways. Instructions for creating a wampum pouch can be found in the Tribal Property section of this manual.

Presentation of Scouting Reports

The scouting reports are an important part of the tribal meeting. Children learn a great deal from presenting a report of something they did, heard, or saw since the last meeting. If the report is about something they did with their parents, so much the better. Children may need to be prompted at first to get started. Talk over the report with your son or daughter before the meeting to encourage him or her to speak.

Watch for subjects that make good scouting reports and point them out to your child. The small and unusual things in nature make the best reports. Encourage your child to ask questions about life, nature, work, mechanical devices, and the like, and then look up the answer with him or her for the report. Perhaps the best kind of report is a parent-child experience, whether a craft, a hike, or even a movie together.

These reports accomplish three important goals:

- Develop poise and speaking ability in a child and give him or her a sense of adding to the value of the meeting.

- Help the child to see what he or she is looking at, that is, to look more closely at nature, to view the very small and the very large, and to muse about what he or she has seen.

- Encourage parents to do more with their children.

The Chief in his or her talk can direct the children's attention to a special subject to help them make a report at the next meeting. Some possible topics are listed here:

Birds	Sign language
Clouds	Stars
Athletics	History of the tribal name
Snakes	Flowers
Growth	Ocean
Favorite Indian	Trips
Fish	Feathers
Rocks	What they want to be
Dogs	Family
Seeds	Trees
Hobbies	

Recognize the children for their efforts in making scouting reports by giving them a bead or feather as a form of encouragement.

Chief's Talks

Immediately following the opening ceremony, the Chief may say a few words to the tribe, giving accurate Indian information, telling of a great Indian or tribe, reminding the tribe of its ideals, or speaking of the Great Spirit or wonders of nature. This provides an opportunity to teach values to sons and daughters. The talk should not be long and should be determined by the children's attention span. If they get restless, bring the talk to a close. The following are examples of ideas to include in the Chief's talks:

- Respect for the family, including things that parents and children can do at home

- Tribal problems: for example, use an Aesop's fable to make a point

- An animal story that encourages good conduct or builds interest in the out-of-doors
- The meaning of the tribal headband and the importance of tribal aims
- An explanation of Indian sign language or sign writing (note the specific tribe that the language or writing is from)
- The wonderful things the tribe has done that it can be proud of
- Interesting facts and stories from magazines
- An explanation of the seasons in terms of Indians and hunters or gatherers
- An invitation for parents and children to talk over their misunderstandings together

Many local Ys have recommitted to teach values and develop character in Y programs. Contact your local YMCA for more information about implementing character development in your program.

Simple examples from nature can make children think about what they see. These are some examples:

- Did you know that ants carry over 100 times their own weight? They need this strength in order to build their homes. If we had the same strength, we could carry over seven tons. Do we need this kind of strength?
- Did you know that one of the slowest, dumbest animals in the forest is the porcupine? In addition, it doesn't have good eyes or claws. But it's protected by quills from enemies. Why?
- Have you ever noticed a sea anemone? It is a little animal that looks like a piece of shell or rock in the shallow pools by the ocean. If you touch it, it closes and looks just like the bottom of the pool. Why is it protected? Have you ever thought about how a grasshopper is like Superman? It has huge legs and big muscles to jump great heights. If we could jump as high as a grasshopper can, we could jump over the Empire State Building in a single bound.
- Have you ever caught a lizard by its tail and then had the tail come off in your hand? Lizards can drop their tails and grow

new ones. Why do they have this special trick? Have you heard about the snowshoe rabbit? It changes color twice a year. In the summer it's brown, but when winter comes it turns snow-white. Why?

- Did you know that there is a spinning wheel attached to spiders? The spider can spin its own web, creating the most delicate designs. Why does it need this spinning wheel?

Tallykeeper's Report

The Tallykeeper has a real job to do in writing up the minutes of the previous tribal meeting in an imaginative way. The Tallykeeper and son or daughter should work on the minutes together, using terms and symbols where possible and bringing in enough humor to interest the other children.

Verbal reports made at meetings should be kept brief. More detailed written reports can be prepared for the tribal history book. The following is a sample report:

TALLYKEEPER'S REPORT

The council fire was held at the home of Strong Bow and Fleet Arrow on Tuesday evening. All members were called to the council by a miniature bow and arrow.

Chief Peacemaker welcomed all members as they entered the home. Using a drum beat, he called the meeting together. After reciting the aims and the slogan of the program, everyone did a sounding rendition of "Friends Always," the program song.

Chief Peacemaker told the tribe about weeds and how they hold tightly to the ground when pulled up. The Great Spirit made strong roots for them so that they might grow tall and strong before they travel to the Happy Hunting Ground. The Great Spirit loves and protects all—even weeds.

The Tallykeeper found all braves present around the council fire.

The Wampum Collector gathered the wampum and heard favorable reports on how the wampum was earned. The

Wampum Bearer found eight dollars and seventy-two cents in the wampum pouch.

Chief Badger Eye said it was time for a big tribal move to the shores of Gitchee Gumie for fishing. A show of hands indicated we would take a trip in twelve suns (days) to Redondo Village Canoe Landing.

Scouting reports showed wide-open eyes and listening ears on the part of all members. Brave Little Dipper was granted "Brave of the Month" for scouting out fossil rock in the Palos Verdes area.

Assistant Chief Bald Eagle praised the members who went to the House of the Great Spirit, saved wampum, made a project, and helped with the annual YMCA food drive.

Braves Big and Little Bear showed the tribe how to make an arm bustle out of small feathers. Little Bear passed out the materials for braves to make these arm bustles before the next council.

Chief Peacemaker told great tales of a far-away Indian tribe of Incas who worshipped the Sun because they thought the Great Spirit was the Boss of the Sun.

The Braves enjoyed a snack of chocolate corn bread and 7-Up.

All members played a game of Scrambled Moccasins (Shoes). Eventually, everyone was able to match up the moccasins that they came with.

Chief Peacemaker closed the council meeting with a prayer.

Good Practices for Interesting Meetings

The Chief and tribal officers should keep effective group practices in mind in their planning and appraisal of tribal development. Remember that the basic purpose of Y-Indian Guide Programs is to increase the number of things parents and children can enjoy doing together during the time when children think their parents are the greatest. Thus it is important that the tribal meeting be interesting to the young children and that they have ample opportunity to participate. The meetings must be oriented toward the children, not the parents. Use the following suggestions as a guide for devising interesting meetings:

- Be concerned about all group members, the shy as well as the outgoing.
- Start meetings on time; close them on time. Opening ceremonies should not spill over into program time.
- Aim the ceremonial parts of the meeting at the children. They should do most of the talking during the meetings; it should be fun for them.
- Focus program activities on the interests and capabilities of the children. Be alert to their needs.
- Plan all phases of the tribal meeting carefully; contact families with special responsibilities in advance. It is the Chief's job to see that the Chief's talk, reports, stories, games, and so on are chosen beforehand.
- Encourage all; share praise where it is deserved. Recognize the progress of all Braves/Princesses/Maidens.
- Allow for a great deal of fun at tribal meetings; support joint participation by fathers/mothers and sons/daughters.
- Pass responsibility around: Know the individual tribal members' interests and experiences. Assign tasks carefully.
- Be wary of parents' talking too much in tribal meetings; use parents' meetings regularly to handle most business.
- Facilitate team discussion and decision making on matters of behavior, program development, and policy for the tribe.
- Be warm, supportive, understanding, and flexible. Be more concerned about the feelings and attitudes of tribal members than with the accuracy of tribal ceremonies or procedures.

Use the following list to troubleshoot problems with your meetings.

STARTING A TRIBE

If you are part of a group that is just entering one of the Y-Indian Guide Programs, this section will give you some vital information. The first part consists of steps to follow in establishing your tribe. The second part is a discussion of the selection of individual and tribal Indian names, and it includes a list of possible names from which to choose.

Initial Steps

Here is a list of steps for starting a new tribe. It may be of help to you and the other parent-child teams in your tribe. The first parents' meeting should take place as soon after the YMCA orientation meeting as possible. Schedule the first tribal meeting as soon as possible after the first parents' meeting.

FIRST PARENTS' MEETING

❑ Select meeting night, set up dates of tribal meetings for next four months, and fill out activity chart for at least the next four months

❑ Decide on wampum and amount and bring to the first tribal meeting.

❑ Choose tribal officers/roles.

❑ Decide on necessary tribal property; make assignments for projects that should be brought to first tribal meeting.

Troubleshooting Problems

If this is happening in your Indian tribe . . .	Do this
Can't get meetings started on time.	Start on time with whoever is present. You'll send a message that the meeting won't wait for latecomers.
Meetings run too late.	Set alarm clock to ring at end of meeting ceremony and at end of program time.
Parents talk too much.	Have one parent keep a record of times each parent speaks and discuss the problem at the next parents' meeting.
Children play while parents watch.	Plan games that call for parents and children to compete on the same team.
Parents talk business during meeting.	Chief stops this by referring matter to the next parents' meeting.
Children are inattentive during meeting, talking and giggling, or running around.	If the meeting is interesting to the children, they'll pay attention because they want to. Give the children things to do. Make the meeting fun.
Inappropriate behavior by children at meetings.	Check meeting and programs for level of children's interest. Decide what positive behaviors are desired and establish them through activities and rewards.

❑ Have each parent-child team pick out Indian names for themselves before the first tribal meeting.

❑ Introduce all tribal members by their new names.

❑ Select Indian tribal name (check with Y office so as not to duplicate a tribal name already in use).

❑ Forward the list of tribal members on the official roster to the Y office along with completed registration forms and fees.

❑ Date for official induction ceremony is set by the YMCA.

Research Indian Names

American Indians name their children for some event in the child's life, for an outstanding character trait, or for a spirit that they hope will guide their child. You can do the same, either using the English or researching an Indian word. This section contains suggested Y-Indian Guide names for parents, children, and new tribes.

Indian Names for Parents and Children

The selection of a name for parent and child should be done with the same respect and ceremony that is practiced by the American Indian. The name should reflect honor, and it should be carried with honor by the bearer.

The American Indians grant names to their children in the following ways, which your tribe can consider in selecting names that have meaning for each specific person.

- The elders' vision of what the child may turn out to be (i.e., a guide for his or her future, such as Silver Bird, Peacemaker, or Straight Arrow).

- Something that stood out in the parents' minds on the day the child was born (Bright Star, Snow Rabbit, Sleeping Bear).

- The hope of the parent or child for his or her future (Strong Heart, Steady Wind, Brave Wolf, Wise Owl).

- The traits of the parent or child (Great Thunder, Tall Cedar, Keen Eyes, Quiet Squirrel).

- An experience of great meaning to the family (Clear Water, Running Deer, Red Sky).

Some suggested English names:

Brave Wolf	Running Rabbit
Bright Star	Setting Sun
Corn Planter	Shooting Star
Dancer	Silent One
Dove	Silver Fox
Flying Cloud	Silver Star
Gentle Breeze	Sky Woman
Great Star	Strong Hand
Laughing Cloud	Sunbeam
Laughing Water	Sunflower
Looking Glass	Swift Cloud
Medicine Crow	Swift Hawk
Morning Cloud	Swift Wind
Peacemaker	Talking Rock
Red Bird	Tall Hunter
Red Cloud	Warm Wind
Red Feather	White Antelope
Red Fox	White Bird
Rising Sun	Wonder Cook
Running Antelope	Young Fox
Running Brook	

Indian Tribal Names

In choosing your tribal name, remember that the careful search for an interesting name will not only be educational, but will result in a selection your tribe will be proud to bear. Some groups prefer a name from the tribes that lived in their areas. Some pick a name because the tribe had particularly admirable qualities or because it's a fascinating name. Some create a tribal name by using the Indian word for a quality they wish to accentuate in their activities. A check with the Longhouse will avoid duplication along with gaining approval of your choice.

To start you thinking, here are a few tribal names and their meanings:

Mohawks	People of the Flint
Oneidas	People of the Upright Stone

Senecas	People of the Great Mountains
Cayugas	People of the Mucklands
Onondagas	Hill People
Tuscaroras	Wearers of Shirts

Listed below are the more familiar authentic tribal names taken from a list based on ten cultural areas of the Indian tribes of the United States. When a tribe adopts a name, they must assume responsibility for researching the tribe and making sure they depict the tribe in an authentic manner. The mixing of tribal names, customs, property, rituals, and ceremonies is not acceptable.

CALIFORNIA INDIANS

Achomawi	Kern River	Purisimeño
Athapaskan	Klamath	Salinan
Atsugewi	Koso	Serrano
Cahuilla	Luiseño	Shasta
Chemehuevi	Lutuami	Shoshone
Chumash	Maidu	Tolowa
Diegueño	Miwok	Wailaki
Fernandeño	Modoc	Wappo
Gabrielino	Mohave	Washo
Halchidoma	Mono	Wintu
Hokan	Nicoleño	Wiyot
Island Chumash	Paiute	Yana
Juaneño	Penutian	Yokuts
Kamia	Pit River	Yuki
Karok	Playanos	Yuma
Kawaiisu	Pomo	Yurok

SOUTHWEST INDIANS
(ARIZONA AND NEW MEXICO)

Anasazi	Isleta Pueblo	Tewas
Apache	Jicarilla Apache	Tiwas
Carrizo	Keresans	Towa
Chemehuevi	Maricopa	Walapai
Cocopa	Mohave	Yagui
Diné	Moki	Yavapai
Havasupai	Paiute	Yumans
Hualapais	Papago	Zuni

LOWER PLATEAU INDIANS
(COLORADO, NEVADA, AND UTAH)

Apache	Kaibab	Uncompahgre
Arapahoe	Kiowa	Ute
Bannock	Monache	Washo
Capote	Navajo	Weeminuche
Cheyenne	Paiute	Yampa
Comanche	Paviotso	
Goshute	Shoshone	

GULF COAST INDIANS (FLORIDA, ALABAMA, MISSISSIPPI, LOUISIANA, AND TEXAS)

Apache	Chitimacha	Seminole
Apalachee	Choctaw	Tawakoni
Apalachicola	Comanche	Timucua
Atakapa	Coushatta	Tonkawa
Biloxi	Creeks	Tunica
Caddo	Houma	Yuchi
Calusa	Muskhogee	
Chickasaw	Natchez	

NORTHWEST INDIANS
(WASHINGTON, OREGON, AND IDAHO)

Bannock	Lummi	Salish
Cayuse	Makah	Sanpoil
Chinook	Nez Percé	Shoshone
Colville	Nootka	Spokan
Duwamish	Paiute	Takelma
Kalispel	Palouse	Umatilla
Kiturahan	Penutian	Wallawalla
Klamath	Quinault	Yakima
Kutenai	Quileute	

INDIANS OF MONTANA AND WYOMING

Arapahoe	Cree	Salish
Assiniboin	Crow	Shoshone
Bannock	Gros Ventres	Sioux
Blackfeet	Nez Percé	Ute
Cheyenne		

PLAINS AND PRAIRIE INDIANS
(NORTH AND SOUTH DAKOTA, NEBRASKA, KANSAS, OKLAHOMA, IOWA, MISSOURI, AND ARKANSAS)

Arapahoe	Hidatsa	Oto
Arikara	Iowa	Pawnee
Assiniboin	Kansa	Ponca
Cherokee	Kiowa	Quapaw
Cheyenne	Mandan	Seminole
Chickasaw	Missouri	Seneca
Choctaw	Moingwena	Shawnee
Comanche	Okmulgee	Sioux
Creeks	Omaha	Wichita
Foxes	Osage	

GREAT LAKES INDIANS (MINNESOTA, MICHIGAN, OHIO, ILLINOIS, INDIANA, AND WISCONSIN)

Chippewa	Kickapoo	Ottawa
Delaware	Mascouten	Potawatomi
Erie	Menominee	Sauk
Foxes	Miami	Shawnee
Huron	Mohegan	Sioux
Illinois	Obibwa	Winnebago
Iroquois	Ojibwa	

NORTHEASTERN WOODLAND INDIANS (VIRGINIA, KENTUCKY, AND ALL NEW ENGLAND STATES)

Abenaki	Massachusett	Penacook
Algonquian	Mohegan	Penobscot
Delaware	Moneton	Pequot
Iroquois	Montauk	Powhatan
Maliseet- Passamaquoddy	Nanticoke Narragansett	Susquehannock

SOUTHEASTERN WOODLAND INDIANS (TENNESSEE, NORTH AND SOUTH CAROLINA, AND GEORGIA)

Alabama	Chickahominy	Powhatan
Apalachee	Chickasaw	Shawnee
Atakapa	Croatan	Tunica
Biloxi	Mattapony	Tuscarora
Catawba	Natchez	Waco
Cherokee	Pamlico	Yuchi

PROGRAM EVALUATION

The tribal evaluation sheet and checklist found on pages 36-39 can be used by program leaders who visit tribes or by tribal leaders to evaluate themselves and set goals for the coming months. Follow these steps in its use:

1. Agree upon a single, one-hour discussion period for parents alone.

2. Have each parent read all questions and decide upon three or four of the most important ones.

3. Tally the top three priority questions of each parent and determine the top five for follow-up.

4. Addressing one question at a time

   a. identify how well the tribe is doing in this area,

   b. agree on one or two steps for improvement, and

   c. assign responsibilities to parents.

5. Seek the help of others in Steps 2 through 4. Involve the Longhouse officer, local schoolteachers or ministers, and/or the YMCA staff.

The YMCA of the USA, Program Development Division, has designed a checklist of suggested practices for local Y-Indian Guide Programs (see the *Leaders Manual*). This checklist is used to comprehensively review the Y-Indian Guide Programs within any YMCA. Tribal chiefs may be asked to serve on a review committee to evaluate the program using this checklist.

Y-Indian Guide Programs
Tribal Evaluation Sheet

How Important as a Goal?					How Well Achieved in Tribal Program?			
Very	Some-what	Slightly	Not		Poorly	Needs improve-ment	Satis-factorily	Very well
				1. Does your tribe get parents and children to spend more time to-gether, in an increasing variety of activities, outside of tribal meetings?				
				2. Do the parents look forward to be-ing with each other in the meetings and activities?				
				3. Do the parents relax and enjoy the time with their children in tribal meetings and activities, with the parents doing a minimum of com-peting through their children?				
				4. Do parents and children talk to-gether more—understand and like each other more—as a result of the tribe?				
				5. Are the other family members in-cluded in some activities in such a way that they are glad the parent and child belong to the tribe?				
				6. Are parents and children proud of the tribe and what it accomplishes?				
				7. Do children get opportunities and encouragement to express them-selves—show what they can do, say what they think of the tribe activi-ties, carry out officer duties?				

(continued)

How Important as a Goal?					How Well Achieved in Tribal Program?			
Very	Some-what	Slightly	Not		Poorly	Needs improve-ment	Satis-factorily	Very well
				8. Do the parents sometimes swap ideas with each other about their children?				
				9. Do parents and children sometimes have experiences in tribal activities that make them aware of spiritual things—God and higher ideals?				
				10. Do all members feel wanted, needed, important in the tribe?				
				11. Is the responsibility for operation of the tribe shared by all the parents?				
				12. Do the children understand and think about the Y-Indian Guide Program's aims?				
				13. Do the parents teach their children new skills?				
				14. Do the kinds of activities and the way the tribe operates give children opportunities to see their parents act as adults?				
				15. Do the parents contribute leader-ship to organize and strengthen other tribes?				
				16. Do the parents feel responsible for helping all the children?				
				17. Do the members feel a part of the Y as a whole and accept its aims?				
				18. Does your tribe conduct research to make sure your actions and activities are authentic to the Indian tribe whose name you have adopted?				

Checklist for Better Y-Indian Guide Programs Tribes

(Local YMCAs are free to adapt this list to reflect the values of their programs.)

Yes	No	
____	____	Our tribe has at least six parents.
____	____	Each parent and child is registered with the YMCA and has paid the fees.
____	____	Each little Brave, Princess, or Maiden has his or her own charter.
____	____	We have 9 dads (or moms, if Maidens or Braves) meeting at least once every other month to discuss business and long-range plans.
____	____	We are represented at all national meetings with a chief and/or one other representative.
____	____	Our tribe has attended the induction ceremony.
____	____	We follow the rule "no boys and girls may attend a meeting without their dads (or moms for Braves and Maidens)" and vice versa.
____	____	Our tribe meets regularly twice a month.
____	____	Our tribe attends most Nation events.
____	____	We meet for not more than 90 minutes per meeting (except for special meetings).
____	____	Members arrive on time.
____	____	All invitations are prepared by parent and child and distributed three to five days prior to a meeting.
____	____	We have an official opening and closing ceremony.
____	____	Each officer knows his or her part in the opening ceremony.
____	____	Wampum or treasurer reports give evidence that Braves, Princesses, or Maidens are earning their wampum.
____	____	The tribe can recite the purpose, slogan, aims, and pledge.
____	____	All Braves, Princesses, or Maidens hold offices for a designated period of time and then rotate.
____	____	Our tribe has at least one copy of *Friends Always*.
____	____	Our tribe has its own program notebook or scrapbook.
____	____	The meetings are well planned with little lapse of time for Braves, Princesses, or Maidens to become restless.
____	____	Each parent takes responsibility for the behavior of his or her son or daughter throughout the meeting.
____	____	Business talk is kept to a minimum while boys or girls are present.

(continued)

Yes	No	
____	____	Our tribe has the prescribed officers. List here:

_____

_____

_____

_____

_____

_____

_____

Yes	No	
____	____	Our tribe has the prescribed tribal property. List here:

_____

_____

_____

_____

_____

_____

_____

Yes	No	
____	____	Our tribe has nominated someone responsible for ensuring that our actions, property, and activities are authentic to the Indian tribe whose name we have adopted.
____	____	Our tribe has conducted research to ensure that we are authentic and respectful to the Indian tribe whose name we have adopted.
____	____	The Tallykeeper is keeping tribe records in an interesting manner.
____	____	The Wampum Bearer is keeping accurate records.
____	____	The tribal program is varied to meet the changing interests and desires of the members.
____	____	The program responsibilities are rotated.
____	____	Refreshments are simple and available when needed to cause little delay. All tribal members are served the same thing.
____	____	Tribe leaves immediately after meeting instead of staying around to "bat the breeze."
____	____	Our tribe follows the "no alcohol" policy at meetings, camp-outs, and events.
____	____	Our tribe carries on a service project for others.
____	____	Our tribe has learned about the YMCA World Service Programs for other lands and has contributed to World Service.
____	____	When asked, we have helped to organize a new tribe and have stayed with them until they have gotten started.
____	____	Our tribe contributes information and items for our Nation's newsletter.

Activity Planning Guide

Activity/Event _____

Date _____ Location _____

Task	Person Responsible	Date Completed

Nation Event Planning Checklist

❑ Select an activity or event.

❑ Set a date and time.

❑ Check the date with other YMCA and community events for conflicts.

❑ Plan activities.

❑ Contact guest, presenter, site director, etc.

❑ Set fees.

❑ Design an invitation, flyer, and/or promotional pieces.

❑ Set up a registration system (format, who, where, deadlines, confirmation).

❑ Assign responsibilities to volunteers and staff.

❑ Purchase supplies and gather equipment.

❑ Enjoy the activities or event.

❑ Clean up.

❑ Evaluate.

Parent-Child Roster

_____ YMCA

Tribal Chief: _____

Assistant Chief: _____

Tribal Name: _____

Nation: _____

Parent and Child Names	Address	Phone	School or Age	Birth-dates	Indian Names	Notes
(P) _____ (C) _____						
(P) _____ (C) _____						
(P) _____ (C) _____						
(P) _____ (C) _____						

YMCA staff contact person: _____

YMCA phone number: _____

Program Rotation Sheet

Tribal Name: _____

Family name	Meeting date										
	H						C	SO	ST	G	H
	G	H						C	SO	ST	G
	ST	G	H						C	SO	ST
	SO	ST	G	H						C	SO
	C	SO	ST	G	H						C
		C	SO	ST	G	H					
			C	SO	ST	G	H				
				C	SO	ST	G	H			
					C	SO	ST	G	H		
						C	SO	ST	G	H	
							C	SO	ST	G	H

Role	Responsibilities
H - Host	Invitation, refreshments, meeting room, atmosphere.
G - Game	Consider space available, number and age of players.
ST - Story	Tell a short story (never read it).
C - Craft	Pre-fab before the meeting. Try making the craft at home first. If the project will need to be completed at home, arrange to have participants bring it back for showing.
SO - Song	Lead a simple song.

Planning a job for every child will make the event more exciting for each of them.

Program Planning

$\mathcal{T}$his section is designed to help you and the other parents in your tribe develop a satisfying program of tribal activities for your group. You'll want to keep in mind that parent-child interaction is the focus of the Y-Indian Guide Programs and that each program's six aims can provide a structure for your program. Later in this section the advantages and disadvantages of prepared versus original program activities are discussed, and there is a list of suggested objectives for tribal programs. As the children change and grow, you will want to change the program; to that end, ideas for projects, recreation, invitations, sports and games, trips, and ceremonies are included. Some tribes may want to dedicate part of their time to parent education, and all tribes should consider carefully whether they want to use award systems as part of their program.

THE PARENT-CHILD FOCUS

Program projects provide a variety of opportunities for you and your children to develop understanding, affection, and mutual respect. Shared experiences, such as working on crafts together, playing games and doing stunts, walking and talking, exchanging ideas, telling stories, and carrying out service projects, are fundamental in building healthy parent-child relationships through Y-Indian Guide Programs. Program projects should be chosen to correlate with the age, abilities, and experiences of the children and to encourage parent-child participation.

Y-Indian Guide Program experiences will further your appreciation of your children's individuality. As you observe your children interacting with others, you will begin to recognize the particular developmental needs of your own daughters or sons. In turn, your children will gain a new understanding of you and other adults from seeing parents have fun together and plan for others. Children are very proud of the special time and attention that parents give them in Y-Indian Guide Programs. They also learn how to get along with other children, and they seem to increase their ability to function within their own families. The Y-Indian Guide Programs offer opportunities for both parents and children to gain new information and insights about their neighborhood, other families, and the larger community.

Program activities and experiences will afford you the chance to share your affection with your children. It will also allow you to help your sons and daughters learn new social skills and master physical challenges. By helping children function effectively in a group, you will support their personal growth among their peers. In addition, you can make a significant contribution to your children's spiritual lives by helping them gain a deeper reverence for God and for basic spiritual values.

THE SIX AIMS

Each program's aims can be focal points for physical, mental, social, and spiritual learning opportunities and skills development. Such structured planning ensures variety and continuity of experience. You and your children can examine the meaning of each aim together through activities and situations designed to help children grow and mature. You can provide a wide range of quality programming through thoughtful appraisal, adaptation, and creative planning.

PROGRAM SPONTANEITY

Every beginning leader looks avidly for tried-and-true programs that can be followed automatically. This is especially true of new adult Y-Indian Guide Program members, who feel shaky at the beginning of the tribe's life about what to do with this vibrant group of energetic children. To help you get started, many concrete program aids appear in this manual. Such prepared programs can also help educate all tribe members about Indian culture, which is a part of this program.

The process of getting organized and learning about the program itself is part of the program at the beginning. All the facets of good programs are inherent in this initial activity—involvement, purpose, creative initiative, group formation, interpersonal interaction and stimulation, socialization, friendship formation, mutual support, and learning about the material that is discussed.

Beyond this, each group itself is a rich program resource for developing its own program ideas. Each parent and child comes to the group endowed with personal interests and skills. Each neighborhood or community has a special character that contributes to the ideas and activities that the group develops. Cooperative efforts utilizing the YMCA staff, local church and school personnel, and community resources can also lead to creative, happy, and worthwhile program experiences for parents and children.

No manual of program ideas can top the quality of programs spontaneously produced out of the natural interests and needs of a specific group. When your group develops activities that are your own, you will find it easier to identify with the activity; it also will be easier to be fully involved. You can derive much fulfillment from creating your own programs or adapting prepared ones to your own needs.

OBJECTIVES FOR TRIBAL PROGRAMS

As you seek to develop a balanced and meaningful Y-Indian Guide Program experience, focus on objectives in the following areas to support the children's growth: understanding of family life, skills development, character development, education for life enrichment, group organization and functioning, community awareness, and spiritual growth.

1. Understanding family life
   a. The adult's role as a mother or father
   b. The distinction between parent and child roles
   c. The fostering of significant communication and relationships among all members of the family
   d. The development of responsibility and mutual concern
2. Skills development
   a. Health and physical fitness
      (1) Motor skills
      (2) Hand-eye coordination
      (3) Physical fitness
   b. Mental skills
      (1) Support in reading and verbalization
      (2) Creative expression
      (3) Development of self-direction
   c. Social skills
      (1) Relating to others
      (2) Expressing concern and having respect for others
      (3) Developing a sense of humor and the ability to listen
3. Character development
   a. Accepting and demonstrating the positive values: caring, honesty, respect, and responsibility
   b. Teaching, modeling, celebrating, practicing, and affirming positive values
   c. Using the values of caring, honesty, respect, and responsibility to guide behavior and decision making

4. Education for life enrichment
   a. Being exposed to new ideas and concepts
   b. Understanding and appreciating American Indian culture
   c. Learning by doing—direct participation and observation
   d. Exploring vocations
   e. Learning about nature and the interdependence of all life

5. Group organization and functioning
   a. Working with others as part of a group
   b. Providing leadership
   c. Assuming responsibility voluntarily
   d. Carrying out tasks for the benefit of all

6. Community awareness
   a. Visiting new and old community institutions
   b. Meeting community leaders
   c. Recognizing the needs of others and providing service
   d. Collaborating with American Indians or American Indian advocacy groups to create a respectful program

7. Spiritual growth
   a. Developing warm, pleasant parent-and-child relationships
   b. Pursuing outdoor nature activities
   c. Participating in sincere, well-prepared, worshipful devotional experiences

PROGRAM PROGRESSION

Because children develop new skills and capabilities as they grow, they can participate in progressively more complex experiences and activities as they move from the Y-Papoose Program to the first through third years of the Y-Indian Guide Programs. The following outlines describe how activities can be changed over time. Although this information will be most directly applicable to tribes composed of children of similar ages, all adults should be aware of the changes that take place in children at different ages.

It is essential to take the time to plan for new experiences that build on children's initial activities and that challenge them to learn new responsibilities. These new activities should also satisfy the different interests and talents of the parents. Plan wisely. Beware of repeating experiences or activities that worked well once—children change quickly.

Y-Papoose Program (Preschoolers)

Projects

Preschool children have limited skills and dexterity, so be sure to choose arts and crafts projects that are not too complicated. Projects should take 20 minutes or less to complete and should not require that the children use any tools that are too difficult or dangerous for them to handle. Find projects that the preschooler can complete with minimal assistance. You want the children to feel good about the projects that they have completed themselves (versus projects that they have watched their parent complete).

Recreation, Sports, and Games

Games should be short and simple, should be noncompetitive, and should have few skill requirements or rules. Preschoolers have not perfected the skills needed for organized sports such as baseball, basketball, or soccer. Instead, rely on an unstructured playtime where children are free to jump, climb, slide, swing, and ride bikes.

Trips

Preschoolers benefit from trips that expose them to new experiences. Trips to the zoo, park, pumpkin patch, or children's museum are examples of appropriate trips. Most trips should be limited to one to two hours. Refrain from scheduling a trip during naptime. Make sure you have snacks available and restrooms close by. Whatever the destination, it should provide children with opportunities for hands-on experiences.

Ceremonies

Keep ceremonies very simple and concrete. Use visuals whenever possible. Refrain from lecturing. Make sure the children are participating.

Y-Indian Guides/Princesses/ Maidens/Braves Program for the First Year (Kindergarten and First Grade)

Projects

During this first year the young Braves/Princesses/Maidens will have limited skills and dexterity. Crafts should be kept simple; you will need to help out a great deal. It is important for you to get to know each other, to tap each other's resources, and to understand the potential of the program. Activities should be related to the abilities of the five- to six-year-old.

Major emphasis should be placed upon making tribal property, such as the tribal drum, totem pole, rattles, and standards. Individual projects should include drawing and painting for decoration and the making of headbands, vests, or household aids.

Recreation

Play is a very important means for children's social and personal development. Games, songs, stories, and other recreational activities should help the children grow and hold their interest. Children need to learn appreciation of rules and the rights of others, and play is the primary arena for this learning. Outdoor hiking, trips, and family picnics are constructive activities.

Invitations

Invitations are very appropriate as a project and program activity. Children should be encouraged to express themselves through simple designs and colorful decorations.

Sports and Games

This is not the time for promoting organized games such as baseball, basketball, and football. Children of this age need to run, jump, and skip. They need help in riding a bicycle and in roller-skating. Focus on informal social recreation games with limited skill requirements.

Trips

Trips should expose children to new experiences and foster new ideas. Destinations should include visits to the zoo, aquarium, dairy, farm, museum, and park. Technical explanations should be kept to a minimum. Learning about animals from firsthand experience is very exciting and attractive.

Ceremonies

Acquiring a feeling for special occasions is an important learning experience. During the first year you probably should adhere closely to the Y-Indian Guide Programs tribal council ceremonies outlined in this manual. Set an example for the children by establishing a climate of dignity and joy in the meetings.

FIRST YEAR

- Members get acquainted and lay the foundation.
- Parents lead the group.
- Children have short attention spans and limited skills.
- Children explore and test relationships.
- The program is oriented toward the individual.

Program for the Second Year (Second Grade)

Projects

The seven-year-old child should be more prepared for actual Indian-type crafts and lore. Projects might include armbands, Indian belts, vests, imitation campfires, new headbands, and anklets. It is important that all projects be done by both parent and child. What young Braves/ Princesses/Maidens do, you should do.

Recreation

Recreation at meetings should start to change. Let the children tell stories as well. Relay games and fun stunts are appropriate to this age group.

Invitations

Continue having the children make invitations as a project. They should be encouraged to take a more active part in planning and working than they might have in the first year.

Sports and Games

Some seven-year-olds are ready for active organized sports; others are not. Play games such as four-square and dodgeball, but don't make the rules too complicated. Don't focus strongly on learning skills. Allow the children to have fun; they'll start to pick up skills automatically. Swimming is an excellent activity for parents and children to share.

Trips

Children this age usually are not ready for long or involved trips. Take them to places where they can keep moving about. Their attention span is short. After a trip, recount what happened that was new or of special interest.

Ceremonies

Change any part of the program that no longer fits a need or interest. Add new ideas and discard the routine things that no longer serve a purpose. Appoint children to participate in specific roles.

Special Events

Family picnics or outings, parent-and-child banquets, fishing derbies, kite-flying events, and camp-outs are wonderful social-learning settings and communication experiences for both second- and third-year tribes.

SECOND YEAR

- Members build on new parent-child relationships.
- Children share in program responsibility.
- Children develop their basic motor skills.
- The group does more community exploration and takes more trips.
- The program is oriented toward nurturing concern for others.

Program for Third Year (Third and Fourth Grades)

Projects

Most children eight to nine years of age can do a fine job at handicrafts. It is important to keep the young Braves/Princesses/Maidens interested by providing a good program. Projects to consider are whittling, woodburning, basket weaving, soap carving, and making Indian costumes, beadwork, gourd rattles, pottery, soft metal crafts, and birdhouses. Parents should be strategic aides and consultants for this age group.

Recreation

Set some meetings aside just for crafts. Skip longer ceremonies and business meetings; try to accomplish a project during the evening. Allow the children to assume some leadership roles by having them tell stories or lead the tribe in songs. Continue encouraging and supporting the children with lots of praise.

It is important to make crafts in homes with adequate facilities. Therefore, decide which homes are suitable and schedule the meetings accordingly. Use the YMCA, parks, and camp for special events.

Invitations

By the third year, this practice may have worn a bit thin. However, the host team should still send out notices of the meeting. Use ingenuity and creativity to make the project of invitations fun for all.

Sports and Games

Some good parent-child games are possible, as long as you keep the emphasis on fun. Relays, bicycle contests, swim events, running and jumping contests, and the basics of team sports are possible activities.

Trips

Children this age may be getting interested in the why and how of things. Trips include more technical subjects, and the children gain real insights into how and why things work. Play to their interests. Visits to zoos or farms, nature centers, airports, docks, and science centers are fun and educational.

Ceremonies

Develop some of your own ideas. Spiritual expression can take on real meaning for the children. Poems, prayers, and music shared by children and parents can provide inspirational experiences.

THIRD YEAR

- Children participate in more advanced projects as their capabilities have grown.
- Children lead games, stories, and songs.
- The group supports peer-group relationships.
- The group has more camping adventures and participates in group service.
- Parents appraise their children's development.

PARENT EDUCATION

Opportunities exist at every step of the Y-Indian Guide Programs for parents to learn new skills. For example, parents may learn more about dealing with children the same age as their own son or daughter; working in groups; developing leadership; becoming expert at crafts; organizing, scheduling, and planning; and handling social relationships.

Tribes can also build into this program a design for more formal education, enlisting the professional help of YMCA staff and community consultants. Fathers, mothers, and families will recognize the areas in which they need more guidance on any specific topic as they continue to meet. Each tribe is best able to diagnose and plan for itself the kinds of educational projects that will be most satisfying.

RECOGNITION AND AWARDS

Recognition is important to children and parents alike. One way tribal accomplishments can be recognized is through words and expressions of praise. A smile from Dad or Mom, a pat on the back, a word of approval from the Chief—all can have real meaning. Another way tribe members can be recognized is through the granting of awards. While awards can be fun for both the giver and receiver, they have some dangers.

Tribes may feel pressured to develop award systems. It may be hard to decide upon fair guidelines and to avoid overemphasizing awards at the expense of enjoying the experience. Awards may become routine; not all games, events, and projects need to conclude with awards. In addition, young children often do not understand the meaning of awards. Honest praise from a parent can be more satisfying to a child than the presentation of a blue bead or feather.

Yet there are times when awards can be useful and necessary. The tribe may truly want to express esteem or appreciation in a concrete way. Honor in giving and honor in receiving is a part of American Indian culture.

Awards, if used in Y-Indian Guide Programs, should be available to all and should reflect personal growth and achievement, service to others, and full support of the tribe. They should not replace the real thrill and excitement of vibrant parent-child relationships and experiences. Honor in giving and receiving should be a crucial factor in any award or recognition ceremony. Parents will want to examine their feelings about recognition carefully before accepting an awards plan.

The following guidelines regarding gamesmanship and awards may be helpful to your tribe:

- In team play, help everyone feel like a winner.
- Do not strive for awards but for involvement.

- Set your mind on the game or project, not on gaining personal attention.
- Be concerned with the value and teachings of the game, not with the score. Acknowledge and celebrate when children display the positive values of caring, honesty, respect, and responsibility.
- Accept an award with honor and present the next award with the same seriousness.

Indian Theme

$\mathcal{T}$he American Indian contributed greatly to our nation's Bill of Rights, introduced western Europeans to many new and important foods, originated new art and craft forms, and provided a living example of the courageous, self-sufficient individual in the wilderness. Yet most parents and children have little knowledge of the significant contributions by American Indians to our nation's history and heritage. The Y-Indian Guide Programs provide families with opportunities to learn about the American Indian culture and way of life. Parents and children will have a common base for interaction and learning, and tribes will gain a sense of unity and a foundation for productive activity.

AMERICAN INDIAN CULTURAL VALUES AND PROGRAM DEVELOPMENT

The American Indian cultural theme gives the non-Indian parent a common interest and learning experience in working with a young child. As parents and children learn about and use Indian arts, crafts, games, songs, and stories, they gain a deeper appreciation for the achievements of another culture. Understanding people who have a different way of life builds strength, tolerance, openness, and wisdom among parents and children alike.

The genuine concern among Indian people for parent responsibility in teaching and guiding their sons and daughters to adulthood is a fine standard for non-Indian parents and children to live by in contemporary society. Teaching values, proper attitudes, fitness, knowledge, and ethics to the child is an integral part of the Indian way of life. Some of their strongest values include the following:

- A profound sense of responsibility for the well-being of all family members. They share their possessions with those who are in need.

- A high moral sense of human dignity and honor. Their given word is sacred, and honesty in all dealings is highly prized.

Tribes should follow these steps as they participate in Y-Indian Guide Programs.

- Take time to learn about American Indians. Visit your local library for accurate information.

- Be sincere and look for the authentic in Indian culture—crafts, symbols, clothing.

- Recognize that Indians live today, not just in the past, and that each tribe is different.

- Solicit American Indian counsel to help you in your studies and tribal activities.

- Respect Indian-based ceremonies and religion.

- Support projects of human need and rights for Indian youth and families.

- Use your best judgment and taste in wearing Indian clothing and jewelry.

- Resourcefulness in using whatever nature has provided and gratitude for the blessings of nature.
- Physical endurance and personal self-control. Children are taught patience and self-control as part of their way of life.
- A high priority on things of the spirit. Their appreciation for the Creator is evident in their religion, traditions, and way of life.
- A deep understanding that all things in nature are interdependent. They realize we must conserve resources and eliminate waste so that future generations will enjoy the natural world the Creator has given us.
- Love of beauty, craftsmanship, and artistic skill. These qualities are honored in every tribe.
- Joy in games and sports. The primary stress is placed on involving all members of the tribe rather than on striving for awards.

The exact nature and content of each Y-Indian tribe's activity will vary considerably as its members seek to develop a program related to the needs and interests of all parents and children. However, there seems to be a certain magic for both parent and child as they share a campfire together; listen to the stories of the Iroquois; sleep in a hogan, chickee, or tepee; share in making Navajo jewelry; paddle a canoe; or play a Choctaw game.

The past and present culture of American Indians challenges parents in two ways: (a) to be aware of their roles as parent, guide, friend, and example for their children; and (b) to develop young boys' and girls' natural curiosity and enthusiasm for life.

THE AMERICAN INDIANS' CULTURAL HERITAGE

The name *Indian* was applied to native Americans by a Spanish explorer who mistakenly thought they were inhabitants of an Asian land. Today, an Indian is a person recognized as such by the Indian tribe with which he or she claims affiliation. A tribe is identified as a group of people, bound together by blood ties, who are socially, politically, and/or religiously organized and who usually speak a common language or dialect. On the basis of this definition, there are an estimated 6,716,000 American Indians living in the United States at this time, with slightly more than one-half of them on reservations and the rest in various cities throughout the country.

According to non-Indian scholars, the American Indian has lived on the North American continent for at least 10,000 years and probably for 35,000 years. At the time of Columbus's arrival in 1492, it is estimated that the Indian population was 834,000, although it had declined sharply to about 243,000 at the beginning of the twentieth century. Some 428 different tribes, bands, and groups have been recorded in the United States, representing a wide diversity of languages and customs.

There have been, and are today, many different American Indian tribes. Each tribe has lived according to its own distinct culture, language, habits, and customs. The food, shelter, arts, crafts, and clothing of each tribe depended on the materials available in their areas.

Six main groups of Indians, present at the time of the Europeans' arrival, have been identified on the basis of how they obtained their food:

- *Eastern Woodsmen:* from Maine to Florida, from the Atlantic past the Mississippi River, and from the Great Lakes and eastern Canada to the Gulf of Mexico.
- *Hunters of the Plains:* west of the Mississippi River to the Rocky Mountains.
- *Northern Fishermen:* along the Pacific Coast from northern California to southern Alaska.
- *Village Dwellers of the Southwest:* Arizona and New Mexico.
- *Nomads of the Southwest:* Arizona and New Mexico.
- *Seed Gatherers:* southern Rockies, Utah, southern California, and Nevada.

At the same time, seven American Indian cultural areas have been identified on the basis of language. (See map above.) These categories are similar to those based on food sources.

Culture areas and approximate location of American Indian tribes. (Courtesy of the Indian Arts and Crafts Board, U.S. Department of the Interior.)

Today, the distinctions among the various American Indian tribes are even more pronounced. They do not form a single, unified minority group. There are important differences among tribes, pueblos, and bands. Variations in customs, language, tradition, attitudes, behavior, beliefs, and values are frequently marked between urban and reservation Indians; traditionalist, Christian, and Native American Church members; and full-blood and mixed-blood Indians.

THE AMERICAN INDIAN TODAY

The family group is the basic unit of American Indian society. Several family groups form a clan; several clans comprise a band. A tribe is usually composed of multiple bands. Tribes are part of a nation, such as the Apache Nation.

A few groups still live much as their ancestors did, whereas others live like their non-Indian neighbors in the city or on a reserva-

tion. Most live with a mixture of traditional and modern ways of life.

Indian children are required to go to school. They attend public schools, mission or private schools, or federal government day and boarding schools.

Although many Indians are bilingual, some know only their tribal language. For some Indian children, it has been difficult to progress in schools where only English is used.

Most American Indians living on reservations engage in farming, fishing, stock-raising, timber production, or arts and crafts. Their average standard of living is very low, however, and unemployment in most areas is high. Contrary to popular belief, Indians do not receive automatic payments from the government.

Indians are United States citizens. They may vote and hold office like other Americans. They work, worship, and travel without restrictions. Many Indian leaders have gained success in government, education, law, art, and business and have made important contributions to this nation.

The American Indian population is increasing in spite of serious health problems, among them infectious respiratory diseases, pneumonia, tuberculosis, and trachoma. Poverty, alcoholism, and a high suicide rate among youth are also serious problems.

All Y-Indian Guide Program tribes will want to acquaint their members with the current plight of the American Indian. Fathers, mothers, sons, and daughters need to understand the serious problems that face Indian families living in the cities as well as on the reservations.

One of the greatest tragedies in American history has been the mistreatment of the Indian. Chicanery, disrespect, and paternalism have marked America's dealings with the Indians and have brought great dismay to many genuinely concerned citizens. Y-Indian Guide Program families can help bring new understanding and change to a persistent problem in our nation's history.

AMERICAN INDIAN ORGANIZATIONS

The Bureau of Indian Affairs in the U.S. Department of the Interior is responsible for the trusteeship over most Indian lands and for provision of public services to Indian people. However, many tribes and reservations west of the Mississippi River are under state jurisdiction. The Bureau of Indian Affairs, through its Tribal Operations Offices (see Appendix for listing), can be a helpful resource for information about American Indian tribes.

In order to advance the rights and culture of American Indians, the following important national organizations have emerged along with many other regional and local units. (Addresses for these organizations are available in the Appendix.)

- American Indian Historical Society
- Honor Our Neighbors' Origins and Rights (H.O.N.O.R.)
- American Indian Movement (AIM)

- National Congress of American Indians (NCAI)
- National Indian Youth Council (NIYC)
- National Tribal Chairman's Association (NTCA)

These organizations can be helpful resources to local YMCAs that are interested in the current struggle, concerns, and needs of American Indian youth and families.

PRECAUTIONS FOR THE USE OF AMERICAN INDIAN CULTURE

Because Y-Indian Guide Programs have drawn heavily on the culture and customs of American Indian tribes, YMCA lay and staff program leaders must try to represent the American Indians' contributions to our nation's life and history accurately and positively. The following guiding principles are presented for consideration and implementation by local YMCA boards and parent-child program leaders. They are designed to strengthen Y-Indian tribal programs, special events, and community interpretation. These principles are fundamental to understanding the American Indian people.*

- *An American Indian is a human being.* Scripts, films, program pageants, and youth activities that portray American Indians and their life-style, culture, and customs should be carefully evaluated for appropriateness. Do they fully express the Indians' humanity?

- *American Indian religion is sound.* Each tribe had its own beliefs, which evolved over many thousands of years. These religious beliefs served American Indians both in times of plenty and in times of need; they were sacred and meaningful to each tribe, and must be treated with respect and reverence.

---

*This statement was adapted from an outline prepared by the Urban Indian Development Association of Los Angeles and presented at the 35th National Longhouse Convention in Pittsburgh on April 23, 1972. Charles C. Kujawa, National Consultant.

- *American Indian morals are of long standing.* The morals of the true American Indians were very idealistic. Each tribe had its own standards, which were strictly observed. The moral decline among some Indian tribes began with the introduction of liquor and dishonorable trading practices by whites.

- *Indian customs have special meaning.* Various Indian tribes observed many colorful and meaningful customs, and each tribe adhered to its own culture and beliefs. Misrepresentation of these would constitute a grave injustice to the American Indian.

- *The languages of American Indians are graphic.* Each tribe spoke its own dialect and took great pride in oratory. The language used was both poetic and expressive. However, it is advisable to use the English language when portraying the American Indian. Today, few understand the Indian languages, and fewer still portray them correctly, thus making the Indian appear inarticulate. Words such as "how" and "ugh" were not part of the Indian vocabulary and should never be used.

- *Indian music and songs portray Indian life.* Music and song played a large part in the lives of American Indians. Through them, Indians expressed their religious beliefs, offered thanks to the Great Spirit, summoned the council, and served their personal and social needs. Music and songs were not taken lightly; thus, whenever used, they should be authentic and should accurately convey the intended meaning.

Indian dances are highly expressive. Dance also provided Indians with recreation and self-expression, relating deeds and events of importance to the Indians. Many dances represent birds and animals from which they were adopted; they were always used with great care and ceremony. Many dances also served to keep the Indians in the good physical condition necessary for their survival.

- *Indian costumes were symbolic.* Costumes were very colorful, with many depicting the birds, animals, and flowers of the area in which the tribe lived. They should be depicted with authenticity.

- *The American Indian has a point of view.* Whenever written materials, scripts, telecasts, and visual aids concerning the American Indian are set forth, they should be made from the Indian point of view. Their values should be considered; their traditions respectfully upheld. Their interpretation of history should also be presented.

- *Indian leadership can create Indian roles.* Society has bypassed the American Indian. Non-Indians make and import Indian crafts, and produce and play the roles of Indians in motion pictures and TV programs about the American Indian. Non-Indians have also written and shaped Indian history and culture. There are many highly skilled and qualified American Indians who could have filled these roles. Unfortunately, the Indians have been alienated while their rich heritage has been exploited.

- *There is a real danger in stereotyping.* Hollywood's stereotype of the American Indian is a gross distortion. Ironically, this image is presented by the mass media to the public, who accept it as the truth. The motion picture industry and other groups, therefore, must take great care to present an accurate portrayal of American Indian heritage. Each Indian is an individual with individual mannerisms, guided by tribal beliefs and customs. YMCA Indian Guide groups should beware of perpetuating stereotypes of Indians in their newsletters, parades, and tribal activities.

- *Indian names should engender respect.* Names such as squaw, buck, and chief are often used as nicknames: The Indian finds this degrading. Indians should be addressed with respect, by their proper names. Titles used in publicity and other materials should be respectful to Indians. Epithets such as "drunken Indian" must be avoided; they tend to label the whole Indian nation. In every case one must be discreet in the use of titles, considering how they relate to the well-being of, and respect for, the American Indian.

- *The Indian was not the aggressor in United States history.* Often American Indians are depicted as the aggressors in pictures, books, and films. It should be remembered that the white settlers and fur traders encroached upon the Indians, threatening their very existence and disregarding their hunting grounds and their rights as the original inhabitants of the land. Indians fought back against these intrusions. It was honorable to defend their homeland, as it is honorable to keep our nation free today. Therefore, it is not accurate to show the Indian always as the aggressor. In contrast, they should be shown as the defenders against white intruders who gave no consideration to the Indian way of life.

- *The American Indian was not a savage.* Many films, TV series, and books refer to the American Indian as a savage race. This abuse of the Indian culture is not accurate, and it should cease. The American Indians had established a very colorful and functional society. Unfortunately, the white race in most cases did not take time to learn and appreciate the Indian way of life.

YMCA lay and staff leaders are urged to use these guidelines in YMCA parent-child programs, policies, and practices; to establish small task groups for developing continuing educational and interpretive program opportunities for children and families, and to open up direct communication with nearby local Indian tribal councils for joint planning and sharing.

Responsible Use of the Native American Theme

A quick reference list: How is your program doing?

Do	Don't
Stay focused on the program's main goal and objectives: to strengthen the relationship between one parent and one child.	Don't make the Indian theme the program's main focus.
If the Y-Indian Guide Program is too controversial for your YMCA, consider alternative parent-child programs.	Don't give up on building parent-child relationships by discarding the programs when they are challenged. Don't restrict the theme to the American Indian culture.
Portray Native Americans as they are today. They have many of the same needs, successes, and problems as caucasians and may be more similar to modern caucasians than their ancestors were. Children have no frame of reference other than what we share with them. They need to know Native Americans are alive and well and living in their communities. Find a balance between the Native Americans of the past and Native Americans today.	Don't focus only on Indians of the past. This tactic often reinforces inaccurate, offensive stereotypes.
If part of your program includes having participants adopt Indian names, make sure it is done with the utmost respect. Be authentic and sensitive and make sure that the names that are selected reflect strong character and set goals. Make the names meaningful instead of mere nicknames.	Don't haphazardly select a name or choose one that mocks the individual or Native Americans. Don't choose a name that is funny, stereotypical, or cute.
Indian costumes are symbolic. Today, Native Americans only use headdresses in ceremonies and always with great respect. If you use costumes, use them sparingly. A vest and headband without feathers may be more appropriate.	Don't make dressing up and "playing Indian" the focus of activities and celebrations. This behavior often backfires, especially in parades and mall events.

(continued)

Do	Don't
Religion is sacred to Native Americans. To some tribes the key to the Indian's being is deep spirituality that permeates the whole life. It is the skein that binds the culture and makes life meaningful. YIG programs must respect the paraphernalia that is connected to religion or has a spiritual value. Using religious items out of context is inappropriate.	Don't make light of or misuse items that have a strong spiritual or religious connotation, such as totem poles, drums, tepees, gourds, medicine bags, medicine men, sacred masks, bear claws and teeth, tribal chants, and the white buffalo.
Select authentic, respectful games and activities. Ask yourself "Does this honor or offend? Does it denigrate Indian culture? Is this a stereotype?"	Avoid stereotypical Indian games and activities from Hollywood: war whooping, tomahawk chops, war dances, war (face) paint, and games like "steal the scalp." Native Americans are no longer at war, and they never were savages or aggressors.
Take time to research the Native American tribes you emulate in your program. Visit the library, museums, schools, and book stores, and go on-line to conduct research. Contact Native Americans or Native American advocacy groups for information.	Don't fall back on stereotypical images. For example, refrain from speaking in broken English or using the words "ugh" or "how." Indians never spoke in such a way. Words or phrases such as "red skins," "restless natives," "wild Indians," "squaw," and "buck" are never appropriate.
If you use costume, dance, or ceremonies, make sure you've done your research and they are authentic and appropriate to the occasion. Too often we mix tribal customs and ceremonies, and the end product is inaccurate and offensive.	Don't combine the dress, traditions, rituals, and ceremonies of different tribes. Select one tribe, research it, and make sure that your portrayal is authentic.
Refer to campfire ceremonies as Y-Indian Guide ceremonies.	Don't refer to ceremonies as "the Sioux nation (or other Indian name) ceremony." It is difficult to be totally authentic and is best not to suggest that the presentation is, in fact, a ceremony of that nation. For example, instead of a "Dakota sweat lodge ceremony," just call it a sweat bath.
Be flexible. Make the program work for you.	Don't feel compelled to run the program exactly as it's written in *Friends Always*. If local Native Americans tell you terms like "lodges" are more appropriate than "tribes," or "elder" is a more accurate reflection of leadership in a small group, feel free to make changes.

Invitations

$\mathcal{E}$very parent-child team gets several turns in the course of a year to make and deliver invitations. This task is often considered a bother rather than a good opportunity to achieve Y-Indian Guide purposes. The following suggestions can help make creating invitations a time for parents and children to work together and to learn more about tribal and Native Indian lore.

- Choose a theme for the invitation that relates to the program or nature. It need not be elaborate or realistic.

- Design an invitation that both you and your child can work on together. For example, a paper tepee that the little Brave/Princess/Maiden has decorated is much better than a real leather one that Mom or Dad created alone.

- Keep the project simple so that the task of making invitations for the whole tribe is not too lengthy or difficult.

- Allow enough time, probably two evenings, so that the project will be fun and the little Brave/Princess/Maiden will have invitations he or she can be proud of.

- Try out invitations that will encourage the other parents and children to work together also, such as putting one bell on a rawhide thong along with a tag telling the meeting time and place. By adding more bells and some fur or leather, parents and children can make this invitation into ankle bells.

- Use authentic Indian sign language and symbols as much as possible (see illustration below).

COUNCIL   (at)   TEPEE   (of)   BIG FOX   and   LITTLE FOX   12th

SUN (DAY)   THUNDER MOON (July)   7:30   (at)   NIGHT.

- If you have exhausted the ideas presented in this manual, additional resources are available at your YMCA or local library.

- Deliver the invitation to each home together with your son or daughter. Talk with your child about what it means to be a host, and the fun you had in making the invitations.

IDEAS FOR MEETING INVITATIONS

Scissors, paper, and crayons can give you an endless variety of invitation designs and do not require much of your time. Here are some good ideas that other tribes have used:

Paint brush	Headdresses
Stretched hide	Leaves
Sun, moon, or stars	Feathers
Animal tracks	Seasonal symbols
Animal that represents Indian name of host	Animal silhouettes
	Pottery
Stick-on stars in familiar constellations	Drums
	Navajo designs
Shirts	Shields
Campfires	Snowshoes
Trees	Peace pipe
Moccasins	Corn
Tools (for handicraft meetings)	Totem poles
	Arrowheads
Indian silhouettes	Wooden paddle
Tepees	Bookmarker
Tomahawks	Birch bark card
Arrows	
Quivers	

If you want to get fancy, you can incorporate some of the following ideas into your own projects: straw bundles, miniatures such as a bow-and-arrow set, moccasins stitched with embroidery thread, wooden knives, and tomahawk or drum cutouts. An inverted, cone-shaped paper cup with a bit of red-dyed cotton batting for a fire makes a realistic tepee. Also, objects from nature such as feathers, leaves, unusual rocks, shells, bones, and pinecones make excellent invitations.

A very successful meeting has been built around a plaster mold invitation that was brought to the meeting and painted. Another good idea was a lollipop with a paper face, and hair attached with tape.

INVITATIONS TO MAKE

The following ideas for invitations have provided parents and children with hours of creative fun and learning opportunities. Try your hand at any one of these designs. They are constructed from materials you may have around the house or can obtain easily such as aluminum foil, balsa wood, boxes, cans, cardboard, cork, leather, paper, pipe cleaners, plastic, rubber, and paper.

Potato Print Invitation

Cut a small potato in half. Have your little Brave/Princess/Maiden draw a design or message on a piece of paper and cut it out to fit the potato. Lay it in the center of the cut side of the potato. Incise the edges of the design about 1/2" deep with a small knife. Remove the background a bit at a time until the design stands out. Color the design using a stamp pad or painting food coloring on the design with a brush. Press the design down on the paper you have selected for printing the invitations; then lift the design straight up.

Remember, designs will print in reverse, so make sure you spell any words on the design backwards so that they read in the right direction. You and your child could each make a design and print them in two colors on paper that has been cut into the shape of an animal pelt or tepee. This is lots of fun and simple!

Cork Alligator

String various-sized corks from head to tail with wire or hairpins. Slit the tail cork to insert a stiff paper tail. Use tacks for eyes and legs. Make a slit in the head cork for the mouth. Put the invitation in the mouth.

Scroll

Split two sticks, each about 3/4" in diameter and 6" long, lengthwise. After inserting the ends of your scroll paper between the two split sides, tack or glue the sticks back together to hold the paper firmly. Write your invitation on the scroll. Decorate the four ends of sticks with colored twine, feathers, and the like.

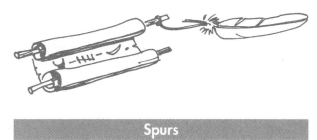

Spurs

Cut two strips from flexible cardboard 1" wide and 13" long. Make a notch at each end of the strips for fastening around the ankle. Have your child make designs and write the invitation on the spurs. You can also paste aluminum foil on the rowel of the spur to make it look more realistic.

The Turtle That Swims

This is an invitation that will have them talking! Draw and cut out a paper turtle from notebook paper. Make a small round hole in the center of the turtle and cut a narrow slit leading from the center hole to the tail. Dip the lower half of the turtle into water. Lay the turtle gently on the surface of the water in a bowl or tub. To make it swim, drop a little oil (1 or 2 drops) into the hole. The oil will start to spread through the slit and the turtle will move forward. In the invitation, your little Brave/Princess/Maiden can promise to make the Indian turtle swim following refreshments.

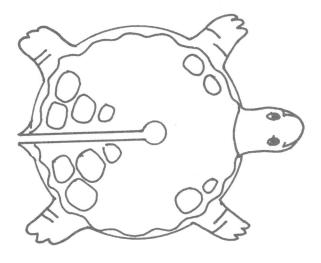

Eskimo Igloo

This can also be a fun short tribal project. Take half of an eggshell or a "L'eggs" (stockings) eggshell package and draw lines on it with a pencil to represent blocks of snow. Paint a little entrance at the bottom. Dip the bottom edge of the shell in glue and place it on a piece of cotton, or have the whole tribe whip up a village on a larger piece of cotton. You can follow with a story about the Eskimos.

Skinning Knife

Get tongue depressors from the drugstore and trace the outline of a skinning knife on the wood. Cut or sand excess wood away and sand an edge on the blade. The handle can be decorated by woodburning, wrapping it in colored string, or painting on designs.

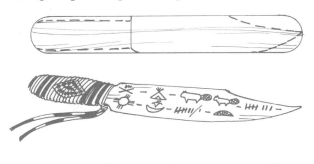

Arrows

Use a small stick or dowel for the shaft of the arrow and cut a slot in one end. Cut out an arrowhead from drawing paper, print the invitation on it, and insert the paper in the shaft slot. Make arrow feathers out of paper, yarn, or bird feathers.

Arrowheads

Cardboard, aluminum sheeting, wood, paper, Styrofoam, or even a rock may be used as the base material for arrowheads. The invitation can be decorated with colorful paints or stamped with a metal punch.

Canoe

For this design you'll need a piece of 4" × 6" heavy paper. Fold the paper in half lengthwise and draw the canoe design on the paper with the bottom of the canoe along the fold. Cut the canoe out and glue the ends together. Have two wooden matchsticks on hand to use as seats. Print the invitation on the outside of the canoe, then glue the two matchsticks near the bow and stern.

Alternative: Use a 6" piece of balsa wood to make a dugout canoe. Instruct your child in the proper use of a carving knife before you begin cutting. You can use a woodburning tool both to decorate and to print the invitation.

Drum

A small can (those used for tomato paste, baby food, etc. are ideal) is the drum base with rubber or leather stretched across the top and bottom. The rubber or leather may be tied or glued on, with the invitation printed on the top or sides.

Feather

This is a good beginning project for children and their parents. You can use paper for drawing or cutting out a feather. Inscribe the invitation with crayons or marking pens. You can also use felt flannel for the feather, with symbols cut out of different colors of felt and glued to the feather.

Headband

Designing a special invitation headband of leather, cloth, or paper can be fun for parent and child alike. The invitation written in Indian symbols provides a warm welcome to neighborhood friends.

Hide or Skin

Cut an 8" × 11" piece of leather, vinyl, or cloth in the shape of an animal hide. Paint symbols for the message in the center. Roll it up and put it in a tube or a wooden napkin ring for carrying.

Alternative: Stretch the hide out flat between 4 twigs and tie them with thread or twine.

Log Chip

Saw a 4"-diameter fireplace log into pieces about 1/2" thick. Inscribe the invitation on the face of the chip with a woodburning tool or paint.

Travois

Obtain a small plastic horse. With small strips of adhesive tape, fasten 2 sticks to the horse (lollipop sticks work well), one on each side. Apply the tape so that it looks like a harness. Cut a piece of paper for the travois, write the invitation on it, and tape or glue the paper to both sticks.

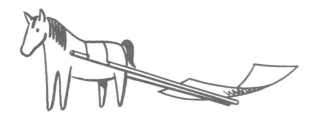

Map

Design an 8" × 11" map that gives directions to the host's home. You can use drawing paper, cardboard, cloth, or plywood. Create a legend to identify the symbols you use, if necessary. Let your imagination run free with this design.

Moccasin

A paper drawing or a 4" leather cutout of a moccasin works well. Decorate the cutout with beads or bells and paint or draw the message on the moccasin.

Necklace

Acorns, beads, or shells that have been collected on a trip to the woods, beach, or store can be strung together on waxed string or twine. Tie a message tag on one end.

Paddle

Cut the shape of a canoe paddle out of a thin wooden stick or shingle; then sand rough edges. Write the date, time, place of meeting, and hosts' names on the paddle blade. You can also use felt, cardboard, or tin in place of the wood.

Pinecones

Take a hike in the woods to collect pinecones or draw your own. Attach ribbon and bells to each pinecone along with a message tag. This design is a good holiday project. You can paint your real pinecones and add glitter to make them look more festive.

Quiver

Make a tube container from a juice can or paper roll. Decorate the outside with magazine picture cutouts or painted designs, felt, flannel, or aluminum foil. Attach a string carrier. Make an arrow from a small stick (see "Arrow" instructions on previous page) and attach the invitation to the arrow.

Snowman

A Styrofoam ball about 2" in diameter serves as the snowman's head. Its hat can be designed from paper or felt. Facial features of shiny colored paper can be pasted into place. The message is printed on small notepaper, folded over, and tucked into the top of the snowman's hat.

Tepee

Design a small tepee from a cone-shaped cup, bright construction paper, or aluminum foil. Insert three twigs or sticks for poles. Decorate with Indian symbols. Glue the tepee to a 4" × 6" cardboard base. Write your invitation on the base.

Tree Leaves

Use scrap pieces of colored leatherette, heavy construction paper, or bristol board for cutting out elm, maple, oak, basswood, ginko, poplar, or ash leaves to actual size. Trace in veins of the leaf. Inscribe the invitation on the leaf's blank side. In some cases, you can use actual leaves.

Animal or Bird Pictures

Use drawing paper, leather, or cardboard and paint or crayons. Draw a picture of a bear, deer, mountain lion, blue jay, or other animal or bird and cut out the design. Print your invitation on the cutout and decorate with Indian symbols or colored designs.

Animal Tracks

Draw beaver, bear, deer, dog, raccoon, or other animal tracks on cardboard, heavy construction paper, or plywood. Print the invitation across the track in bright colors.

Bookmarker

This is a good beginning project. Cut the bookmarker out of cloth, leather, or plastic. Depict the message on the bookmarker with Indian symbols.

Tribal Property

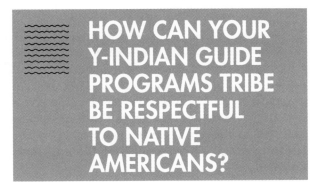

HOW CAN YOUR Y-INDIAN GUIDE PROGRAMS TRIBE BE RESPECTFUL TO NATIVE AMERICANS?

*P*revious editions of *Friends Always* have included suggestions for tribal property, dress, customs, dance, sign language, symbols, and activities. Many of these suggestions were based on the culture of the Plains Indians and were not applicable to all tribes. The result was that Y-Indian Guide participants adopted a tribe from the South, Southwest, West, or New England area and tried to fit Plains Indian customs and traditions into their tribal activities. This resulted in Y-Indian Guide tribes that were made up of a collection of customs from several tribes and were not true to any one particular American Indian tribe. This was inaccurate and disrespectful.

In writing this newest edition of *Friends Always*, we have left out some of these customs sections. It was impossible for us to anticipate which tribes local participants would adopt. Also, the number of American Indian tribes is vast; there was no way we could research and provide in this manual all of the genuine property, dress, customs, and dances for each tribe. Therefore, we encourage Y-Indian Guide tribes to take time to research the particular tribe they have adopted. This is a wonderful project for a meeting early in the program year. Here are

some suggestions for keeping your tribal traditions accurate:

1. Check with your local YMCA. The staff responsible for Y-Indian Guides may have reference materials for you to review. Staff members might also have the experiences of past participants to share with you. Many YMCAs have a Y-Indian Guide library and will have resources to offer.

2. Have your young Guides/Princesses/Maidens/Braves take some responsibility for the research by asking their school librarian for ideas and suggestions. The children can bring summaries of their research or reference books to a tribal meeting. Working together, parents and children can determine what tribal property would be appropriate, what customs are authentic, and what names or structure would be applicable for their particular tribe.

3. If your child strikes out at the school library or if you want to make it a family project or a tribal meeting, take the group to the public library. Review the resources and speak with the librarian.

4. The appendix of this manual includes a list of Native American organizations and Native American advocacy groups. As a tribal project, write to these organizations to ask for advice, information, and resources.

5. Another tribal event might be a trip to the bookstore. Using money collected in dues, purchase books about the tribe you have adopted.

6. Some museums have a Native American section, and some communities have

museums dedicated only to Native American people and culture. A parent-child visit or even a full tribe visit to the museum could give the tribe a chance to gather information it needs to make its program authentic and respectful.

7. It is amazing what you can access through the internet. Log on to the world wide web and visit the home pages of Native American organizations, the Library of Congress, other Y-Indian Guide Programs, and many other helpful resources.

8. Many of you may already know Native Americans from your communities, schools, and places of business. Ask these Native American friends, neighbors, and coworkers for help. Explain that out of sensitivity to the Native American culture, you want to make your use of the Native American theme respectful and accurate. Ask if they'd be available to speak at a tribal meeting or participate in a Nation event or camp-out. See if you can get the support of your Native American friends. You may find that they have quite a bit to offer to your tribe.

9. If you use the theme sparingly and are not interested in doing extensive research, you can probably get by if you assign someone in your tribe the responsibility for ensuring that your actions and activities are authentic and respectful.

Every Y-Indian Guide Programs tribe should make its own tribal property authentic to the tribe it has adopted, purchasing the material with the tribal wampum. Property is usually kept in the tribal property box. Following each meeting, the next host takes the property box to his or her home so that tribal property is always on hand at the site of each successive meeting.

Each parent and child should share some of the responsibility for making part of the tribal property. For example, the Tallykeeper makes the tallykeeper's book, the Wampum Bearer makes the wampum pouch, and so on. Two families might work together on the larger items. You can decide how the property is to be made in the parents' meetings. The important point is to get your property made as quickly as possible, with everyone sharing some of the responsibility.

BASIC TRIBAL PROPERTY

The basic tribal property for each tribe **may** include the following:

Totem pole	Council fire
Ceremonial Indian shield	Tribal property box
Wampum (money) pouch	Tallykeeper's book
Talking stick or rock	Coup stick
Tribal drum	Tribal standard

Totem Pole

Although original totems were carved out of huge tree trunks, in the Y-Indian Guide Programs, simpler methods are used. **First, we suggest that you do some research to find out exactly what design or styles were used by the Indians from whom your tribal name was adopted.**

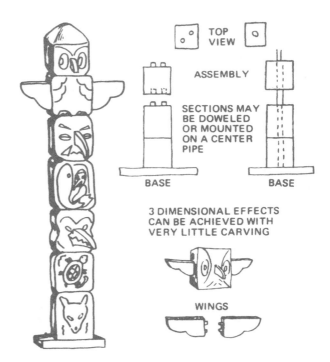

The totem pole may be one of the most important tribal properties (depending on the tribe your group has adopted). Each family decorates its own section. This section is taken to and from the council meeting by each family and placed on the totem at the beginning of the meeting. By placing your block on the totem, you indicate your presence at the council.

Totem poles can be made quite easily from one-gallon cans. These cans, when decorated, stand supported by a central dowel, and make a good first totem. As your tribe becomes more interested in crafts and wants to make a more ambitious totem pole, you might consider the following project.

One parent should take responsibility for going to the lumberyard and purchasing a piece of 6" × 6" lumber long enough so that each family in your tribe will have a section. We recommend a soft wood, like pine or redwood, that is easy to work with. If the parent does not have an electric saw, he or she should have someone at the lumberyard cut the wood into uniform lengths. The next step is to drill a hole 1/2" deep and 3/4" to 1" in diameter in each end of each length. A 3"-long dowel is then glued in the bottom hole so that the pieces can be stacked one on top of the other, with the dowels holding them in place.

Each family then receives its section. The son or daughter in the family should sand down the four sides for finishing. The totem is now ready for decorating. You may want to include your Y-Indian Guide Programs tribal name on one side of the totem, one letter to each block, if possible. Use your imagination in decorating the other sides with a woodburning tool or paints.

Make a base as a stand for the totem. The tribe may decide later to make a top piece, such as a spread eagle. We suggest that families not try difficult carvings. It is best to keep the totem pole simple and complete it as quickly as possible. Each family should bring its totem pole section to each meeting, even if they are still in the process of decorating it, so that members can share ideas and see how each family is progressing.

It is not essential that each tribe use the same materials or follow the patterns described above. In some cases, tribes have used nail kegs, lard cans, large (No. 10) vegetable cans, and many other items for totem poles. Originality is important in constructing tribal property.

Ceremonial Indian Shield

The following materials are needed for this project: stiff white cardboard (enough for a 16"-diameter circle); plywood circle of the same size; colored sand; four 6" feathers; fluff feathers; a large stick; dyed horse hair or colored yarn (optional); a drill or punching tool; a large stapler or hammer and nail; string; and glue.

Cut out a cardboard circle and glue it to a plywood circle for strength. Draw symbols representing tribal designs, individual names, or the seasons. Some tribes have each child draw out a representation of one of the six aims and explain in meetings what it means to him or her.

Cover the designs with bright sand painting (see instructions for sand painting in the "Crafts" section). Finish the shield by decorating it with feathers. Holes are punched to tie the feathers at the four corners, with 3" intervals between them. Four 6" feathers represent the four directions, the colors of which are North—yellow; East—red; South—blue; West—white. Smaller fluff feathers are hung from the holes between the four corners. Glue a tuft of dyed horse hair or colored yarn to the center of the shield if desired. Fasten a handle to the center of the back with a staple or nail.

You can also make these shields from canvas and paint them with oil paints. They are very colorful and add dignity and color to public affairs, particularly inductions, where they are mounted on tripods to be displayed. The National Longhouse has suggested that tribes may make these shields instead of totem poles.

Wampum (Money) Pouch

This is a container for holding the tribe's funds. Usually a drawstring is inserted to close the pouch. Decorate the pouch with beads and paint, using original designs created by both parent and child. The pouch can be either fastened on the belt or carried in the hand.

You can use chamois, imitation leather, or heavy felt to make the pouch. Sew the edges together with heavy thread. Insert cord or leather thong for the drawstring. Fringe the bottom, then decorate as desired. Other pouch designs are possible. Several types are suggested below.

Talking Stick or Rock

No two talking sticks or rocks are alike. This project can tap the creative imagination of the tribe. Using a stick or a strong, round rock found on a tribal hike, parents and children proceed to paint and decorate it with feathers, beads, leather, or other decorating materials.

The purpose of the talking stick or rock is to grant a tribal member permission to speak at a meeting. The person who is speaking holds it in his or her hands. Everyone else must listen until that person finishes. The talking stick or rock is then passed on to the next speaker. The stick or rock can also be placed in front of the member who is to speak.

Tribal Drum

The tribal drum is an indispensable piece of equipment for the tribe. Tribal participation in

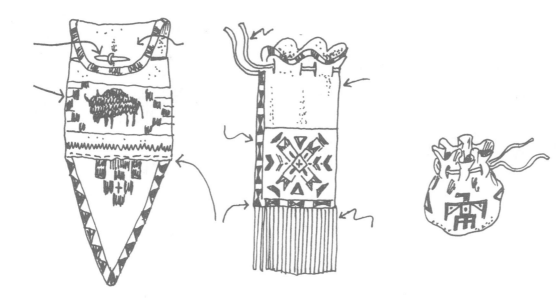

making the drum builds a strong feeling of ownership and teamwork. The drum is used regularly in meeting ceremonies, and it should not be considered a toy. The tribe should make and use it with care, for it is one of the principal Native American musical instruments.

There are several ways to make a tribal drum. You can make a good body for the drum from a clean, tight wooden nail keg, a round cheesebox, or a large tin can. Be sure to make the drum small enough to fit into the tribal property box (described later). Rawhide makes a good drum head. The rawhide should be about 2" or 3" larger than the diameter of the body. You can use any scraps left over from the head for thongs.

The body of the drum should be smooth; pad the ends over which the head will be stretched with a thin layer of cloth or soft leather. Seal any holes or leaks through which air may escape as tightly as possible in order to preserve the good tone of the drum.

Soak the rawhide in warm water for about 4 to 6 hours. Frequently changing the water helps remove dirt and other matter left on the hide. Cut two circles out of the rawhide that are a few inches larger in diameter than the diameter of the drum body. Then cut a series of small holes around each circle of rawhide 1" from the edge and 3" apart. These holes should be in the shape of a narrow "V" with the point facing the edge of the circle.

Place the body end down on one of the heads and cover other end with the other head. With thongs cut from scraps of wet rawhide, begin lacing diagonally through the holes cut in the heads. When the lacing reaches around to where you began, have someone hold the two thong ends together while you go back around and take up all the slack in the thong. Tie the loose ends together with a secure square knot.

Let the drum dry slowly and evenly. Coat the uncured rawhide with a protective layer of clear varnish to retard deterioration. Decorate the drum with Indian symbols or other designs.

Make a beater for the drum at the same time. First wrap cotton cord or gauze bandage around a supple stick about 12" long. When finished, wrap the cotton or gauze with strips of adhesive tape; then cover with a piece of soft leather. Decorate the stick with feathers or beads.

Council Fire

Gather some small sticks, 10" to 14" long and 1" to 2" in diameter. They may be live or dry, depending on what you can find. (Do not cut down a live tree or bush for this purpose.) Take six to ten sticks and stack them in the form of a tepee, a log cabin fire, or a combination of both. Screw, nail, or tie the sticks together.

Mount a light socket in the center of a 1/2" to 3/4" plywood base, and make sure the cord runs underneath the wood. Attach the sticks over the light socket. Use a small 25-watt red bulb to simulate a fire. The electric cord should be at least 12' to 14' long so that it will reach the center of any tribal council room. You can hold council around a campfire indoors with this device.

Tribal Property Box

This box should be large enough to hold all tribal property, yet small enough to handle easily. It should be a hinged, covered box with a latch so that it can be decorated. This box holds most of the tribal property, including totem pole, drum, campfire, and headbands. We recommend that you use plywood to construct this box. Even an old footlocker, painted and decorated, will make a very satisfactory chest. You may want to purchase a lock for the box as well.

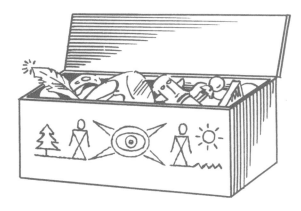

Tallykeeper's Book

Keep records of councils and meetings in this book. It can be constructed easily by the Tallykeeper and his or her child. Use 2 pieces of 1/2" plywood about 9" × 12" for the covers of the book. Drill two or three 1/4" holes along one side of both covers to accommodate loose-leaf sheets. Bind the covers together with leather thongs. Decorate the covers with a woodburning tool or paints and inscribe the tribal name on the front.

This book can also be used as the tribal scrapbook. Collect pictures of trips, outings, family events, and special activities to keep as a history of the tribe. It will grow in value as the months and years go by.

Coup Stick

Some Indian tribes used the coup stick to welcome guests and show them hospitality. It was displayed *outside* the home. To others it was used to touch the enemy during a battle. Research how coup sticks were used by the tribe you have adopted. If appropriate, make the coup sticks by securing a 3' to 4' dowel or stick. The coup stick should be pointed at one end. Decorate the stick with a totem head, feathers (6" long), colored yarn, fur, painted designs, and the like.

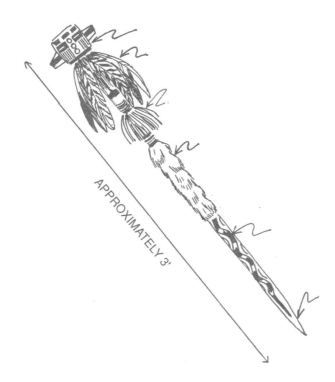

APPROXIMATELY 3'

Some Indians also used these sticks to indicate ownership. When moving from one hunting ground to another, they would drive the stick into the ground to mark their hunting areas as well as places where they had left their possessions. Other Indians, seeing the coup stick, knew at once by the decorations the name and tribal affiliation of the owner.

Tribal Standard

Some tribes use the tribal standard to identify themselves at Longhouse events, special ceremonies, and camp-outs. Each parent and child can help make and decorate the staff and shield or banner. Select a pole or sapling about 4' long for the standard and banner. Attach a plywood shield or cloth banner; then paint tribal emblems and history on the standard. A colorful, attractive standard is a symbol of the tribe's unity.

DRESS AND ACCESSORIES

Although costumes are not mandatory, they establish a sense of unity in the tribe and help participants get into the spirit of the program. Each tribe may decide on a costume, material, and style, and each parent and child can then make their own. The costume itself is not as important as the sharing and enjoyment that parents and children experience in making it.

The costumes may include vests, dresses, shirts, decorations, shields, and jewelry. The clothing may be full dress with beads, fringe, and feathers or a simple cape or vest cut out of a gunnysack. You can also use a cotton-polyester blend or muslin (unbleached) as costume material. Try to choose a fabric that is easy to sew and that requires little or no ironing.

Vest

To make the vest, you will need 1 yard of material for each parent and child—use either flannel, denim, canvas, rayon, suede, leather, or wool. Use 3 yards of 1/2" red flannel or bias tape for seam binding. Obtain yarn or embroidery cotton for designs and fringe (optional).

Trace a vest pattern on wrapping paper to fit each parent and child, one piece for the back and two for the front of the vest. Pin the pattern together and fit it to the wearer, making adjustments where needed.

Trace the pattern onto the material and cut it out. Pin the pieces together and add the red flannel or bias tape as a seam binder. Decorate the vests and add fringe as desired. Each parent-child team can have its own design and pattern, or a tribe may develop similar vests to build unity in the group.

Trophy Shirt

Get 1/2 yard of brown denim or flannel, flannel scraps for designs, 12 grommets, and 24" of leather thong for fringe (optional).

Trace a pattern on wrapping paper and cut out to size, including a center head space. Pin the pattern on the material and cut out. Insert 12 grommets along the lower sides for lacing. Sew on Y-Indian Guide emblem, name patch, or other designs. Add fringe on the bottom if desired.

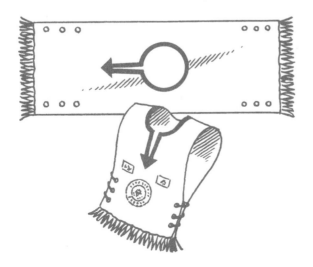

Name Badge

You will need leather scraps, a ballpoint pen or woodburning tool, scissors, and a safety pin. Make a pattern for your tribal emblem out of cardboard (e.g., arrowhead, tomahawk, animal). Trace the pattern on leather and cut it out. Decorate and put the tribe's or child's name on the badge with either a ballpoint pen or a woodburning tool. Sew the safety pin on the back. You can also cut two slits in the top of the badge and thread a leather thong through them to drape the badge around the neck.

Pendant

Pendants are similar to name badges. To make them you will need water-based clay, a pencil or pointed stick, and a 10-penny nail. Roll the clay until you have a round ball about the size of a large marble. Flatten the ball on a smooth, hard surface such as a kitchen countertop or cutting board. Smooth the edges with a wet finger. Draw an animal head or Indian symbol on the top surface.

When the design is finished, wet the nail, and gently push it through the clay to make a hole for the leather thong to pass through. Let the pendant dry, at least overnight. Paint the pendant with bright colors, if desired. The pendant also can be fired in a kiln to make it stronger.

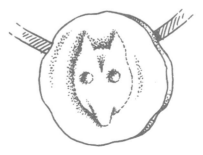

Rattles

Good rattles can be made out of cow horn, gourd, tin cans, or turtle shell. You will also need 1"-diameter doweling 12" to 18" long, one dozen dried peas or small pebbles, leather or other material for covering the rattle, leather thong for lacing, glue, paint, yarn tassels, and feathers. Drill holes in the tin can, gourd, or shell to insert the dowel handle. Insert pebbles or dried peas and the dowel. Glue or lace the cloth or leather rattle covering over the tin can, gourd, or shell. Decorate with paints, tassels, or feathers.

Costume Belt

You can make a decorative belt of leather, plywood, or metal. You will also need twine or a leather thong, paint, and a woodburning tool or metal or leather stamping tools. The material should be cut into enough squares to encircle the wearer's waist. Punch or drill 4 holes in each square. Paint, burn, or stamp a design on each square; then lace them together.

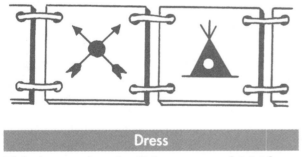

Dress

This is a project for Princesses and Maidens. The dress requires approximately 3 1/2' × 36" material, preferably something durable such as bleached muslin, burlap, denim, or sail-cloth. The material should be twice the length from the wearer's shoulders to her calf or ankle. Choose a bright color like red, blue, or green.

Start by making a pattern from a simple kimono-sleeved dress, or use an extra large paper bag. Cut a hole in the bag large enough to slip over the wearer's head easily; also cut out armholes in the sides of the bag. Check and mark the width of the shoulders for comfort. Add enough width on each side to make the sleeves the desired length. Cut and fit the pattern to the wearer from under the arms to the hemline. All Indian dresses should fit loosely.

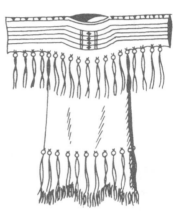

Lay the entire pattern out on the full length of the material. Then cut the material 1" wider than the pattern to allow for seams.

Fold the material at the shoulders and sew the seams on the wrong side. Sew from the end of the sleeves to the hemline on both sides before turning the dress right-side out.

Hem around the neck, sleeves, and bottom of the dress. Sew 6"-long fringe of soft leather, leatherette, or plastic to the bottom of the sleeves and the skirt.

Sew decorated bands to form a triangle on the front of the dress at the neck. If fringe is desired on the decorative bands, sew it on the bands before sewing them on the dress.

Ceremonies

*C*eremonies add drama and interest to programs, highlighting points of commitment or recommitment to program principles. To be effective, ceremonies should be short and should require those involved to participate actively. They should be predictable, and all participants should prepare beforehand so the ceremony can proceed as smoothly as possible.

The following ceremonies include prayers, installation and induction ceremonies, campfire and candlelighting ceremonies, and graduation and camp-out ceremonies. All are appropriate for both Y-Indian Guide Programs and the alternative parent-child programs included in the last section of this manual. Feel free to modify the ceremonies to reflect your own terminology and customs, substituting for the words in the brackets as needed and changing or adding other wording as desired. For example, substitute "band" for "tribe" when inducting new members into the Voyagers program.

PRAYERS

As with the ceremonies, feel free to modify prayers to reflect your group's terminology and customs, substituting the words in the brackets as needed or otherwise changing the wording to fit your situation.

[O Great Spirit], do not keep us from your sight. Teach us your way on this day. Make this [Nation] and its [tribes] full of strength and wisdom. Show us our most productive path. Make our hearts aware of your presence here among us. Maker of all life, spark the lives of those around us.

_ _ _ _ _ _ _ _ _ _ _ _ _ _

[O Great Spirit], the [fathers] and [sons] of this [tribe] offer you their thanks for the opportunity of meeting here in a spirit of companionship. We pray for your guidance in the leadership of this [tribe]. May these [Guides] be blessed with wisdom, patience, sacrifice, and acceptance so they may recognize each other's worth as people. May the circle of their [tribe] be as strong as the sacred circle of their families. May they live in mutual harmony with their community and seek a world pleasing to your sight.

_ _ _ _ _ _ _ _ _ _ _ _ _ _

[Great Spirit], be with us during this ceremony. Watch over us and bless us as we [trade our kernels of corn], [father to son] and [son to father], showing each other our love, as you show your love through all creation.

_ _ _ _ _ _ _ _ _ _ _ _ _ _

(Facing North) [O Great Spirit], Grandfather of the North, from whence comes the long nights and white snows, make smooth the paths of all those who voyage. May they reach the end of their journey in health and achieve the wisdom they need. Send your buffalo to sustain them.

(Facing East) [O Great Spirit], Grandfather of the East, where the sun always rises, send your vision that they may see far and wide. May they be illuminated through their travels. Send your golden eagle to guide them on their way.

(Facing South) [O Great Spirit], Grandfather of the South, from whence come warm breezes, grant them perception of the nature of the hearts. May they feel the obvious and see what is just in front of them, in innocence and trust, like a child. Send your mouse in the green field as an example to them.

(Facing West) [O Great Spirit], Grandfather of the West, where the sun always sets, remind them to spend a time in their looks-within place before each sunset. May they review and reflect on their daily voyage. Send them your black bear of introspection.

(Slowly turning right and left) [O Great Spirit], Grandfather of all that is, we thank you for your four great gifts, and ask that we be balanced with

them. May we have wisdom and balance with feeling, touching, and compassion. May we have illumination and insight and vision, and may we balance these with introspection.

_____

(Close the ceremony with the following thought or with one more appropriate to the specific celebration or time of the year.)
[Great Spirit], this year has come to an end, and it was a good year. The events with our children will always be remembered, and we thank you for giving us this time to share together.

_____

This day we may have [Guides] leave our program and go on to other activities. Help them find the time to do things together. Help them continue to be ["Pals Forever"].

_____

We have many [Guides] returning to our [tribe]. Help those returning to keep our activities productive, respectful, and fun.

INSTALLATION AND INDUCTION CEREMONIES

Use these models to help you kick off the year with the appropriate balance of joy and solemnity. As always, feel free to adapt the details to fit your needs, inserting your group's terminology as appropriate and adding or changing other wording to reflect your customs.

Installation Ceremony

Ceremony preparation: Use two candles in this ceremony. Many prefer to use candles of two different lengths for symbolic significance. Bring a patch for each parent and child and a safety pin for each. Obtain a list of the members of the group names in advance.

Gather together, around a fireplace, if available. Turn your back to the fire. Have the group members stand or sit in two concentric semicircles, children in front of their respective parents, facing you. Keep the room dark with the exception of one dim light or the light from the fire.

1. Ask the group to please stand, and then offer a prayer to [the Great Spirit]:

[O Great Spirit], the father and children of this, the _____ [Tribe] offer to you their thanks for the opportunity of meeting here in a spirit of com-

panionship, one person with another. We pray for your guidance in the leadership of this [tribe]. May these [Y-Guides] be blessed with wisdom, patience, sacrifice, and acceptance so they may realize each person's worth. May the circle of their [tribe] be as strong as the sacred circle of their families. May they live in mutual harmony with their community, and seek a world pleasing to your sight.

2. Have all take their places again, then explain the symbolism of the candles:

[Y-Guides], you see before me two candles. *(Light the first, longer candle.)* This candle represents the parent. *(Light the second, the shorter candle.)* This candle represents the child. Notice how each puts forth its own flame and is bright individually. Notice, however, how the glow from the two candles grows when brought together. *(Bring the flames together.)* As the parent and child grow and do things together, so too does their flame grow, casting a glow of warmth and affection, kindled by their communication.

3. Now hold up a program patch and explain the symbolism.

4. Call up, by name, each parent-child pair, one at a time to stand before you. Pin the patch on the child and tell him or her that this patch signifies that he or she is now a member of the _____ [Tribe] of the _____ [Nation] of the _____ Program.

Then give the child his or her parent's patch and ask the child to pin it on the parent, to signify that he or she too is a member now. Shake the hands of the parent and child in turn, then ask them to return to their places.

5. Close the ceremony by extending a word of welcome to the new [tribe].

Induction Ceremony

Let all tongues be silent, let all eyes be watchful, let all ears be attentive, and let all hearts be joyful.

Ladies and gentlemen, boys and girls, welcome to the [year] Induction Ceremony of the _____ [Nation] of the _____ YMCA. The induction ceremony is a very important tradition, for it gathers all returning [tribes] together to be counted and recognized, and it is also a time to welcome new [tribes] into the [Nation].

One of our traditions is the relating of the history of the program so that all might understand its roots and appreciate its value. The first program was started by Mr. Harold S. Keltner, a

St. Louis YMCA director. While on a hunting trip to northern Canada, Mr. Keltner had an Ojibwa Indian as a guide, a man by the name of Mr. Joe Friday. One evening, as Mr. Keltner and Mr. Friday sat around their campfire, Mr. Friday said, "The Indian father raises his son. He teaches his son to hunt, to track, to fish, to walk softly and silently in the forest, to know the meaning and purpose of life and all he must know, while the white man allows women to raise his son." These comments struck home with Harold Keltner. Upon returning to St. Louis, he made arrangements for Joe Friday to follow him at the end of the hunting season and to work with him at the YMCA.

Mr. Friday spoke before groups of YMCA boys and dads in St. Louis, and Mr. Keltner discovered that fathers and sons had a keen interest in the traditions and ways of Native Americans.

Taking to heart the words of Joe Friday, and being greatly influenced by the work of Ernest Thompson Seton, a great lover of the outdoors, Harold Keltner conceived the idea of a father and child program based on the strong qualities of Native American culture and life. These qualities included dignity, patience, endurance, spirituality, feeling for the Earth, and concern for the family. Thus, in 1926, he organized what was then called the first Y-Indian Guide tribe in Richmond Heights, Missouri. This first group was led by Mr. William H. Hefelfinger.

The rise of the family YMCA following World War II, the genuine need for supporting young girls in their personal growth, and the demonstrated success of the father-son program nurtured the development of other YMCA parent-child programs: Princesses, Maidens, and Braves. These programs have flourished all over the country.

(If you are offering an alternative Y-Indian Guides parent-child program, share the history of your program here.)

The purpose of the _____ Program is to foster understanding and companionship between a parent and child.

The six aims of the program are as follows:
_____

Our pledge is as follows: _____
_____

Our slogan is _____, meaning that a parent and child have a close, enduring relationship in which there is communication, understanding, and companionship. The _____ Program encourages such a relationship by providing a means for parent-child pairs to share enjoyable experiences, to observe and learn about one another, and to develop mutual respect.

The years encompassed by this program are crucial years. At this point vital communication links between a parent and child can be created and built on. But the initiative to keep communication open lies with the parent. The parent must be willing to invest the time, patience, and effort.

[Fathers], by being here tonight, you are taking an important step in the journey toward the world of your children. You must, however, remember not to dominate the world. You must treat your child with dignity and respect.

Now I see many faces here that I recognize; they are the established [tribes] of our [Nation]. I wish to recognize them.

As I call your [tribe] name, please stand and greet the [Nation] loudly with our slogan, _____.

Now I see faces here that I do not recognize. These must be new [tribes] desiring to join our [Nation]. I wish to welcome them.

As I call your [tribe] name, please stand and greet the [Nation] loudly with our slogan, _____.

(Call each new group in turn, greet them with the slogan, and have them return it warmly.)

You will all notice that there are no strangers here, although there may be some friends you haven't met. It is good to have new friends in our [Nation]. Please return to all our [Nation Gatherings].

Now parent and child take the [necklace] you were given when you arrived here, and turn to face each other. [Fathers] first, place your child's [necklace over her] head and repeat our slogan.

By these simple acts of understanding and companionship, I declare you all members of the _____ [Nation] of the _____ YMCA.

I close this ceremony by having all of you join hands and repeat our program pledge.

Induction of a New Leader

Old [Chief]: As our program year comes to an end, we have one remaining important task before us. Let all eyes be watchful, let all tongues be silent, and let all hearts be joyful in this night as we induct a new [Chief]. Will [parent's and child's names] please come forward?

Do you [parent's and child's names] pledge yourself to give us your wholehearted support?

New [Chief]: Yes!

Old [Chief]: Will you give your best efforts to help our parents and children find the values and joys of our _____ Program?

New [Chief]: Yes!

Old [Chief]: Will you attend all meetings required by your office and carry out those responsibilities?

New [Chief]: Yes!

Old [Chief]: Will it be your aim to be ["Friends Always"] with your children and to be a living example of the _____ Program?

New [Chief]: Yes!

Old [Chief]: O Spirit of the North, from whence come cold and long nights, make smooth the paths of all those who travel. May they reach the end of their journey in good health and good spirit.

O Spirit of the West, where the sun always sets and where the buffalo roam, do not remove us from this Earth until all things that should be done by us are done.

O Spirit of the East, where the sun always rises, lift up the hearts of all mankind that might feel discouraged. Send wisdom to the hearts of all humankind. May each rising sun instill in them the desire to be a friend to all they meet.

O Spirit of the South, from whence come warm breezes, may they clear the minds of all humankind. Help them make broad and lasting decisions for the welfare of all humanity.

[O Great Spirit], we ask your blessing on this new [Chief]. Please give us a sign of your acceptance. *(Flash from the igniting of the fire)*

[Y-Guides], the time has come for all of you to accept your challenge. You have heard [names of new Chief and child] pledge themselves to you. If it is your decision to accept their pledge, signify by saying "Yes."

[Names of new Chief and child], we have heard the gathering accept you. You are hereby inducted as the [Chief] of the _____ YMCA _____ Program! *(Applause.)*

CAMPFIRE OR CANDLE LIGHTING CEREMONIES

Lighting of the Campfire

[Chief]: [O Great Spirit], we ask your blessing on this gathering. Please give us a sign of your acceptance. *(Nothing happens.)*

[Chief]: I feel [the Great Spirit] is with us. The Voice of the Campfire, I beseech you to light our campfire tonight. Light it now! *(Nothing happens.)*

We are cold and it grows dark. We need your help to keep away the creatures of darkness. Light our fire now! *(Nothing happens.)*

We need the Magic Campfire. Let us all unite and yell out our slogan, ["Friends Always"], three times.

All: ["Friends Always, Friends Always, Friends Always!"] *(Nothing happens.)*

[Chief]: Repeat the slogan three more times.

All: ["Friends Always, Friends Always, Friends Always!"]
(Light fire!)

Candle Lighting Ceremony

At this time, would all parents please come forward to light your candles from our council fire and then return to your place next to your child? Please do not light your child's candle yet.

As two candles are held together, you will notice that they give off the same color of light and quickly become one light. Together they shine much brighter than one alone. This is the same for parents and children. Together they are stronger and brighter than they are alone. This is the purpose of the YMCA _____ Program. The light of both parent and child becomes one. They work together, play together, and share their love together.

[Fathers], please repeat after me:

[Daughter], I pledge . . . as your [Father] and member of the _____ Program . . . to give up my selfishness. . . . I promise to spend time with you . . . love you . . . teach you . . . guide you . . . and play with you . . . even when there are other demands on my time . . . be it work, recreation, or other interests. . . . [Daughter], you are worth my time. . . . I love you!

[Fathers], please light your [daughter's] candle.

[Daughters], you hold in your hand the magic of light. Your [dad] has just told you that [he] promises to spend time with you in both fun and teaching. Part of being a [Princess] is being thoughtful, understanding, and patient. [Daughters], hold your candle close to your parent's candle so the families become one and repeat after me:

[Dad], I promise . . . to listen to you . . . respect you . . . be patient with you . . . and to show my love and thankfulness. . . . [Dad], I am lucky . . . to be a [Princess] . . . with you. . . . [Dad], I love you!

Please blow out your candles and give each other a hug.

Lighting of the Induction Fire

Each of you has come here because of the love you have for each other. It is the love that will bind you together, and it is the love that we honor here tonight. The wood before you is nothing now but a cold, simple pile of wood. It is, however, possible for it to become fire, becoming a tool that burns brightly and is wonderful to those who use it right.

So it is with the relationship between a parent and a child. It can be a simple unkind comment at breakfast or before bedtime. It can be a negative exchange between a parent and a child when his or her grades at school are bad or a hug for a parent only when receiving a birthday present. This is the kind of relationship that is like the cold, unlit fire.

A parent and child can also have the kind of relationship that is like the flame that burns brightly and brings warmth to all those around it. In this kind of relationship, both parent and child choose to spend time together. They do not need a special occasion to hug each other. In this kind of relationship, a parent may discipline the child, but then is able to let him or her know he or she is still loved. By being here tonight, both parent and child are saying to the world that they want, or already have, the kind of relationship that is like the burning flame. Let the induction fire be lit!

Corn Ceremony

Greetings and welcome to all of you. I greet you as brothers and sisters. Turn now and face the center of the council circle. You will see our harvest of friendship. This [Nation] is a symbol of each [Brave] here. For the [father] it is meant to show you love your child. You are a [Guide] so that you may join in enjoyable experiences, observe and learn about each other, and develop mutual respect. Through greater understanding, acceptance, and appreciation you can better guide your child to adulthood. These are wise and timely goals, for the communication you establish today will last well into the future, as long as you continue to protect and nourish your relationship. There are dangers, however, and you must eliminate them. These are character traits that may limit and perhaps stop your success as a [Guide]. For the [fathers], this trait is selfishness. For the child it is impatience.

When we came together, each of you was given a kernel of corn. For decades corn has been a staple of life in this country. We will use the kernel of corn as a symbol of sacrifice and as a reminder to guard against selfishness and impatience.

[Fathers], by being here you have taken another step in the journey toward the world of your children. This is a different journey, and you will be tested many times. You must remember not to dominate this world and to treat your children with dignity and respect. Your own selfishness, a selfishness that makes all of us at some times think first of our own wants, our own work, our own pleasures, must be sacrificed. As your part in becoming a [Guide] of our [Nation], you must rid yourself of this selfishness. Therefore, take your selfishness and put it all into your kernel of corn, every bit of it. When you have done this, cast your selfishness into the council fire.

Young [Braves], you have seen your [father] sacrifice [his] selfishness. This means that [he] will endeavor to spend more time with you. You, too, must make a sacrifice. You must learn to be thoughtful and patient—patient enough to wait when you cannot do or say something right when you want to. By being patient, you will help yourself, your [father], even your family to have better relationships. As your part in becoming a [Brave] of our [Nation], you must rid yourself of this impatience. Therefore, take your impatience and put it all into your kernel of corn, every bit of it. When you have done this, cast your impatience into the council fire.

You have all done well. Now all take your second kernel of corn and turn to face your [father or child]. Take each other's hands and repeat after me:

This kernel of corn is like our friendship.
It can only grow if we water it with love,
fertilize it by spending time together,
and give it sunshine by having fun together.
[Fathers] only, repeat after me:
[Son], I give you this corn with my promise
. . . to spend time with you . . . guide you . . . and love you . . . during this year and for many years to come.
[Sons] only, repeat after me:
[Dad], I give you this corn with my promise . . . to listen to you . . . to obey you . . . and be patient with you . . . during this year and for many years to come.

You may all hug each other if you wish.

Let us close this ceremony by singing "Kum bi ya."

GRADUATION CEREMONIES

SPRING CAMP-OUT CEREMONY

Option #1

(If possible, have children stand on chairs, benches, or the like in order to be approximately eye to eye with the parent. As an alternative, ask parents to get down on their knees at the children's eye levels.)

At this time, I would like to ask all parent-child pairs who are graduating out of the _____ Program, to please stand and face each other.

Please take each other's hands and repeat after me, parents first:

[Daughter], I'll never forget . . . the special times . . . the fun we had . . . the things we learned about each other. . . . These great times will always be with me. . . . You're the greatest. . . . I love you!

Now children:

[Dad], I'll always remember . . . the meetings, the outings, the activities . . . these special times we had together. . . . Let's not stop now. . . . Let's keep doing fun things together. . . . You're the greatest. . . . I love you!

Congratulations to all of you. We are going to miss you.

It's OK to hug if you want.

Option #2

I now call upon each [tribe] to tell us the story of its journey since the fall camp-out. *(Have the groups spend three to five minutes sharing highlights, taking turns among each group so that each telling is a group effort.)*

You have heard much of what each [tribe] has done. Together these experiences help make us a great [Nation]. Part of that greatness is the leadership provided by our Senior [Guides]. I will now call upon each [tribe's] [Chief] to recognize [his] Senior [Guides] who are concluding their participation in the program. We will award _____ to each of them as a token of our appreciation for their service to the _____ [Nation].

Let's give [three cheers] for our Senior [Guides].

To conclude our council fire, I call upon the [Chief] and [his] Senior [Guides] to lead a march around the council fire. After two times around the fire, they will be joined by all members of the [Nation] in a show of unity and support.

Welcome to the council fire of the _____ [Nation]. The [Great Spirit] has blessed us richly this year. As parents and children, we have come closer together in bonds of friendship that will last forever.

I, [Chief] _____, call upon _____ *(the officer assigned responsibility for leading the prayer)* to offer a prayer of thanksgiving to the [Great Spirit] that he may look upon this council fire with favor.

(Have someone offer an appropriate prayer.)

In the spirit of unity that makes our [Nation] strong through the combined efforts of our many tribes, I call upon the [Chiefs] to step forward under the gaze of the [Great Spirit] to light the council fire in unison.

I now call upon each [tribe] to tell us why the _____ Program is important to them. *(Have each [tribe] step forward, one at a time, to state why the program is important.)*

_____ [Tribe]. [Y-Indian Guides] teaches us *togetherness*. [Parents] and [children] have spent time together, sharing experiences and getting to know one another better. We lift up the importance of *togetherness* to this council fire.

_____ [Tribe]. [Y-Indian Guides] teaches us *cooperation*. [Parents] and [children] work together unselfishly to accomplish tasks in the spirit of teamwork. We lift up the importance of *cooperation* to this council fire.

_____ [Tribe]. [Y-Indian Guides] teaches us *understanding*. [Parents] and [children] become closer and more sensitive to each other's needs. We become more caring and better able to provide love and support when needed. We lift up the importance of *understanding* to this council fire.

_____ [Tribe]. [Y-Indian Guides] teaches us *respect*. [Parent] and [child] learn mutual respect for each other through increased togetherness, cooperation, and understanding. We come to appreciate each other for who we really are. We lift up the importance of *respect* to this council fire.

_____ [Tribe]. [Y-Indian Guides] teaches us many good things, but perhaps the most important is *friendship*. [Parent] and [child] truly become ["Friends Always"]. We lift up the importance of *friendship* to this council fire.

All these important values help build stronger bonds and relationships between parents and children. That is what makes the [Y-Indian Guides Program] so worthwhile. We thank [the Great Spirit] for the time we can spend together.

Crafts

Craft projects are recommended for tribal meetings and play an important part in the life of every well-organized tribe. As parents and children participate in craft programs, they develop a sense of achievement and pride in their handiwork. Crafts afford children opportunities to

- use their hands to make various items;
- discover new areas of interest and satisfaction;
- share activities with their parents; and
- create items that can be displayed during tribal meetings, in public, or at home.

At the same time, parents have a chance to share their skills with other families, to work closely with their own children, and to tap some new interest or skill areas of their own.

KEY FACTORS IN CRAFT PROGRAMS

Select projects with great care, taking into consideration the children's ages, skills, and development. Start out with simpler projects that younger children can do, then work up to the more difficult crafts as the children's abilities develop. Pay attention to the children's reactions to the project you have selected. The pleasure they take in doing it, and the problems they may have, will indicate whether the next project is more challenging, more simple, or in a different category. Avoid encouraging competition among the children in making projects. Remem-

ber these are projects for both adults and children: Emphasize parent-child teamwork. Finally, vary the types of projects from meeting to meeting.

Advance preparation is the secret to a successful project for the Y-Indian tribal meeting. The attention span of the five- to nine-year-old child is short. Plan projects that are about fifteen minutes long. For the best results, follow these simple guidelines.

- Know the craft well yourself. Complete a sample prior to the meeting so that you know how long the craft takes to make.
- Have all materials ready in advance, divvied up for each parent-child team.
- Arrange distribution of materials for a quick start.
- Plan teaching steps carefully, involving all parents and children in the process. Explain the craft as clearly as possible (diagrams sometimes help).
- Be alert to safety factors and group behavior so that no one gets hurt. This is particularly important when using any cutting tools or electrical equipment.
- Allow time to display completed projects if possible and/or help parents and children work together. Be alert for parents who take over their children's tasks in the project or who sit back and let the children do everything.
- Expose the children to a variety of craft media—paint, wood, paper, plastic, clay, leather, metals, plaster of paris, and so on.
- Evaluate the craft program in terms of success and need for improvement.

PROGRESSION IN EXPERIENCE

The skills of parents and children vary widely in any tribe. Five-year-olds need a great deal more help than nine-year-olds, and you will need to adjust the complexity of crafts to the age and skill level of the children.

For *first-year tribes*, making nameplates and armbands is appropriate. Drawing, painting, and displaying animal, bird, and fish pictures are also feasible. Simplicity is the key.

Second-year tribes likewise need to have simple projects that take a fairly short time to complete. Avoid spending a lot of money on craft materials. Parents' imaginations and good planning will spark some creative ideas for anklets, breechcloths, leaf displays, bird feeders, plywood cutouts of animals, holiday decorations, and beanbag tosses.

Third-year tribes require creativity and a change in craft projects if you want to maintain their interest. Tap the skills and hobbies of the parents. Use authentic American Indian arts and crafts for worthwhile projects. Try new materials besides wood and paper.

In the following sections, we divide the crafts into seven categories: Indian Decorations and Accessories, Holiday Crafts, Household Items, Nature Crafts, Gifts, Games and Toys, and Art. The projects listed in each category vary from simple to complex and should provide hours of fun and a sense of achievement for the parents and children in your tribe.

DECORATIONS AND ACCESSORIES

These craft projects enable you to create decorations for your tribal meetings and to add to the costumes of parents and children.

Cut-Straw Necklace

Materials: Plastic straws, scissors, colored yarn or leather thong, masking tape.

Cut plastic straws at various angles and in various lengths. String the cut pieces on colored yarn or a leather thong. To thread the yarn through the straws more easily, wrap a piece of masking tape around one end of the yarn.

Dyed-Macaroni Necklace

Materials: Macaroni, food coloring, waxed dental floss.

Dip pieces of dry (uncooked) macaroni into water tinted with food coloring. After they have absorbed the color, remove and let them dry on a paper towel. String the macaroni on waxed dental floss.

Dried-Vegetable Necklace

Materials: Carrots and potatoes, knife, toothpicks, waxed dental floss, varnish or craft sealer.

Cut carrots and potatoes into chunks. Poke a hold through the center of each chunk with a toothpick and string all the cut vegetables on waxed dental floss. Hang necklace in a cool, dry place for several days. Once the vegetables are dried, they can be varnished or sprayed with sealer.

Necklace

Materials: Bleached chicken bones (leg bones work well), acorns with tight-fitting caps, drill, string or leather thong.

Scrub several chicken bones and leave them for several weeks in a sunny place to bleach. When they are well dried and bleached by the sun, drill holes through one end. Gather acorns with tight caps and drill one hole through the body of each acorn. Starting at the center, alternate acorns and bones as shown in the picture; then string acorns for the rest of the necklace. Tie in back.

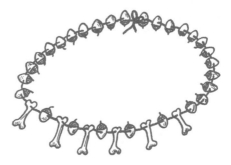

Ankle Bells

Materials: 1 1/2" wide piece of leather or vinyl, hole-punch, leather thong or shoe lace, small bells.

Cut a 1 1/2" wide strip of leather or vinyl that is the length of the wearer's ankle or upper arm. Punch 4 evenly spaced holes in the strip for the bells and 1 hole at each end. Insert a leather thong or shoelace down through the first hole, up through the second, through a bell, and down through the second hole again. Next, thread the thong up through the third hole, through a bell, and down through the third hole.

Do the same for each hole until all bells are in place and the leather or shoelace comes up through the last hole. Leave the leather or shoelace long enough to tie on the anklet or armband.

Masking Tape Wampum Dish

Materials: Small paper bowl, masking tape, cotton balls, shoe polish (wax or paste), rag.

Cover the small bowl completely with small pieces of masking tape that have been ripped from the roll, not cut. Be sure all edges overlap so that none of the bowl shows through. Dip a cotton ball in shoe polish and rub into the grain of the tape. Pass the wampum dish around at meetings.

Paper Beads

Materials: Colored-print section of the newspaper, glue, toothpicks, leather thong or string, varnish or craft sealer.

Cut triangles about 1 1/2" at the base and 8" on each side from the colored-print section of the newspaper. Apply a few drops of glue to one side of the paper and roll it neatly around the length of a toothpick. Remove the toothpick immediately and let dry. String the beads when you have enough. They can be varnished or sprayed with a craft sealer.

Arrowhead Emblem

Materials: Leather scraps, scissors, holepunch, plastic thong, woodburning tool or leather-working tools.

Cut out a 3" to 4" arrowhead from leather scraps. Punch holes around the edge and interlace with colorful plastic thong. Burn or mark child's name and tribal name on the arrowhead.

Clay Bead Jewelry

Materials: Water-based clay, toothpicks, paints, string or leather thong, varnish (optional).

Roll or press clay into beads of different shapes (squares, balls, diamonds, rectangles, circles, etc.) about 1" thick. Pierce a hole through each one with a toothpick. Remember, clay shrinks when it dries, so the hole must be big enough to thread a string through when the bead is finished. Allow the clay beads to dry thoroughly, then paint them. You can add a final coat of varnish if you wish. String the beads when the paint and/or varnish is dry.

Salt Dough Beads

Materials: Saucepan, flour, salt, water, measuring cup, food coloring, nails, shoelace or leather thong.

In a saucepan, stir together 1/2 cup of flour, 1 cup of salt, 1/4 cup of water, and 3 drops of food coloring.

Cook over medium flame until the dough thickens, then let it cool. When you can hold it in your hands, roll bits of dough into balls and punch a hole through the middle of each with a nail. Let them dry overnight, then string them on a shoelace or leather thong. You can make several batches of dough in different colors, and your beads can be many different shapes.

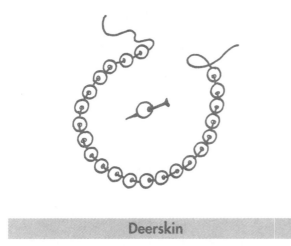

Deerskin

Materials: Grocery bags or brown mural paper, crayons (or markers, water colors, etc.), tape.

Have each parent-child team draw the shape of a deerskin on a large piece of brown mural paper or opened-out grocery bag (you can find pictures of deerskins in library books). Have each parent-child team draw symbols, objects, people, ideas, or anything else on the deerskin with crayons. Ask each pair to tape its deerskin to the wall and explain what the pictures mean.

You can also do this project on pieces of leather, as long as you can purchase the leather at a reasonable cost. This material is more permanent and can be kept as a record of a trip, council, or other memorable event in the life of the tribe or of a particular parent-child team.

Tepee

Materials: 5 pieces of cardboard, 55" × 25" wide at the base and 5" wide at the top; paints; yarn (leather thongs or shoelaces work as well); punching tool.

Cut a 20" long door that is 18" wide at the bottom and 11" wide at the top out of one of the pieces of cardboard. Decorate each piece with Indian designs, the tribal name, events

from tribal activities, and so forth. Punch holes in the edge of the cardboard pieces and tie the 5 pieces together with 10" pieces of yarn, leather thong, shoelace, or other strong material.

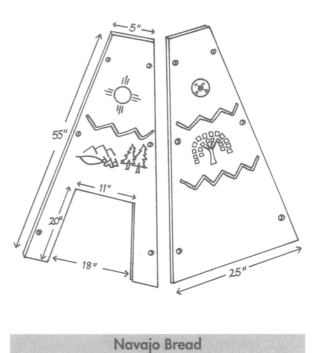

Navajo Bread

Materials: An electric fry pan, large and small mixing bowls, mixing spoons, measuring spoons, rubber spatula, measuring cup, egg beater, small platter or tray. Ingredients: Corn oil, dry yeast, water, eggs, salt, flour, honey.

Measure 6 cups of flour into a large bowl. Measure 2 cups lukewarm water (100°F) into a small bowl. Add 1 tablespoon salt, 1/4 cup honey, 1/4 cup corn oil, and one envelope of dry yeast. When yeast is thoroughly dissolved, add 1 beaten egg to liquid mixture. Pour this mixture into 6 cups flour in the large bowl. Mix. Knead by turning bowl with left hand and manipulating dough with the right hand.

At the end of 8 to 10 minutes of kneading, you will have a ball of dough weighing about 56 ounces. It should be smooth and elastic. Divide the bread into 1 1/2-ounce pieces (about 1/4 cup) and, with your thumbs, shape each piece into a flat circle, about 4" or 5" in diameter.

Pour corn oil into the electric fry pan and heat to 375°. Once the oil is well heated, place 4 circles of bread at a time into the hot oil. Fry until golden brown, then turn and brown the other side. Add more oil each time you fry another batch. Butter each piece while it's hot.

To store the bread, put it in a plastic bag in the freezer. When you want a piece, take one out, put in the toaster, and eat it while it's piping hot. Yield: about 38 pieces.

Story Mural

Materials: Newsprint, markers or crayons, brown mural paper, tape.

This project requires two meetings to complete. At the first meeting, use the newsprint to record ideas generated by a group discussion on the group's purpose, history, background, and members. Discuss what the members know about the Indians for whom the tribe is named. Brainstorm as many ideas about the identity of your group as you can and list them on the newsprint.

At the next meeting, explain that you as a group will be creating a story mural using ideas brainstormed at the previous meeting. (Make sure you have the newsprint from that meeting on hand.) You might point out that what you are creating is much like the American Indian wall designs. Roll out the brown mural paper so that every parent-child team has some space on which to draw. Decide who will draw which part and begin.

You can take the mural with you on campouts and from meeting to meeting; add to it as your tribal history continues.

Coloring Cloth With Natural Dyes

Materials: Variety of white fabric, samples of fruits (blueberries), vegetables (beets), parts of a tree (red sumac leaves), pan, strainer, stove.

It was everyday work for Indians and pioneers to dye materials with vegetable and fruit juices. You can dye fabric the same way. Be sure the floors and tables are protected with newspapers. Give each parent-child team one piece of white cotton, white rayon, white linen, white wool, and white nylon. Chop leaves, grind roots and stems, or crush berries. Soak the plant pieces in enough water to cover. Boil until you achieve the desired color or until the color is bright. Strain the dye, removing the plant material. Dip cloth samples in water and wring

them out. Put the cloth in the dye bath and cover. Simmer slowly until material is the desired color. The color will lighten as the material dries. When the cloth is almost dry, smooth it out.

Other colors: light brown from onion skins; orange from carrots; green from spinach; rose from beets or pokewood berries; yellow from goldenrod flowers or wood sumac; red from red sumac berries or red raspberries; brown from coffee or the hulls of black walnuts; black from red sumac leaves; blue from red maple or blue ash bark; purple from red cedar roots.

HOLIDAY CRAFTS

Holiday crafts are especially popular with young children. These projects give them a chance to learn new skills and to create thoughtful gifts or decorations for others.

Jack-O'-Lanterns

Materials: Pumpkins, carving knives, Jackknives, spoons for scooping out pumpkin seeds, candles, newspaper.

If the tribal meeting falls in October, carving pumpkins for Halloween is lots of fun despite the mess involved. Parents will need to help the children with doing the artwork, carving, and placing the candle. Spread newspaper to make cleanup easier.

Halloween Spiders

Materials: Large black pom-pom, three 4" black chenille stems, glue, plastic eyes, elastic thread. Another type of spider will require a large wooden bead, three 6" black chenille stems, paints, paint brush.

the can. Using various sizes of nails, punch holes in the can to outline the design. Remove the paper and let the ice melt so that you can pour out the water. Spray paint the outside of the can and, when dry, place a candle inside. The flame will illuminate the punched design.

To make the pom-pom spider, glue the sticks to the bottom of the pom-pom and bend for legs. Add plastic eyes and tie elastic thread around the pom-pom so the spider bounces when hanging.

To make the bead spider, select a wooden bead with a hole big enough to pass through the 3 chenille sticks. Bend stick ends to form 6 legs. Paint eyes on the bead and use elastic thread to suspend the spider from the ceiling.

Sour Ball Ornaments

Materials: 30–60 unwrapped sour ball candies, 1 muffin tin, oil, string.

Place 5 unwrapped sour ball candies in each section of a lightly greased muffin tin. Bake in a 375° oven for 6-8 minutes, being careful not to let the candy bubble and turn brittle. Remove from oven and immediately poke a hanging hole at the top of each candy ornament with a wet toothpick (not too close to the edge). When the candies have cooled, invert the pan and pop them out by pressing on the back of each muffin well. String the candies and hang them on a tree or in the window.

Coffee Can Luminaria

Materials: A 1- or 2-pound coffee can, pencils, brown paper, tape, pencil, various sizes of nails, hammer, spray paint, candles.

This project is perfect for winter holidays. Fill a 1- or 2-pound coffee can with water and freeze it solid. Cut a piece of brown paper to fit perfectly around the outside of the can. Lay the paper out flat and draw a design on it, preferably something simple; then secure it around

Christmas Angels

Materials: Disposable aluminum pie plates, stapler or paper clips, pencil (optional).

Cut out the bottom of the pie plate. On half of the circle, cut out an angel pattern (see illustration). Bend the halo and the wings forward. Roll the body of the angel into a cone shape. Fasten the back with a stapler or paper clip. If you are using the angels for invitations, print your message with a dull pencil before you roll the body into a cone. This imprints the lettering into the aluminum.

Christmas Ornaments

Materials: Aluminum frozen food plates, brightly colored wrapping or construction paper, stapler, hole-punch, string or ribbon, scissors.

Have everyone save aluminum frozen food plates and bring as many as possible to the meeting. You will also need some brightly colored paper—Christmas wrapping paper or construction paper will do. Cut out 2 circles of aluminum and 1 of colored paper, all the same size. Put the paper between the aluminum like a sandwich. Staple all 3 together on the center line (see illustration). Bend the aluminum flaps so the color will show. Punch a hole at the top for a string and hang the decoration on your tree. Try other shapes such as diamonds, squares, and triangles.

Christmas Garlands

Materials: Popped popcorn, cranberries, macaroni, construction paper, aluminum frozen food plates, scissors, large darning needle, heavy thread.

Your tribe can make garlands and chains to go on your tree. Prepare a bowl of popcorn, and buy fresh cranberries and a box of macaroni. Cut some small circles from colored construction paper and aluminum frozen food plates. String the various items on the thread to make a gay and colorful chain or garland to hang on the tree.

String Ornaments

Materials: Balloons, household string, white glue, spray paint, ribbons, newspaper.

Ordinary household string wound around small balloons makes a lovely ornament. Inflate each balloon. Soak the string in white glue, then wrap around the balloon. Hang the balloon over newspaper or other covered surface while drying. When the string is dry, prick the balloon and remove it. Spray paint the resulting ornament, and tie or glue a ribbon on the top as a hanger.

Decorated Glue Disks

Materials: Lightweight cardboard, white glue, aluminum foil, dried corn (or cloves, peppercorns, etc.), food coloring, small paper cups, tweezers, toothpicks, assorted ribbons, nylon fishing line.

Glue disks can be decorated with corn, spices, or food coloring; they make attractive ornaments. Cut strips from cardboard 1/2" wide and 8"-11" long. Glue the ends of each strip together so that each forms a circle. Let dry, then shape to make the circle completely round. Lay circles on aluminum foil and pour in glue. Spread with a toothpick, making sure the glue touches the cardboard all the way around.

You create the spice ornament before the glue has dried. With the tweezers arrange spices to look like a flower. Press in place, dry.

For the painted designs, mix glue with food coloring. Use separate paper cups to mix colors. When glue circles are completely dry, lightly draw in designs, using your own or tracing from greeting cards or coloring books. Fill in the designs with glue-paint—using one color at a time and letting each one dry before applying the next. Glue-paint is applied by pouring a few drops, then spreading with toothpicks.

To complete ornaments, lift from foil and glue ribbon around cardboard circles and a flat ribbon bow on top. Tie with fishing line for hanging.

Light Bulb Snowman

Materials: used light bulb, Styrofoam ball, black and red construction paper or felt, jar lid, plaster of paris, white tempera paint, paint brush, glue.

Paint light bulb with white tempera paint. When paint is dry, glue the Styrofoam ball on the tapered bulb end for the snowman's head. It may be necessary to scoop out a bit of the ball so it will fit. Mix plaster of paris and pour into jar lid. As it begins to set, stand light bulb on it and hold until firm. Cut hat from black paper or felt and glue to head. Cut features from black paper or felt and glue to face. Cut scarf from red paper or felt and glue around neck. Try this same idea for other holiday figures such as Santa, pilgrims, ghosts, and the like.

Clothespin Reindeer

Materials: 3 flattop clothespins, 2 plastic circles for eyes, red and green felt scraps, nylon fishing line, glue, stain, white felt scraps, tiny bell, gold thread (optional).

If you wish to stain clothespins, do so ahead of time so they have a chance to dry thoroughly. For the reindeer body, glue 2 clothespins together. Glue a third one with open end pointing up, but make sure the groove on the side of all the clothespins lines up, as shown in the picture. Glue on nose of red felt, plastic eyes, and holly antlers made out of green felt. You can add a white felt tail and tiny bell on a gold thread around the neck.

Crystal Icicle

Materials: 6" white chenille stem, 5 crystal paddle wheel beads, 11 crystal tri-beads, four 10-mm multifaceted crystal beads, four 6-mm multifaceted crystal beads, nylon fishing line.

Loop and knot nylon fishing line to make a hanger for the icicle. Bend and crimp one end of the chenille stick over the center of the hanger. Thread the beads onto the chenille stick from the bottom in this order: all paddle wheels, all tri-beads, all large multifaceted beads, all small multifaceted beads. Bend the bottom end of the chenille stick snugly around the last bead to finish the ornament.

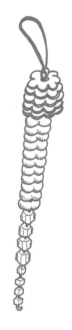

Cylinder Cardholder

Materials: 1 large can (2-pound coffee can or potato chip can), yarn.

Remove the top and bottom lids from the can, Drop one end of the yarn through the can, bring it up on the outside, and tie it so that it forms a snugly fitting loop. Pull the knot around so that it is on the inside of the can. Continue to tie loops around the can, remembering to pull tightly as you go. Fit each strand snugly to the one before it so that none of the container shows through. Slide a Christmas card onto the strands so that each strand fits in the fold of the card. If a card is too tall, trim it down so that it fits on the can.

Novelty Candles

Materials: Molds, wax, wicks, color (crayon pieces), double boiler or 1-pound coffee can and saucepan, match (or nail, pencil, or piece of wood or metal).

The most important part of the candle is the wick. Single strand ordinary string does not burn correctly. For home candlemaking, buy wicks from a craft supply store, melt down cheap candles, or braid string. Molds may be tin cans, dessert molds, muffin tins, cardboard milk containers, wet sand, or anything that will contain hot wax. Using a real wick, you can make adequate candles from ordinary paraffin wax. For slower burning candles, add to the paraffin approximately 20 percent stearic acid and 5-10 percent beeswax, found in drugstores or craft stores. Color the wax by adding pieces of crayons.

After you choose the mold, melt the wax in a double boiler over a slow fire. A 1-pound coffee can may be placed inside another pan with water in it to make a double boiler. Bend the can to make a spout. To hold the wick in the center of the mold while pouring, tie one end of it to a match, nail, pencil, or piece of wood or metal and set it over the edge so the wick hangs straight down in the mold. Let the wax harden thoroughly, then remove from the mold.

HOUSEHOLD ITEMS

Projects to make household items give parents and children an opportunity to make practical, useful objects that contribute to family life. Children particularly enjoy making things that other family members use and value.

Napkin Rings

Materials: Cardboard tube, scissors, glue, yarn (or braid or rick-rack).

A paper towel or toilet paper cardboard tube works well for this project. Slice the tube into 1" lengths to make the napkin ring base. Glue one end of the yarn, braid, or rick-rack to the inside of the ring. Loop the material around the ring until the entire surface is covered. Make enough rings for everyone in the family plus 2 or 3 guests.

Windproof Napkin Holder

Materials: 1-gallon bleach bottle, knife, stapler, coat hanger, wire cutter, glue, beads.

Cut the bleach bottle as shown in the picture, removing the top as well. Cut a slot, 1/8" wide, down each side, starting about 2" from the top. Staple the ends together at the top, covering the staple with a 4" flower cut from bottle scraps. To make the bar that holds the napkins in place, cut an 8" length of coat hanger wire. Glue a bead at each end of the wire. Place napkins inside the holder and lay the wire on top of them to keep them in place on windy days.

Camp Pillowcase

Materials: Carbon or dressmaker's paper, plain pillowcase, ballpoint tube paints or colorfast magic markers.

Using carbon or dressmaker's paper, trace a design, name, or picture onto a plain pillowcase. Paint the picture with ballpoint tube paints or colorfast magic markers. Allow the paints to dry for 1-2 days before washing the pillowcase.

Dishcloth Placemats

Materials: Dishcloths, large blunt plastic needle, colored yarn.

Reproduce the woven design of the dishcloth by running pieces of yarn in and out of the fabric. Use the large, blunt plastic needle to weave the yarn. The yarn does not need to be secured but can extend 3" to 4" on either side as fringe.

Decorated Soap Dish

Materials: Plastic soap dish, acrylic or ballpoint tube paints.

Use the paints to decorate a plain plastic soap dish with designs, patterns, pictures, or names.

Furry Refrigerator Magnets

Materials: Drinking glass, scissors or art knife, fake fur, magnetic tape strip, small pompom, wiggle eyes.

Trace the rim of a drinking glass on the back side of a piece of fake fur. Cut it out, being careful not to cut through the fur but just the backing. Brush the fur outward. Glue the pom-pom nose and wiggle eyes in the center. Apply magnetic tape strip to back after removing adhesive backing.

Plaster of Paris Refrigerator Magnets

Materials: Plaster of paris, plastic bottle caps (1 7/8" in diameter), emery board or sandpaper, paints, paint brush, decals, magnetic tape strip, scissors, petroleum jelly.

Mix plaster of paris according to directions. If exact proportions are not available, use 1 part water to 2 parts plaster. Add the plaster to the water and mix until smooth. It sets quickly, so make a small batch at a time.

Lightly coat the plastic caps with petroleum jelly and pour the plaster into them. Do not make them too thick or the magnetic tape will not hold them onto the refrigerator. After the plaster has dried, remove it from the plastic caps and sand the edges smooth. Paint the circles

after they are absolutely dry. Apply the decals at this time as well. Then cut a piece of magnetic tape, remove pull-off adhesive backing, and stick on the back.

Alternative: Use metal cookie cutters for molds and make Christmas tree ornaments. Pour plaster about 1/4" thick. Place molds on a surface covered with foil or waxed paper. If they do not rest flat, place a weight on top. Make a hole for the hanger before plaster is completely set. Use a toothpick or small nail, but don't leave it in the plaster or you won't be able to pull it out.

Refrigerator Decorations

Materials: Coloring book, scissors, sheets of art foam, sequins, braid, trim, glitter, markers, magnetic tape strip.

Art foam comes in an assortment of colors. Children's coloring books offer simple and good-sized patterns. Cut out the patterns and glue them onto the foam. Trim the designs with glitter, trim, sequins, and braid. Draw features or other detail with markers. Cut and fix piece of magnetic tape to back.

Drinking Glasses

Materials: Jelly glasses, paper, pencil, enamel paints, tape, brush.

Draw a design on a piece of paper that will fit inside the jelly glass. Tape the picture in place so it can be seen from the outside. Paint the design on the outside of the glass with colorful enamels. Place the glass on a cookie sheet and put into a 225° oven for 20 minutes.

Birch Mementos

Materials: Length of white birch 4" to 6" in diameter, ring or other type of hanger, woodburning or woodcarving tools or paints and paint brush, natural materials (pinecones, fungi, shells), varnish.

Slice the white birch diagonally into 1/2" thick slabs, like a loaf of bread. Parents with power tools can do this easily or you can ask the local lumberyard operator to slice the wood. Decorate the slabs with woodburned, carved, or painted designs or use natural materials such as pinecones, fungi, or shells. Complete the project with a ring at the top (or other device for hanging) and a coat of varnish.

Bookmarker

Materials: 1 1/2" × 10" leather, paper, or cloth strips; pencil; paint or leatherworking tools.

Draw a design on the surface of the material, then paint the design or use leatherworking tools if you are working with leather. Personalize the design with something that has meaning to both parent and child.

Shoeshine Kit

Materials: 3 pieces of 1/4" plywood for bottom and side pieces, 3 pieces of 3/4" pine board (2 for ends and 1 for handle), sandpaper, hammer, nails, glue.

Cut out plywood pieces before the meeting, as shown in the picture. Sand the rough edges. Assemble the pieces with glue and nails. Have parents and children take their unfinished kits home to paint or varnish them.

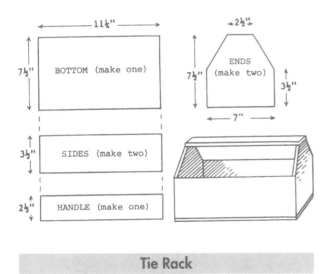

Tie Rack

Materials: 1/2" plywood or composition board, 1/4" dowel and small cleats (or metal crossbar), hammer, nails, decals or paints and paint brush, varnish.

Cut out plywood before the meeting, as shown in the diagram. Attach dowel with small cleats or use a purchased metal rack crossbar. Paint or apply decals for an artistic finish. Varnish finished project.

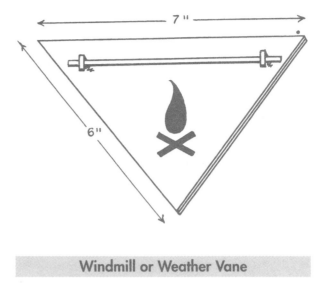

Windmill or Weather Vane

Materials: Stiff paper, 18" stick or dowel, scissors, knife, nails, hammer, glue, mounting stick.

Cut out a paper propeller from stiff paper and a triangle with rounded corners for the tail piece. Nail the paper propeller onto one end of the dowel so that the propeller spins freely.

Cut a slit in the other end of the dowel and insert the paper triangle, securing it with glue or a nail. Nail the dowel to the mounting stick so that it swings freely with a change in wind direction.

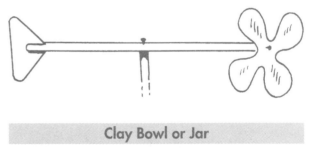

Clay Bowl or Jar

Materials: Water-base clay, pictures of Indian bowls, sticks or other tools for drawing designs in clay, paints and paint brush.

Secure water-base clay from your hobby or craft store. Ask for clay that does not need to be kiln-fired in order to harden. Mold the clay into bowls, following pictures you have gathered of Indian bowls. Use sticks or other objects with various blunt, pointed, or flat ends to etch designs into the wet clay. Place the bowls in a sunny or warm place until they are thoroughly dry and hard. Paint Indian designs around the sides.

Paper Pottery

Materials: Paper rolls, white glue, scissors, tape, paints and paint brush or markers.

Paper pottery, created with paper and glue, can look very much like clay products. Start with a roll of paper. The size of the roll will determine the type of shapes you can make. A thick but small-diameter paper roll can make a bud vase; a thick, large-diameter paper roll can make a bowl.

Ready-made rolls are easy to find. Just purchase adding machine or cash register tapes or shelf paper rolls. If the rolls are wound too tightly to press out the center with your thumbs, you may have to unwind and rewind them more loosely. If the paper roll is too thick, cut it down by unwinding it to the proper size and cutting off the excess paper.

You may also want to make your own paper rolls. To do so, cut even strips of paper from newspaper, a paper pad, or typing paper. Slightly overlap the strips and tape or glue them end to end. Wind the paper strip to make a spiral roll and tape the end so the roll won't unravel.

To make the pottery, press the center of the roll out with your thumbs and fingers, and ease the sides up and out. Don't go up too far or the whole form may fall apart.

When you have created the shape, mix a small cup of white glue with a little water. Spread the glue evenly with your finger or a paint brush over the entire surface, inside and out. When the glue has dried, paint the pottery as you wish.

Corn Planter

Materials: Wide-mouth jar, pebbles, loose earth, a packet of corn or bean seeds.

First put about 1/2" of pebbles in the bottom of the jar (a peanut butter jar works well). Add about 2" of loose earth. Plant 5 or 6 corn or bean seeds about 1/2" deep where they can be seen through the sides of the jar. Water them according to instructions on the packet. Soon you will be able to see the tiny roots grow out of the seeds. As they grow larger, you may want to transplant them to a larger pot or to a garden outside.

Pellon Banner

Materials: Pellon (5 yards cut into 10" × 12" pieces), 12" long wood dowels, black and red marking pens, patterns, stapler or glue, crayons, yarn, sequins and glitter, pencil, paper (optional).

Cut pellon into 10" × 12" pieces before the meeting. Select a pattern and trace the picture onto the pellon with a marking pen. Fill in the picture with crayons, pressing hard for a more brilliant effect. Staple or glue the banner onto the dowel. Tie yarn to the dowel to hang the banner. You can also add decorative touches by putting fringe on the bottom or gluing sequins and glitter on the material. If the children wish to draw their own designs, suggest that they draw them first on paper and then trace the patterns onto the pellon.

Wind Chimes

Materials: 3 clay pots (3" in diameter), 1 yard of heavy macramé cord, 3 ceramic beads (1" in diameter), acrylic paints and paint brush, drill (optional).

Paint the pots with colorful designs. If pots do not have drainage holes, drill holes in the center of the bottom of each pot. Make a hanging loop in one end of the macramé cord. Slide 1 pot up the cord to within 10" of the loop and make a knot on the inside of the pot to hold it in place. Slide 1 of the ceramic beads up the cord until it is just inside the rim of the pot. Tie a knot to hold it in place. Repeat with 2 other pots and beads, leaving a 10" space between each pot. Hang the wind chime in a place where it will sway in the wind. The ceramic beads will strike the sides of the pot and create a soft, ringing sound.

Old-Key Wind Chimes

Materials: Tin can rim or metal ring, yarn or twine to cover rim, nylon fishing line, old keys.

Wrap a tin can rim with yarn or twine to cover the metal surface. (To remove rim, place it into the can opener head on after removing top.) Tie varying lengths of nylon fishing line through holes in keys. Tie opposite ends of lines to metal ring. Keys should be grouped in 3s or 4s at 1 or 2 different levels so they will touch each other at the slightest breeze or movement. Tie 4 more strands of fishing line to the ring at evenly spaced intervals. Holding the ring in the air, pull the ends of the strands together above it and tie them in an overhand knot. The ring should hang straight.

Kitchen Wreath

Materials: Heavy cardboard or Styrofoam wreath; brown florist's tape; various spices, beans, dried peas, popcorn, birdseed; spaghetti; glue; spray varnish; hanger; ribbon and bow.

Cut small wreath shape (7" diameter) from double thickness of heavy cardboard or purchase a small Styrofoam wreath. Wrap completely with brown florist's tape. Gather various kitchen spices and dried seeds, popcorn, birdseed, and the like. Determine how many sections you want on your wreath, and mark them by gluing 2 pieces of spaghetti on the wreath to make the divisions. Glue different arrangements of spices and seeds into each section until the wreath is completely covered.

When the glue dries, spray on varnish for shine. Glue hanger on the back of the wreath and add a bow or ribbon around the outside edge.

Carryalls From Soda Pop Cartons

Materials: One 6- or 8-pack soda pop container, art knife, paints and paint brush, decorations or wallpaper scraps, glue, small fruit cans (for tool carryall).

This project can be made to carry household items or tools. For household items, paint the carton and remove the dividers on one side. Finish the outside by painting on your own decorations or gluing on cutouts from magazines, wallpaper scraps, and so on. Use the open side for carrying paper plates and napkins and the other side for silverware and condiments.

To make a tool carryall, follow the same steps as above, but, instead of removing dividers, insert small painted fruit cans into each section. Use these cans to hold screwdrivers, pliers, and the like.

Sunburst Hot Pad or Wall Decoration

Materials: 39 popsicle sticks, 39 wooden beads (3/8" in diameter), 3/8"-diameter heavy-duty string or thread, 6" ruler, pliers, 3/32" diameter drill, large blunt needle, scissors.

Drill 2 holes in each popsicle stick (see illustration). Thread the needle with the string, then use the needle to thread the end hole of all 39 sticks. Tighten the string as much as you can and make one loop of a square knot. Have someone hold the loop tightly with pliers. Finish the knot and clip the ends.

String the wooden beads at the second hole, alternating sticks and beads until you have 39 of each to form a circular design. Tighten the string so that the mat lies flat and knot the thread. Clip the ends to finish the sunburst hot pad or wall decoration.

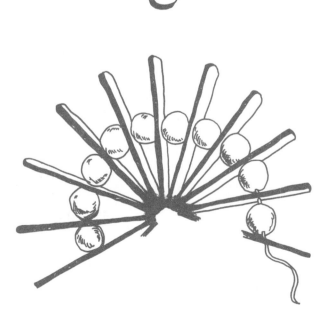

NATURE CRAFTS

Nature craft projects provide hours of fun and enrich parents' and children's appreciation of the natural beauty around them. Hikes, fishing trips, boat trips, and camp-outs provide many opportunities to collect natural objects and observe nature. These projects emphasize using what is available in nature and adding only a minimum of ready-made materials.

Animal Tracks

Materials: Plaster of paris, knife, pencil, plywood plaque, screws or glue (optional).

This craft project provides multiple learning opportunities. You can take a trip to the forest or beach to discover wild animal or bird tracks. Of course, you can also look for dog, cat, and squirrel prints closer to home.

When you find a set of clear prints, mix the plaster of paris in a container, stirring it to a smooth, spreadable consistency. Pour mixture into the animal track, and let it dry for 20 minutes before lifting. Trim the plaster with a knife to remove excess matter; then label the mold with the name of the animal that made the track. Later, you might want to add the place where the track was found, the date it was found, and other information about the animal. You may want to mount the plaster cast on a plywood plaque with glue or screws.

Pinecone Bird Feeder

Materials: Large pinecone, peanut butter, birdseed, string.

Tie a string on the pinecone for hanging. Then cover the pinecone with peanut butter and roll it in birdseed. Hang it up in a tree.

Corn Cob Bird Feeder

Materials: 4 corn cobs, 4 large spikes, 2 sticks, nails, hammer.

Drive the large spikes through 1 stick at equal intervals. Stick a corn cob on each spike. Nail this stick to the top of the other one in the shape of a "T." Post the bird feeder in the ground and watch the birds come.

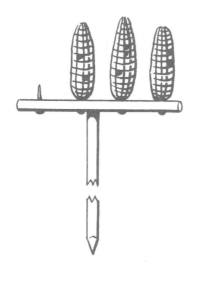

Coat Hanger Bird Feeder

Materials: Coffee can, 2 pie tins, coat hanger, can opener, nail, hammer, wire cutters, dark paint, paint brush, rubber tubing (optional).

Cut a row of "V"-shaped openings around the open end of the coffee can. Punch nail holes in both pie tins and through the closed end of the can as shown in the illustration. Cut the coat hanger in the center of the bottom wire and put ends through first pie tin, can, and second pie tin as in the illustration. Twist the ends to hold the bird feeder parts tightly together.

If you use aluminum pie tins, thread the coat hanger up over the outside of the can and through the "V"-shaped openings before passing it through the bottom pie tin.

Paint the can a dull color to avoid frightening the birds. You may want to place a piece of rubber hose around the wire that rubs against the tree limb to protect the bark.

When you fill the bird feeder with seeds and hang it on a tree limb, the seed will automatically feed through the "V"-shaped openings.

Suet Log Bird Feeder

Materials: Log that is 1-3' high and at least 6" in diameter, suet, grain, large bore drill, large eye screw, thong or wire.

This is an easy nature project. Make holes in the small log. Fill the holes with melted suet mixed with various grains. Attach a screw with an eye to one end of the log and thread a thong or wire through it to hang the log.

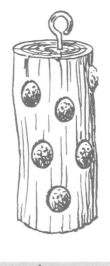

Weed Creatures

Materials: Dried weeds/pods, driftwood or smooth rock, paints and paint brush, decorative materials (wiggle eyes, feathers, pipe cleaners), glue.

Glue dried weeds and/or pods to driftwood or smooth rock in the shape of various creatures. Add features such as painted faces, wiggle eyes, tails, and feathers.

Alternative: Use pinecones as the base for the creatures' bodies. Fashion woodland creatures from a combination of pinecones, small shells, beans, pods, seeds, fungi, feathers, and other natural materials. Use quick-drying glue or cement (such as tacky glue or epoxy) to fix the materials together. Pipe cleaners can serve as legs and necks.

Compact Campfire

Materials: 1 tuna can, tin can and saucepan for heating, bar of wax, cardboard, 1 wick.

Line the tuna can with a cardboard strip. Set the wick in the middle of the can. Heat the wax in a tin can set in a saucepan half filled with water; pour melted wax over cardboard and wick, filling the tuna can to the top. Allow wax to cool. The campfire is ready to warm coffee, cocoa, or food. Handy to have on the trail.

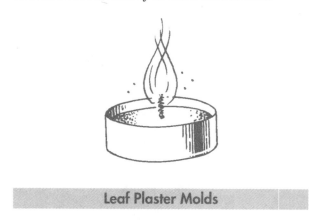

Leaf Plaster Molds

Materials: Plaster of paris, aluminum pie tins, petroleum jelly or vegetable oil, leaves, pencil.

Mix the plaster of paris. Cover each leaf with petroleum jelly or oil and lay it in the bottom of a pie tin, making sure the leaf is lying flat with no bulges or air pockets around the edges. Don't let the plaster get under the leaf or it will be hard to remove from the plaster when dry.

Pour the plaster into each pie tin. Be sure not to make the mold too thick—about 1/2" to 3/4" is fine. Allow the plaster to dry thoroughly before removing from the pie tin. The leaf should peel off, leaving a fine impression in the plaster. Label each mold with the name of the tree and the date the mold was cast.

Mystery Propeller

Materials: 10" stick; small shingle nail; wood (or plastic or aluminum) propeller 1/8" thick, 1/2" wide, 2 1/4" long; a rubbing tool stick or old ballpoint pen; file, saw, or knife; drill.

Notch the 10" stick as shown with a file, saw, or knife, making each notch 1/8" wide at the top. Drill a hole in the end of the stick for the shingle nail to prevent splitting; attach the propeller with the shingle nail.

Rub the notched stick back and forth vigorously with the rubbing tool and watch the propeller. The propeller can also change directions.

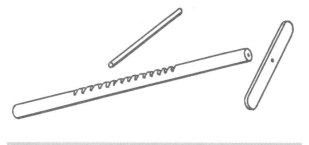

Hummer Button

Materials: 2" wooden disk or large button, heavy string, short sticks for handles, drill.

Drill 2 holes in the wooden disk (or use button) and thread heavy string through the holes. Fasten each end of the string to wooden handles. Pull back and forth to make the disk hum.

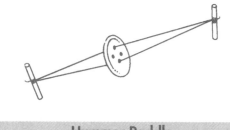

Hummer Paddle

Materials: 1 strip of wood 1/4" × 1 1/2" wide × 8" long, 1 dowel 1/2" diameter and 8" long, string, drill.

Drill a hole in one end of the paddle wood and tie it to the dowel, leaving about 1' of slack between the two. Grasp the dowel and swing the paddle vigorously in a circle; listen to it hum.

Terrarium

Materials: 2-liter plastic soda bottle, small plants, potting soil, small stones, small figurines, colored gravel, scissors.

Pry the black plastic bottom carefully from the empty 2-liter bottle. With sharp scissors, cut off the top of the bottle at the neck where it starts to narrow. Fill the black base with potting soil, several small plants, and so forth. If there is any glue remaining on the clear portion of the bottle, run hot tap water over it and the glue will peel off. Attach the clear dome of the bottle to the black bottom. Water your terrarium and set it in a warm place.

Waterscope

Materials: Large tin can, clear plastic bag, heavy rubber band, can opener, tape.

Cut top and bottom from can, and slip the plastic bag over one end. Hold the bag in place with a heavy rubber band. Tape the other end, which is used as the viewing edge, for safety. Hold the covered end underwater and look into the open end.

Crystal Jewels

Materials: 1 ounce of alum, 1 measuring cup, spoon, large jar, saucepan, glass or plastic funnel, cotton or clean cheesecloth, shallow dish, glass jar of alcohol or cleaning fluid or plastic box with cotton covering the bottom.

Put alum in a large jar. Add 1 cup of water and stir. Most of the alum will dissolve. Place the jar in a saucepan 1/3-full of water and heat it slowly over low heat. This dissolves the remaining alum in the jar.

When the chemical is completely dissolved, set the jar in a cool place where it is protected from dust and will not be disturbed. Slow cooling forms better crystals.

When the crystals have formed, pour off the remaining solution *slowly* through a filter so that it just drips through into a shallow dish. To make the filter, stuff cotton or cheesecloth into the mouth of a glass or plastic funnel so the liquid will drip through.

Pick out one of the larger, well-shaped crystals remaining in the jar. Place it in the dish containing the solution. The crystal will grow larger as the solution evaporates.

Store the finished crystals in a glass jar of alcohol or cleaning fluid or on a cotton ball in a plastic box.

Natural Window Hanging

Materials: Cardboard furnace filter, clear plastic Contact paper, scissors, wildflowers, tiny leaves and seeds, nylon fishing line.

Cut a piece of furnace filter into desired shape. Lay the piece onto the sticky side of a piece of clear plastic Contact paper. Place 1 leaf, flower, or other decoration in the center of each space in the filter. Lay another piece of Contact paper over this, sticky side in. Trim off excess paper neatly around the edges. Make a small hole at the top for a fishing line hanger.

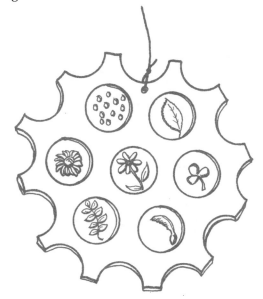

Dried Food Picture

Materials: Poster board cut into 4" × 6" or 5" × 7" pieces, white glue; pencils; paints and paint brush; dried food such as peas, popcorn, beans, tea leaves, sesame seeds, sunflower seeds, and powdered spices; hanger. (Each parent-child team should bring 2 or 3 dried foods.)

Draw a picture with pencil on a poster board—a tribal scene, a landscape, a series of designs or Indian symbols, animal pictures, or something each parent and child have done together. Paint any background work first; then, working on one section of the picture at a time, outline and fill in your designs or picture by gluing on dried foods. Attach a hanger to the back of the picture.

Rubbish Monster

Materials: Litter, glue, tape, paints and paint brush or markers.

This craft is a good ecology lesson. Ask everyone to bring some rubbish from home or collect litter on a tribal hike and use the materials for this project.

Assemble a monster using a large carton for its body and assorted cans for its arms and legs.

Think of additional ways to decorate the monster by adding egg cartons, meat trays, pie tins, bottle caps, lids, and so on. When the monster is complete, put an environmental message on it with paint or markers.

GIFTS

The crafts in this section are ideal for birthday or holiday gifts or as tokens of appreciation for people to whom parents and/or children feel especially close. Children can learn the value of showing their gratitude or affection for others in ways that also allow them to develop self-expression and new skills. The projects suggested below range from simple, easy-to-make items to more complicated gifts.

Ribbon Bookmarker

Materials: 2 large wooden beads, 15" piece of 3/4"-wide velvet ribbon, sequins or small glass beads (optional).

Tie a knot about 2" from each end of the ribbon. Make the knots large enough so the wooden beads will not slide over them. Thread the beads onto the velvet and tie a knot at each end of the ribbon to hold the beads in place. Decorate by sewing sequins or glass beads on the velvet. This project makes a great stocking-stuffer at Christmas.

Felt Bookmarkers

Materials: 9" × 12" felt, scissors, paper pattern, pencil, glue, material scraps.

Select a pattern for the bookmarker, such as those shown in the illustration. The pattern should be about 2"-3" wide, so you can make 3 bookmarkers from 1 piece of felt. You should provide paper patterns for the craft or have the parent-child teams make them before the meeting.

Place the paper pattern on the felt and trace around it with a pencil. Cut out the pattern. Repeat the process for the remaining 2 bookmarkers, using the same or a different pattern. Decorate the bookmarkers with scraps of felt or other material, adding eyes, spots, stripes, names, and so forth. You can also fringe the ends by making cuts 1/4" wide and about 1" long in the felt.

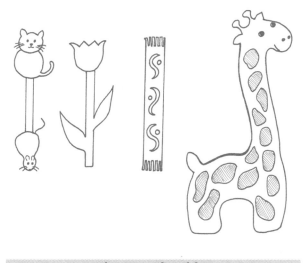

Clay Pencil Holder

Materials: Water-base clay, pencil, tempera paints and paint brush.

Mix the clay according to directions—make sure it does not have to be fired in a kiln. Roll the clay between your hands into a ball about the size of an orange. Whack it down on your worktable to flatten the bottom.

Using a pencil, press 5 or 6 holes about 1" deep and 3/4" apart into the clay. Make the holes near the top end of the clay. Widen the holes slightly because the clay often shrinks when it dries.

Carve or cut designs into the clay base with a stick, pencil, or other tool. Allow the clay to dry thoroughly and paint with tempera paints.

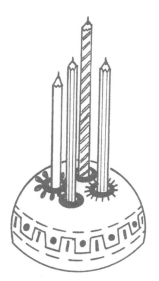

Bookworm Pencil

Materials: Pencil, 15" colored pipe cleaner, glue, wiggle eyes, small plastic hat.

Wind the pipe cleaner tightly around the end of the pencil. Glue wiggle eyes and the small plastic hat to the end of the coil to make the bookworm.

Frustration Pencil

Materials: Pencil, craft fur (1" × 3"), small plastic eyes, 10" length of yarn, red felt (circles cut with paper punch for mouth), glue.

*When things make you nervous and upset
And you're so frustrated you don't know what to do,
Just twist this pencil between your palms
And let it blow its top for you!*

Part the craft fur before cutting so you can keep the strands long. Wrap fur tightly around pencil, glueing as you go. Leave eraser exposed so it can still be used. Tie securely at neckline with yarn. Glue on eyes and mouth. Stroke fur upwards and follow poem. Include a copy of the poem when you give the pencil to someone.

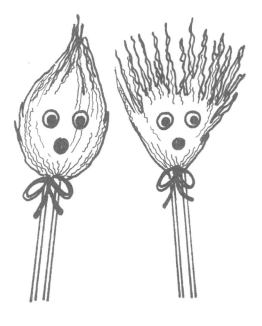

Clothespin Key Chain

Materials: Wooden clothespin, fine sandpaper, paints and paint brush or markers, screw eye hook, key ring, pliers.

Remove any protective wax coating from a wooden clothespin with fine sandpaper. Decorate the clothespin with paint or markers. Apply the eye hook and key ring to the top. Close up the hook with pliers.

Buoy Key Ring

Materials: Pill bottle, cork to fit bottle, spray paint, reflective tape, key chain, waterproof glue, drill.

Spray paint a pill bottle. Remove the cap and glue the cork in its place with waterproof glue. Drill a hole through part of the cork that sticks out and insert a key chain. Add reflective tape so that you can find the buoy key ring in the dark.

Fabric Crayon T-Shirt

Materials: T-shirt, Fabric Crayons, plain paper, iron.

Color a picture on plain paper using Fabric Crayons. Remember, the picture will come out in reverse on the T-shirt, so if you use a name or numbers as part of your design, draw them backwards!

Lay the picture wax-side down on a T-shirt, and put a layer of newspaper inside the shirt. Iron for 30 seconds at a hot setting. Your picture will transfer to the T-shirt. Let the pattern set 1-2 days before washing.

Macaroni Name Tags

Materials: ABC macaroni (No. 18), glue, balsawood, art knife, food coloring, pin back closure.

Cut balsawood to the size name tag you want. Use the macaroni as is or color it by dipping it into water dyed with food coloring. Allow the dyed macaroni to dry thoroughly. Spell out the names for the tags with the macaroni before glueing them down. Once you have the spacing worked out on the name tag, glue the macaroni to the balsawood. When the glue has dried, glue a pin back closure to the back side of the name tag.

Super Stones

Materials: Smooth stones or rocks, poster paints, brushes, white glue, clear varnish spray.

Gather smooth stones or rocks on a tribal hike or beach outing. Prepare stones for painting by washing and drying them thoroughly. Mix poster paint with white glue, using 2 parts paint to 1 part glue to make an adhesive paint that will stick well to the stones.

You create super stones by first painting a background color on the stones and, after the color has dried, adding a design. Or you can just paint the design on the stone, using the stone's natural color as the background.

Spray the stone with a clear varnish for a glossy finish when the paint has dried. Super stones are good paperweights and decorative table pieces.

Weather Guide

Materials: 5" × 5" piece of wood for base, 3 straight sticks about 8" long, small rock, string or thong, glue, drill, scissors, marker, paper (optional).

Drill 3 holes in the base about 1/2" deep. Glue the sticks in the holes and tie them at the top in a tepee fashion. Tie the string or thong to the rock and hang it from the middle of the sticks. Write the following instructions on the base or on a piece of paper that you glue to the base.

Place outside on a level surface. If rock is:

Wet—It's raining.

White—It's snowing.

Hot—It's hot outside.

Cold—It's cold outside.

Moving—It's windy.

Hard to see—It's foggy.

Shaking—There's an earthquake.

GAMES AND TOYS

These projects can be done at tribal meetings. They not only provide an opportunity to teach parents and children new games and skills but also can be used for parent-child interaction at home.

Acorn Toss

Materials: Paper cup, paints and paint brush or crayons, 15" piece of yarn or string, acorn, drill, large needle.

This game is easy to make and easy to play; however, it takes a little practice. Decorate the paper cup with Indian art designs. Punch a hole at the top edge; tie on the yarn or string (the yarn is springier). Drill a hole through the acorn and thread the other end of the yarn through it using a large needle; then tie a knot. Hold the cup in one hand, and try to flip the nut into it.

Ball Catch

Materials: 1 yard of rubber line, small ball, ice pick, a flat 1' stick, small juice can, screw, leather thong, drill.

Poke a hole through the rubber ball with an ice pick. Push one end of the rubber line through the small ball and knot it. Drill a hole at each end of the stick. Tie the other end of the rubber line to the stick. Fasten the small juice can to the end of the stick with a screw. Tie the leather thong in a loop for a handle at the other end of the stick.

Try to flip the ball into the can. You can decorate the various parts of this game if you wish.

Scoop Catch

Materials: 2 round cereal boxes, knife, tempera paints and paint brush, small rubber ball, tape (optional).

Cut part of one side of the boxes away to make a scoop. Paint both boxes with Indian symbols, designs, or other decorations. You may want to tape the rough edges. You and another player can toss a small rubber ball back and forth with the scoops. Start a few feet apart and gradually increase the distance.

Beanbag Toss

Materials: 18" × 24" piece of 1/4" plywood or cardboard, several 6" squares of cloth in different colors, dry beans, needle, thread, paints, paint brush, saw or art knife.

Draw a picture of a bear's (or wolf's) head on the wood or cardboard. Cut 4 holes at least 5" in diameter for eyes, nose, and mouth. Paint the animal's head on the board and place point numbers of 5 under each eye, 10 under the nose, and 5 under the mouth.

After the paint dries, stand board up against the wall or on a chair. Sew cloth squares together with needle and thread, leaving one side open, and fill the bag with dried beans. Sew remaining side closed. Decorate bags with paints. Toss bags at the board, trying to get them into the holes.

Tic-Tac-Toe

Materials: 2" × 4" wood beam, sandpaper, colored golf tees, drill, markers.

Cut square blocks of wood from 2" × 4" beam before the meeting. Sand the edges smooth. Draw 6 boxes in a tic-tac-toe pattern and drill a hole in the center of each box. Use colored golf tees for the markers.

Clothespin Wrestlers

Materials: 2 round wooden clothespins (not the spring type); large, wide rubber bands; markers, paints and paint brush, or crayons.

Have the children decorate clothespins to resemble wrestlers. Loop a rubber band around a pair of the clothespins and twist them in opposite directions. Toss them onto a table and let them spin, jump around, and unwind. The one on top is the winner. Landing side by side is a draw.

Indian Stick Dice

Materials: 3 pieces of wood or cardboard (1 1/2" × 4" × 1/4"), paints and paint brush or watercolor markers, varnish (optional).

Indians have played with dice for at least 2,000 years. Indian dice have only two sides: One is blank and the other is carved, painted, or decorated with different shapes.

Decorate one side of each piece of wood or cardboard with Indian designs and geometric shapes. Leave the other side blank. If desired, varnish each side.

To play, toss all 3 sticks in the air at once. Score as follows:

3 designs = 10 points

2 designs and 1 blank = 2 points

1 design and 2 blanks = 3 points

3 blanks = 5 points

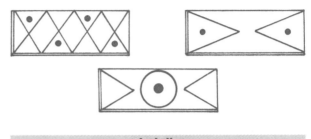

Jar Lid Skill Game

Materials: Large, clean jar lid; postcards, greeting cards, or wrapping paper glued to a lightweight cardboard; hole-punch; BBs or small ball bearings; clear plastic wrap; tape; glue; scissors.

Choose an appropriate picture and cut it to fit the inside of the lid. Punch several holes in the picture. Glue it in place. Add the same number of BBs or small ball bearings as there are holes. Cut a circle of plastic wrap a little larger than the lid. Stretch and tape it tightly over the lid. Try to land a ball bearing in each hole by tipping the lid back and forth.

Bottle Cap Snake

Materials: 4' of heavy string, needle, 100 bottle caps, 2 pieces of soft wood 1 1/4" in diameter, drill, punching tool, carving tool.

Punch a hole in the center of each bottle cap. Using the 1 1/4" blocks, carve a snake head from one block and a tail from the other. Drill a hole through the snake head lengthwise from the back of the head out through the mouth; drill a hole through the large end of the tail. Tie one end of the string to the tail and thread the string through the bottle caps, tying a knot before and after each one to hold it in place. Pass the thread through the snake head. Tie a knot at the end of the snake's mouth, leaving 1" of string for the tongue.

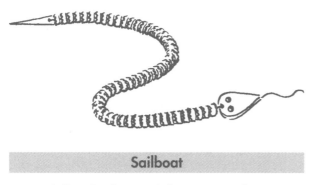

Sailboat

Materials: Cork, straight pin, tack, paper, scissors.

Use the pin for the mast, the cork for the hull, and the tack for the ballast on the bottom of the cork. Cut a triangle out of paper and fasten it to the pin for a sail. Children can race their sailboats in a dishpan of water, with all of them blowing to provide the wind.

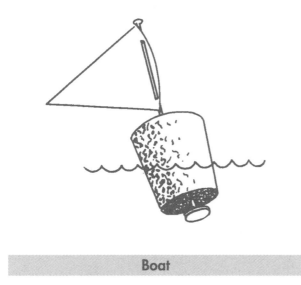

Boat

Materials: Milk carton, knife, string, paper plate, crayons.

Use a paper milk carton—either the quart or half-gallon size. Rinse it out well. With a knife,

cut down one long edge of the milk carton diagonally across the top and bottom. Hinge open the carton until it lies flat. The top of the carton will be the front of the boat.

Make another knife cut about 1/3 of the way back from the front of the boat to accommodate the paper plate sail. The slot should go halfway down through the 2 thicknesses of the carton and be angled slightly to match the angle of the paper plate edge.

With crayons, draw a design on the paper plate. Fit the plate into the slot for the sail. Tie a length of string to the front of the boat so you can tow it to shore.

Talking Cans

Materials: 2 juice cans, 15' string coated with resin, buttons, drill.

Remove the lids from one end of each can and drill a hole in the center of the remaining lids. Insert string and fasten securely to a button on the inside of the can. Use 15' of string coated with resin between the cans. Stretch tightly and talk into one can while someone else listens at the other can.

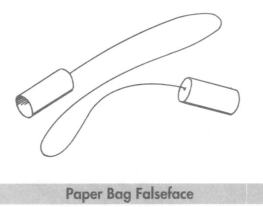

Paper Bag Falseface

Materials: Paper bags, pencils, crayons, glue, colored paper, scissors, drinking straws.

Slip the paper bag over your head and pinch the bag lightly or mark with a pencil where your nose and eyes are. Remove the bag and cut openings for the eyes and nose. Try on the mask again to check all the openings. Color in features or cut out colored paper and glue them on; the more color the better. Drinking straws make stiff, straight hair.

Animal Race

Materials: Stiff cardboard 10"-12" high, 10' string, pencil, scissors, crayons.

Each person makes an animal that he or she can race at the end of the project. The animals don't all have to be the same, but they should all be about the same size.

Take a piece of stiff cardboard, roughly 10" to 12" high. Draw the animal shape on the cardboard; be certain that the rear legs of the animal are extended back farther than the body or tail. Cut out the shape and punch a hole through the cardboard a little below the animal's head—about where the neck would be (see illustration). The hole should be as big around as a pencil. Decorate the animal any way you wish, making sure to color both sides.

Cut a piece of string about 10' long. Tie one end of the string to a chair or table leg about 10" up from the floor. Thread the other end of the string through the hole in the animal. Hold the loose end of the string in your hand, then

pull it tight. By slackening the string a bit and then giving it a small jerk, you can make the animal walk. When the animal gets to the other end of the string, jerk the string up slightly and the animal will flip over and be ready to race back. Have fun with your races!

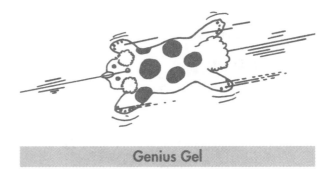

Genius Gel

Materials: Cornstarch, water.

Genius Gel is a substance that is both liquid and solid at the same time. To make Genius Gel, measure 5 parts cornstarch and 4 parts water. Mix this together with your hands. After the cornstarch is totally dissolved in the water, explore all the unusual things that you can do with this mixture. If you pound your fist on the mixture, it's hard. But if you place a relaxed hand on top of it, the hand will sink as if in quicksand! A chunk of Gel can be broken off as with other hard materials. But if some of the mixture is placed on your hand, it begins to drip off—just like liquid! Genius Gel can be poured like water, and, as it's pouring, you can crack off the drips like a solid.

Snow-Snake Derby for Winter Powwow

Materials: Piece of wood 1 3/4" wide, 1 1/2" high, and 3 1/2' to 4 1/2' long (make sure it is a soft wood); pocketknife; sandpaper; paint, polyurethane varnish; paint brush; 2 round-head upholstery tacks.

During the winter months of heavy snow and cold weather, Indians had several ways to keep themselves amused. One way involved contests with snow snakes. A snow snake is a long, straight piece of wood carved to resemble a snake. The Indians would throw this snow snake down a long trough made of snow and ice. The Indian who threw the snow snake the farthest was the winner. The game inspired great competitions among the tribes and gave

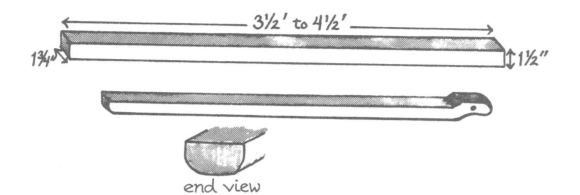

end view

the Indians some of the basic skills they needed to survive in the wilderness. It has been reported that some Indians could throw their snow snakes as far as a mile down this iced track.

The track is a long, straight, narrow bank of snow about 2' high, 1' wide, and as long as needed. The top of the bank is flattened and a chain link is dragged over the flat surface of the bank to make a trough or track in the snow. This trough is then iced to make it as slippery as possible.

Before you can play this old Indian game, you must make a snow snake. Carve your piece of wood into a shape similar to the one in the illustration. Round the bottom corners. If the head is *too high* the snake will roll over when tossed. Make sure it is not top-heavy. This is important so the snake can fit into the icy trough.

Use your imagination to make unique heads. Put upholstery tacks in for eyes. Paint your snake with Indian designs and, last of all, varnish the wood.

Regulations for Snow-Snake Derby

- The snow snake must be made of wood.
- Regulation size is 4 1/2' maximum length, 3 1/2' minimum length; 1 3/4" maximum width; 1 1/2" body height; and unrestricted head height.
- The snow snake must be similar in shape to the one shown in the instructions above. Spears or pointed sticks are not allowed.
- The snow snake must be painted.
- Any kind of wax, ice, or snow may be added to the snow snake.
- There are no restrictions on weight.
- The snow snake must be thrown underhand.

- Competition is divided according to age and sex.
- Runners are not allowed on the snow snake.
- This is a parent-child project—both should be involved in making the snow snake and playing the game.

Backyard Kite

Materials: Trash bags, 1/2" flat wood moulding, string, kite string, glue, knife.

Each parent-child team will be able to produce this kite during one long activity session. Take 2 pieces of the lightest weight moulding you can buy—1 piece longer than the other. Place them perpendicular to each other in a cross. Lash them together at the crossing and cut a slot at each of the 4 ends.

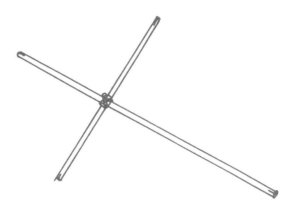

Pass string through the slots all the way around the kite frame until you have created a kite shape without the fabric. Tie another piece of string to the top of the kite, stretch it to the bottom, and tie it off. Do the same for the crosspiece. Where these 2 strings cross, tie on your kite string.

Spread out a heavy plastic trash bag. Lay the kite frame face down (string up) on the plastic. Fold over the edges, trim, and glue together. Happy flying!

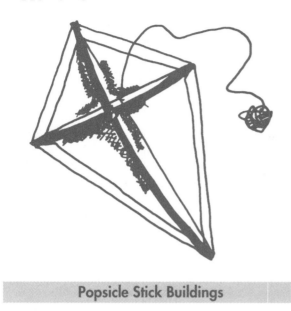

Popsicle Stick Buildings

Materials: 24" piece of aluminum foil, Popsicle sticks (6 for each group), paper clips (10 for each group).

Divide the group into 4 or 5 teams with at least 2 adults per team. The members of each team sit together in a circle. Give each team the same set of materials (foil, sticks, clips). Each team puts the materials given it on the floor in the middle of its circle.

Without touching the materials, they have 3 minutes to discuss as a team how they are going to build something out of these materials. Remind them that they need to develop a good plan, because when the time comes for them to build their object, they aren't going to be able to talk. Urge them to plan carefully and to try to involve everyone on the team.

Then give each team 3 minutes to build the structure with no talking. When the leader calls "time," ask each team to look at the structures of the other teams. Then ask the members of each group to discuss how they felt about their team, teamwork, planning, and execution.

Jigsaw Puzzle

Materials: Picture, scissors, white glue, measuring cup, mixing bowl, spoon, 10" × 12" sheets of waxed paper.

Choose a picture you would like to make into a puzzle. Your choices are broad—road maps, postcards, posters, magazine covers, book jackets. Cut the picture into puzzle-shaped pieces, taking care not to make them too small.

Mix 1/4 cup water and 1 cup glue in a bowl. Stir until smooth. Alongside the bowl, put a number of smooth sheets of waxed paper. Dip the puzzle pieces one by one into the glue. Gently hold each piece up and let the excess glue drip off. Then lay the piece down flat on the waxed paper. After about an hour, lay another piece of waxed paper over the top and weigh it down with books. The glue will dry hard and clear overnight.

Ship in a Bottle

Materials: Small jar with tight-fitting lid, half of a cleaned-out walnut shell, blue and brown modeling clay, white tagboard, toothpicks, contact paper, permanent felt markers, scissors, glue.

Using the tagboard, cut figureheads for the front and back of the boat and then color them. Fill the walnut shell with brown clay, and stick in the figurehead at the pointed end of the shell. Cut a sail from the tagboard and color it. Stick the toothpick through the tagboard in two places. It may be helpful to poke a tiny hole in the tagboard to get the toothpick through. Stick the toothpick into the modeling clay in the center of the walnut. Cover both the figurehead and the sail with contact paper and trim the edges. In the lid of the jar, place and shape the blue modeling clay to look like waves. Place the walnut ship into the blue clay. Fill the jar with water and put the lid on tightly. The jar rests on the lid.

These projects are selected to give parents and children opportunities to explore their artistic talents. The finished products can be framed, put in a scrapbook, or displayed at the meeting or at home for all to see. Children and parents should let their imaginations go.

Finger Painting

Materials: Finger paints, finger painting paper, aprons to protect clothes, newspapers or other covers to protect tables and floors.

This is great fun for both parents and children. Allow plenty of time for cleanup, though, because the young artists tend to get fully involved in their work. This is a good project to encourage those children and parents who are shy about their abilities.

Painting

Materials: Paper, watercolors, markers, rags, brushes, glasses or paper cups to hold water.

Youngsters love to draw and paint with watercolors as well as enamels. Be sure to have plenty of paper available and keep rags handy for any emergency spills. Painting pictures of camping trips, family scenes, and animals are all worthwhile efforts that allow parents to help their children while encouraging maximum creative expression.

Sand or Salt Painting

Materials: Pencil, colored sand or salt, glue, colored poster paint, paint brush, heavy cardboard or board.

Pencil in a design on the board, then fill in the design with selected materials. If you use *colored sand*, paint adequate glue on all areas needed for a single color. Pour sand on these areas, allowing them to dry for a few seconds. Then tip the board to eliminate all loose sand. Paint glue on the next areas requiring a different color sand. Repeat procedure until project is completed.

If you use *salt*, generously paint all the areas that will be the same color. Immediately pour salt on the wet surfaces. Let the paint dry for a few seconds, then shake excess salt off the picture. Repeat this process with remaining colors until the project is completed. Salt glistens more than sand.

Note. The poster paint dries very fast. If necessary, paint a small area, pour the salt on it, and continue painting and salting small areas at a time until the project is finished.

Cellophane Stained Glass Window Decorations

Materials: Construction paper, scissors, cellophane (various colors), clear Contact paper, white glue, tagboard patterns to trace (optional).

Place 1 piece of construction paper on top of another, or take 1 piece and fold it in half. Trace a design—animal shape, star, diamond, circle, and so forth—on 1 piece or side of the construction paper. Either cut the design outline within the pieces of paper or cut out two identical design silhouettes and make matching holes in the center.

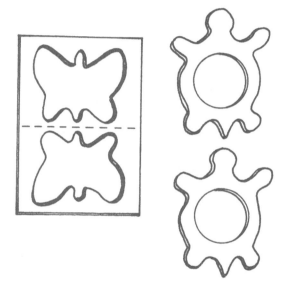

Cut colored cellophane into small pieces, no larger than 1" across. Cut a piece of clear Contact paper slightly larger than the hole in your original design. Peel off the back of the Contact paper and place it on the table with the sticky side up. Arrange the cellophane pieces side by side, leaving no space between, until the entire piece of Contact paper is covered. It is helpful to leave a small sticky border around the edge.

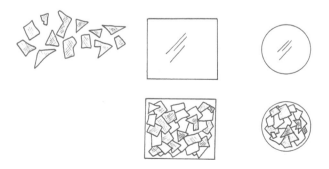

Stick the decorated Contact paper between the construction paper outlines to fill the precut hole. Glue the construction paper edge together to frame the cellophane. This will give the craft the look of stained glass. To display, hang the design near a light or in a window.

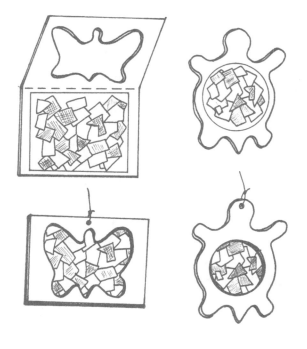

Wood or Soap Carving

Materials: Well-sharpened knife or carving tools, soap or soft wood, sandpaper.

Instruct the children in the safe use of carving tools before you attempt this project. Draw an outline of a small animal on the soap or soft wood (cedar, basswood, white pine, ash, and sumac are good carving materials). Carve out the animal in as much detail as you wish. Smooth off the rough edges with sandpaper.

Lanterns

Materials: Rectangles of construction paper, scissors, tape, or stapler.

To make the lanterns, fold a rectangle of paper in half lengthwise. Cut slits from the fold to within 1/2" of the open edges. The slits can be of varying sizes. Open and form into a cylinder. Tape or staple the edges together.

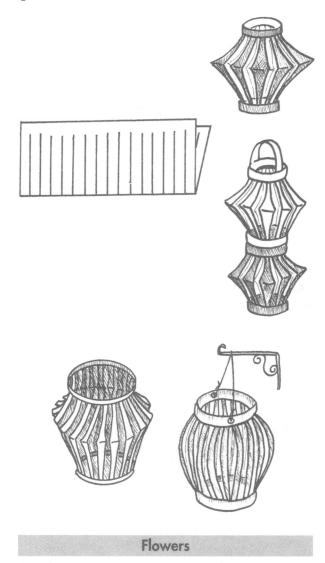

Flowers

Materials: Rectangles of construction paper, scissors, glue, stapler.

To form flowers, fold and cut construction paper as for lanterns. Fold the uncut edges under and paste together. Then form the rectangle into a circle and staple the circle closed. Link several flowers together with paper chains.

Fabric Mural

Materials: Colored felt squares, burlap, glue, needle and thread, pins, pencils, fabric scraps, scissors, 2 dowels, construction paper, cord; colored yarn, yarn needles, glitter (optional).

The fabric mural makes an excellent group project for a tribal meeting. This is a large project, and each parent-child team should be responsible for a section.

Design the entire mural on construction paper first. Use this as a pattern to cut out design elements from felt or fabric scraps.

Pin fabric pieces to the burlap, then either glue or sew them in place. Sew on colorful yarn and use glitter or other materials to add detail. Sew in a casing at the top and bottom to hold the dowels. Attach a cord for hanging.

Paper Straw Chains

Materials: Embroidery thread or yarn, needles, white or colored milk straws, colored construction paper, scissors.

Cut straws into various lengths. Cut out fancy shapes from construction paper (flowers, triangles, wings, etc.). Thread the needles with yarn and string straws and paper shapes in alternating sequences. The chains can be used to decorate for a tribal meeting, a birthday party, or other special occasions.

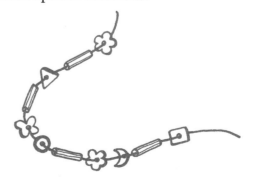

Paper Straw Art

Materials: Paper straws, colored construction paper, glue, scissors.

Cut out geometric or abstract designs from colored construction paper and glue them down on a piece of larger construction paper. Cut up straws and glue them on top of design or overlap the ends, as shown below.

String and Nail Design

Materials: Hammer; 10"-square wood boards; 1" nails; string, yarn, or rubber bands; sandpaper.

If the wooden board is rough, sand down the surface and edges first. Next, randomly hammer nails into one side of the board, keeping them at least 1" apart. The nails should be hammered in far enough to hold firmly, leaving about 1/2" of the nail sticking out. Now begin weaving the yarn or string among the nails in any desired pattern or design. Let your imagination go!

Ribbon Butterfly

Materials: 1 yard of #40 cotton ribbon of any pattern, cloth-covered wire, 2 chenille stems, scissors.

Cut the ribbon in two 9" and two 7" pieces. Fold each piece in half and cut the parts according to the pattern shown in the following illustration. Unfold the cut pieces.

Place Top #2 on Top # 1. Gather the 2 pieces up in the center and wire them together. At-

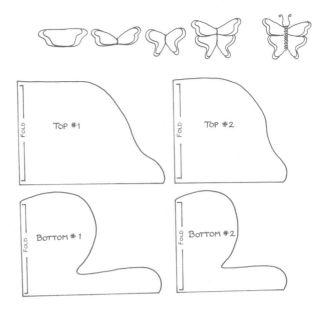

tach Bottom #1 and Bottom #2 in the same way. Wire the assembled bottom of the butterfly to the assembled top.

Cut a chenille stem in half. Fold one half into a "V" shape around the center of the butterfly, twist to secure, and shape to form the antennae. Wrap the other chenille stem around a pencil to form a coil, leaving 1" on each end to attach to the butterfly for a body.

Pipe Cleaner Model

Materials: Pipe cleaners of different colors, scissors.

The simple but imaginative use of pipe cleaners to depict animals, birds, fish, and other creatures is a good overnight project.

Games

Games are an important part of all tribal meetings. Children look forward to and enjoy games, and parents often have as much fun as the children. Parents find that playing games with their sons or daughters provides an excellent opportunity to understand their children better.

Games selected for tribal meetings should be well planned, related to the children's skill level, and tested by the host before being introduced at the meeting. Involve your own children as much as possible in the selection of games.

Games provide opportunities for fun as well as teach coordination and teamwork. They foster a friendly and informal atmosphere at meetings. If games are planned after the formal portion of the meeting, they allow children to let off steam and can make the rest of the meeting easier to manage.

CHECKLIST FOR ORGANIZING AND LEADING GAMES

The following guidelines can help you organize and lead games successfully without losing either the children's interest or control of the meeting.

❑ For best results and the most fun, choose a game in which parents and children participate actively.

❑ Consider the skill level of all the children in the tribe. Make sure that the game will not put any player in a bad light because he or she cannot physically manage the skills required. Games should help participants feel successful at what they do.

❑ Understand the game and know the rules.

❑ Be ready to bend or adapt the rules if necessary.

❑ Have all the equipment or materials needed on hand ahead of time.

❑ Mark off boundaries and goals—use masking tape indoors, use flour outdoors.

❑ Demonstrate the game to the group. Make sure everyone understands the rules of play.

❑ Don't play the game too long. Stop when the interest and excitement is high—the memory of the fun will last longer.

INDOOR GAMES

These games can be played at meetings during rainy or winter weather, on camp-outs when there is adequate space inside, or in other indoor locations. They are easy to learn and play and can help you get the meeting started.

Pick-Up-Wampum

Materials: Large bowl, kitchen spatula, 25 marble-sized cotton balls, blindfold (optional).

Set the bowl on the floor or on a table and scatter the cotton balls around it. At a given signal, either parent or child takes the spatula and tries to get as many cotton balls into the bowl as possible in 20 seconds. For more fun, blindfold the person trying to get the balls into the bowl.

Scrambled Birch Bark

Materials: 2 identical newspapers.

Divide the tribe into 2 teams and give each a scrambled newspaper. The object is to be the first to reassemble the newspaper in proper order within a given time limit. Teamwork is needed.

Scrambled Moccasins

Materials: 1 shoe from each adult.

Place all the shoes in the center of the room and scramble them up. At a signal, the children rush to find their parents' shoes. The first child to get the shoe back on the parent's foot is the winner.

Alternative: A noncompetitive version of the game is to see how long it takes the children to get all the shoes back to the parents. Repeat to see if the first record can be broken.

Indian Rooster Fight

Materials: Masking tape, ribbons, safety pins.

Mark a 4' circle with masking tape. Pin different colored ribbons to the backs of 2 persons. Turn them to face each other in the circle. They cannot leave the circle. The object is to be the one who finds out the other person's color first.

Ghost Guess

Materials: 1 sheet.

Divide into teams. One team leaves the room, then sends 1 member back into the room under a sheet. The other team tries to guess who it is. Only 1 guess is allowed. If they are right, they get a point. If wrong, the point goes to the other team. Hint: Encourage the players to switch shoes, change height by crouching down, or try to look heavier or thinner.

Crazy Artist

Materials: Paper, crayons or markers.

Provide each team with a crayon or marker. The object is for the whole team to draw a house on a piece of paper. The catch is that each person can only draw 2 straight lines at a time. The house judged the neatest or best is the winner.

Ring Toss

Materials: Clothespins, rubber jar ring.

Each parent holds a clothespin while his or her son or daughter tries to ring the clothespin with a rubber jar ring. Parents may move the pin to try to catch the ring.

Clever Feet Relay

Materials: 2 chairs, 2 pop bottles.

Set chairs about 3' apart. In front of each chair draw 2 circles about 1' apart and 4" in diameter. Put a soda pop bottle in each circle. Divide the tribe into 2 teams, 1 for each chair. Have a starting line about 10' to 20' from the chairs. At a signal, the first person from each team runs forward, sits in a chair, and tries to move the bottle from one circle to the other using only his or her feet. Once the bottle has been moved and is upright, the person runs back to his or her team and the next person goes. The first team to finish is the winner.

Paper Cup and Plate Balancing

Materials: Paper plates and cups.

Each parent, taking turns, sits on the floor with feet extended and head back. The parent's child then tries to balance as many plates and cups on the parent's forehead as possible. Start with a plate and then alternate cups and plates. Select someone to keep track of how many cups and plates are balanced before they fall. Once they fall, the parent and child reverse position and balance more plates and cups on the child's head. The parent-child pair with the most points (1 per plate/cup) is the winner.

Balloon Volleyball

Materials: String, balloon, 2 chairs.

Divide the room lengthwise and tie a string between 2 chairs to use as the net. Divide the tribe into 2 teams that sit on the floor on opposite sides of the string. Use a balloon as the volleyball; no spiking is allowed. All players must remain seated at all times.

Newspaper Cutouts

Materials: Newspaper.

Give each parent-child team a sheet of newspaper. Have each team fold and tear out pieces, making a design. Give a prize for the best parent-child design.

Flying Feather

Materials: Downy feather.

Parents kneel so that their heads are no higher than their children's heads when the children are standing. Players face each other and join hands, and the leader throws up a downy feather between them. The parent and child, holding hands at all times, try to keep the feather in the air by blowing.

Alternative: Divide the tribe into 2 teams. Each team forms a circle, holding hands. See which team can keep the feather up the longest.

Tin Can Toss

Materials: Tin can, nail, plywood board, bottle caps.

Nail a tin can onto a board. Have the children toss bottle caps into the can for points. Set the distance from the can with one line for the children and another line that is farther back for the adults. This is a good game to play before the meeting.

Guess Who

Materials: Pictures from magazines, safety pins.

Cut out animals, buildings, cars, and the like from magazines, and pin the pictures on the backs of children and adults. By asking questions of the others, parents and children discover who or what they are.

Potato Bowling

Materials: Newspaper, masking tape, potatoes.

Spread a sheet of newspaper on the floor and mark with masking tape one line 6' away and another 10' away from the paper. Children stand at the 6' line and try to roll a potato so that it stops on the paper. Adults try to roll from the 10' line. Each member has 3 tries.

Eagle Beak's Nose

Materials: Large cloth or sheet with small holes in it.

Hang a large cloth or sheet with a small hole cut in it across a doorway. Each parent puts his or her nose through the hole and the children try to identify which nose belongs to which parent. You can have the parents guess the children's identities as well.

Balloon Battle Royal

Materials: Inflated balloons, string, scissors.

Tie inflated balloons to the waists of the parents and the children. At a beat from the drum, everyone tries to burst everyone else's balloon and protect his or her own. Both bumping and grasping balloons are permissible. The one who keeps his or her balloon the longest wins.

Follow the Sachem

The tribe forms a circle with chairs fairly close together. The tribe then chooses a person to be IT; that person leaves the room. After this person leaves, the group decides upon a person to be the sachem or leader. The leader then begins to make body motions (e.g., slapping hands on knees, moving head up and down, moving feet), and the person who is IT is brought back into the room.

The leader must change motions every 15 seconds or so, and the group must follow. The idea is for the person who is IT to find out who the leader is. The followers should be careful not to give away the leader by looking directly at him or her, but rather should look out of the corners of their eyes or watch someone across from them who is watching the leader. IT has 1 guess for the leader each time the motion is changed.

Do This—Do That

The leader takes a position for directing drill movements with arms, legs, or body, and tells the group to follow him or her whenever a motion is preceded by "Do this" but not to follow the movement when preceded by "Do that." The group holds the former position when a "Do that" command is given. The exercises should be snappy.

Alternative: Substitute the words "Simon says" for "Do this." For example, "Simon says touch your toes." Any command given without "Simon says" should not be followed.

Drum Chairs

Materials: Drum, chairs.

This is a variation on musical chairs. Substitute a drum for the music; otherwise the game is the same. Set up a line of chairs, 1 less than the number of members in the tribe. The tribal members walk around the chairs to the drum beat until the beat stops, then all scramble for a chair. The person who does not get a chair is out, and 1 additional chair is removed from the circle. Changes in tempo and abrupt stops in beat give the game added suspense.

Alternative: Place cards with various instructions for movements, noises, and so forth on all the chairs. Make sure there are as many chairs as there are members. When the drum stops, each person takes a seat and then does whatever his or her card instructs (e.g., pushups, jumping jacks, duck walk, animal noises, etc.). No one is eliminated from this game.

Almond Race

Materials: 2 bowls of almonds, 2 nutcrackers, 2 chairs.

This is a relay race using a bowl of almonds and a nutcracker. Divide the tribe into 2 teams.

Place a bowl of almonds and a nutcracker on each of the chairs at the other end of the room. At a signal, the first person in each line races to the bowl, shells a nut, eats it, and then returns to tag the next one in line. The first team to get through the line with each member's having shelled and eaten a nut wins.

Magic Noise

A person is chosen to be IT and goes out of the room. The group selects an object and hides it around the room. IT returns to the room and starts to search for the object, getting clues from the buzzing of the tribe. The farther he or she is from the object, the softer the buzz; the nearer, the louder the buzz.

Keen Eyes

Divide the tribe into 2 teams. The teams start out by facing each other in straight lines. Each team studies and tries to memorize how members of the other team are dressed. The teams then go into separate rooms, and the members rearrange their appearance by moving, changing, or swapping articles of clothing. For example, they might exchange vests, untie shoes or put them on the wrong feet, or remove glasses. The teams then get together again. Each person on the team takes a turn pointing out something different about any member of the opposing team. A scorer keeps track of right and wrong observations.

Balloon Relay

Materials: Balloons, 2 chairs.

Blow up enough balloons in advance so there is 1 for each person. Place the chairs at the end of the room. Line up the players in 2 lines for relays. Give each player an inflated balloon.

At the starting signal, each player in turn runs to the chair and breaks his or her balloon by sitting on it. When the balloon is broken, that player returns to the line and the next player has a turn. The first team to break all of its balloons is the winner.

Ring on a String

Materials: Strong string or twine, ring or washer.

Use a string long enough to make a circle that all members of the tribe can hold on to at the same time. Choose 1 person to stand in the center of a circle formed by the rest of the group. Pass the string around to form a circle on the inside of the group circle.

The person in the middle closes his or her eyes while the ring is placed on the string and passed from person to person. If the string is held tight enough, the ring cannot be seen. The person who is in the middle opens his or her eyes and has 3 guesses to find out where the ring is. If the person finds the ring, he or she trades places with the person who has it. If the person does not find the ring, another player is chosen to stand in the middle of the circle.

Dog and Bone

Materials: Object to be used as bone.

Choose one person to be the "dog." This person is blindfolded and seated on a chair with his or her back to the others. The object of the game is for someone to sneak up to the "dog" and place any object (the "bone") under the chair without being heard by the "dog." If the "dog" hears someone, he or she shouts "bow-wow," and the person who is caught returns to his or her seat. Anyone who places the bone without being caught becomes the "dog."

Balloon Rocket Contest

Materials: Balloons, markers.

Each person chooses a balloon and marks it with his or her initials. All line up on one side of the room with a deflated balloon in hand. Each person then inflates the balloon, holding the open end tightly. On a signal, all balloons are released at once. The person whose balloon travels the farthest is the winner.

Ditto

The tribe sits in a circle. One person starts by making a particular motion such as clapping. The person to the right immediately makes the same motion. The next player continues the motion until everyone around the circle is doing it. Once the motion has gone completely around the circle, the leader changes the motion to start a new one going around the circle.

Ping-Pong Blow

Materials: Table, Ping-Pong ball.

Divide the group into 2 teams, placing 1 team of adults and children on each side of a table. Place a Ping-Pong ball in the center of the table. The object of the game is for each team to blow the ball off the table on its opponent's side. Only blowing is permitted; hands must be kept out of play. Each time the ball goes over the opponent's side of the table, the other team scores 1 point. Set a total of 5, 7, or 10 points as the winning score.

This Is My Nose

The leader stands in the center of the circle of players. He or she spins around and then stops in front of 1 person, points to some part of his or her own body, and calls it by the name of another part. For example, the leader says, "This is my nose," pointing to a knee.

The person addressed has 10 seconds to point to the part of his or her body named and call it by the name of the part to which the leader pointed. In response to the same example above, the person says, "This is my knee," pointing to the nose. If the person does not do this by the count of 10, he or she becomes the leader.

The Boiler Burst

Everyone in the group except the storyteller sits on a chair in a circle. The storyteller stands in the center of the circle and starts a story. Somewhere in the tale this person says, "The boiler burst," at which point everyone must change seats while the storyteller tries to get a seat. The person left without a chair becomes the next storyteller. He or she can either start a new story or continue where the previous one left off.

7-Up

Materials: 7 erasers or other objects.

Choose 7 or fewer people to be IT. The leader asks everyone else to sit down, close their eyes, and put their heads down. Those who are IT quickly tiptoe around, placing the 7 objects in front of 1 or more persons.

When all objects are placed and the 7 players have returned to the front of the group, the leader calls "7-Up." All those with objects in front of them must stand up. The leader then asks those standing to identify, one at a time, who gave them the object. If they are correct, they change places with the person they identified and become part of the IT group. If they are wrong, they sit down. When all have guessed, those who are IT pick up the objects and the game begins over again.

Pantomime

Materials: Wristwatch or stopwatch, slips of paper, 2 pencils.

Divide the group into 2 teams. Each team selects 4 or 5 popular songs and writes each name on 1 slip of paper. A person on one team draws one of the slips, then has 2 minutes to act out the name of the song for his or her team to guess. The person may not sing it or say any of the words. The team may ask only those questions that can be answered by yes or no by the person acting out the name. The 2 teams take turns acting out the song titles until all of them have been solved. The team that took the least amount of time to guess the song titles wins.

Name Game Bingo

Materials: 1 ruled chart for each player, 1 pencil for each player, slips of paper for the names, bowl or box, colored construction paper squares or unpopped popcorn.

Name Game Bingo is a handy way to introduce people to one another and to speed the learning of each other's names during the first tribal meeting. You can play the game with as few as 9 and as many as 40 members.

Have each person write or print his or her name on a small slip of paper, which is collected and put into a box or bowl. Then give each participant at least one 8 1/2" × 11" sheet of paper marked off in squares.

All the players, armed with their charts, go around the room asking for the other players' first names. They write or print these on their charts in any box, obtaining as many different names as there are squares. Allow adequate time for this name collecting. The whole idea is for group members to get to know one another. When the name collecting is completed, hand out colored construction paper squares to each person. Each square should be the size of 1 square on the chart. (You can use unpopped popcorn instead.)

When the charts and colored squares are ready, the leader draws out one of the slips from the box and calls out the name written on it. The person whose name is called identifies himself or herself. Any player who has that name on his or her chart places 1 of the colored squares (or popcorn kernels) over it. The leader continues to draw until at least 1 player covers all the names in a row, either vertically, horizontally, or diagonally, as in Bingo. When this happens, the winning player shouts "Name Game!"

To play the game again, players simply clear their charts and the leader puts the name slips back into the box.

Alternative: During the name-collecting period, have the members write down not only the person's name but also 1 particular thing about him or her. This activity helps each person to remember the others and may initiate later conversations.

Scavenger Hunt

Divide the group into 2 teams. Each team forms a circle, and a leader stands between the circles at an equal distance from each. The leader calls for an article such as a comb, belt, penny, white shoe, green shoe, and so forth. The adult or child who finds the article hands it to the player next to him or her, thus passing it around the circle so that all players handle it. When the article returns to the first player, he or she hands it to the leader. The team that gets the article to the leader first scores 1 point. Play to as many points as you wish, or set a goal of 7 points for the winner.

Paper Airplanes

Materials: Paper, pencils.

At the end of a camp-out or a tribal outing, ask parents and children to write down on paper what activities they liked best and what they liked least. After they have finished, have everyone make a paper airplane out of the sheet of paper and "air mail" it to someone else. When this has died down, ask parents and children to get out another sheet of paper and write down what they like best, or what they are proudest of, in their parent or child. When they have finished, have the parents and children "air mail" their messages to each other.

Cracker Race

Materials: Crackers.

Divide the group into 2 teams facing each other. At the "Go" signal, the first person on each team eats two crackers. As soon as he or she is finished, he or she whistles. The next teammate begins, but not until the previous teammate has whistled. The first team through wins.

Huckleberry Beanstalk

Hide a small object while the players are outside of the room. Call them into the room to hunt for the hidden object. Anyone seeing it takes his or her seat and calls "Huckleberry Beanstalk!" The object of the game is to not be the last one to find the object. Children will learn quickly not to look at the object as they say "Huckleberry Beanstalk!"

Peanuts on Knife Relay

Materials: Unshelled peanuts, table knives.

Place a bowl of unshelled peanuts on each of two chairs at one end of the room. Each player is given an ordinary table knife. On the "Go" signal, the first person in each of two lines puts as many peanuts as possible on his or her knife and carries the knife and peanuts to the other end of the room. When the first person finishes, the next person in line follows the same procedure. Teams continue in this manner until everyone in line has had a turn. Any peanuts dropped on the way cannot be picked up. The winning team is the one that gets the most peanuts to the other end of the room.

Photo Guessing

In the invitation to the tribal meeting, ask each parent and child to bring a picture of themselves as a baby. Number the pictures and pass them around the room. Have each parent-child pair try to identify who the other "babies" are in the photos. See who had the most correct guesses.

Blind Obstacle Course

Set up an obstacle course with chairs, shoes, tables, etc. Begin by having the parents ("coaches"), one by one, lead their blindfolded children through the course. The coach should be very specific with instructions so that the child doesn't touch any of the obstacles. Examples of instructions are "go," "slow," "stop," "over," "under," "big step," "little step," "right," or "left." When all the "coach"-child pairs get through the course, they should switch roles and have the children become the "coaches." Rearrange the course and begin again. When parents and children have all had turns being the "coach," discuss how it felt. What directions were clear? What instructions could have been clearer?

Paper Bag Skits

Divide the tribe into 2 groups. Give each group a paper bag with miscellaneous items (such as combs, ball, toothbrush, newspaper, toy, wig, dress-up clothes, food, etc.). Each group's task is to make up a 5-minute skit using each item in the paper bag and involving every member of the group. Each group performs its skit for the other group.

Balloon Rocket

Materials: Balloons, drinking straws, tape.

Parent-child pairs tie one end of a long piece of string to a high place in the room, like a curtain rod. This is the moon, or Mars, or wherever each group wants their rocket to go. Thread the string through a drinking straw. Blow up the balloon. Tape the straw to the balloon. With one hand, hold the inflated balloon and with the other hand, hold the string so it is stretched tightly. Then let go of the balloon. As the air escapes from it, the balloon rocket races up the string to its destination.

OUTDOOR GAMES

These games are great for outdoor fun, and they teach children and parents teamwork, coordination, and new skills. Use them on camp-outs, at meetings held during warm weather, on weekend trips, or during any other time when the tribe is outdoors.

Treasure Hunt

Materials: Objects to serve as treasure, paper, markers.

Form teams of 3-5 members each and name each team. Write each team's name on a piece of paper, and put the names in a hat. Each team draws 1 name from the hat so that there are pairs of teams. First the teams each decide on a "treasure" and have 15 minutes to hide it. They then create a treasure map to give to their partner team to help them find the treasure. When each team has hidden its treasure and created a map, the leader gives the signal and the great treasure hunt begins. Set a limited time to find the buried treasure.

Steady Head Race

Materials: 1 empty can for each player.

Give each player an empty can. Without using their hands, players must walk to the finish line with the cans balanced on their heads. If a can drops off, the player must start over. The race can be an individual, team, or relay event.

Crows and Cranes

Materials: Flour for marking a playing field.

Divide the players into 2 teams: the "Crows" and the "Cranes." Mark a field of play in the following manner:

A = Crows' goal line
A' = Crows' starting line
B = Cranes' goal line
B' = Cranes' starting line

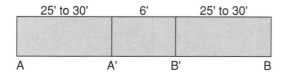

The members of each team line up on their starting line with one foot touching the line. The leader calls either "Crows" or "Cranes." Members of the team called must try to get to their goal line before being caught by pursuing members of the other team. If they are caught, they become members of the opposing team. Play continues until only 1 team remains.

Steal the Moon

Materials: Handkerchief or other article.

Form 2 lines about 15' apart. Both lines should have an equal number of players. Number the members of each line from left to right, and have them face each other. Draw a small circle in the center between the 2 teams, and place a handkerchief or other article in the circle. The leader calls out a number, and the players with that number rush toward the circle.

The object is to grab the handkerchief or article first and make it back to your own line without being tagged by the other player. Two points go to the team if the player gets back without being tagged; 1 point is given to each team if the player gets tagged. The leader can call more than 1 number.

Pass the Grapefruit (or Orange)

Materials: Grapefruit or orange.

Form 2 circles. Choose 1 person to be the leader in each circle. The leader from each team is given a grapefruit or large orange. He or she passes the fruit to an adjacent player without using hands by clamping it to the collar bone with the chin. The fruit is passed from player to player. If the fruit is dropped it goes back to the leader and the game starts again. Alternate parents and children, trying to place parents next to their own sons or daughters.

Nail Driving Relay

Materials: 2 hammers, nails, 2 blocks of wood.

Divide the group into 2 teams, and give each team a block of wood in which an equal number of nails have already been started. Give the first player on each team a hammer. On a signal, the player hits the nail, but is allowed only 1 blow. After 1 hit, he or she passes the hammer to the next player, who also hits the nail with only 1 blow. The team continues to pass the hammer around until all the nails are driven into the board. Only nails driven in straight count, so encourage the players to continue even if the other team drives in all their nails first.

Over-Under Relay

Materials: Object (beanbag, basketball, etc.) to be passed.

Divide the tribe into 2 teams. Alternate the parents and children in each team in a straight column, one behind the other. The first player hands the object over his or her head to the player behind him or her. The second player passes the bag or ball through his or her legs to the third player. The team members continue over-and-under passing until the bag or ball reaches the last player. That player runs to the front of the column and starts the relay all over again. Play continues until all players are back in their original order. The first team to finish wins. You can also play the game by passing overhead only or under only.

Duck, Duck, Goose

The group sits in a circle. Choose 1 person from the group to be IT. He or she runs around the outside of the circle tapping each player on the head and saying "duck" until he or she picks 1 player and says "goose." The one who is called "goose" jumps up and chases IT around the circle. If he or she makes it back to the open space without being tagged, then the other player becomes IT and starts the game again. If IT is tagged, then the other player sits down and IT begins again.

Shadow Tag

One person chases the other players. This is similar to conventional tag, but instead of tagging another player, the person who is IT must step on that person's shadow.

Crawler Tag

Mark a large circle. One person is IT. None of the players can leave the circle. The tagger must crawl on all fours to catch another player. Once

tagged, the player also becomes a crawler. Play continues until all are crawlers. Encourage the taggers to use teamwork.

Glue Tag

This is a conventional tag game except that the boundaries of the game are marked and any player who is tagged sticks to the tagger by hanging on to him or her. Eventually all players are stuck to the tagger like glue. Teamwork by the glued players helps trap those who are not yet stuck.

Dodgeball

Materials: 1 soft rubber ball or volleyball.

All players form a circle. Then 4 players move into the center. Those who form the circle have a soft rubber ball or volleyball with which they try to hit (below the waist) the players in the circle. Players who are hit join the circle. The last one remaining in the center is the winner. Repeat the game until all players have had an opportunity to be inside the circle at the beginning. If the ball goes outside the circle, a nearby player recovers it and passes it to another player in the circle.

Crossover Dodgeball

Dodgeball is a competitive game that can be transformed into a cooperative one. Play the game the same way you would traditional dodgeball, except that every time a player gets hit by the ball, or every time a thrown ball is caught, the player crosses over to the other team. The object is to get all the players on 1 side—then everyone wins.

Sardines

One player hides while the rest of the players come together in an informal group and count to 100. When the counting is done, they set out to hunt. When 1 player finds the hider, the player secretly joins the hider and both hide from the rest of the group. This continues until all players are hidden with the original hider and are packed in like sardines. When the last hunter discovers the spot, the game starts over and the first finder becomes the hider.

Call Ball

Materials: Volleyball (or similar ball).

All players are in a circle around 1 player in the center who is holding a volleyball. The center player throws the ball high into the air and calls out another player's name. The player whose name was called then must catch the ball before it bounces more than once. If the player does, he or she replaces the caller. If not, the same caller repeats.

Stalking (Blindman's Buff)

A player who is IT is blindfolded and placed in the center of a circle formed by the rest of the tribe. The object is to sneak up and touch the center player without being caught. This can be played while sitting or standing. Anyone caught trying to touch the blindfolded player switches places with him or her.

Bull in the Ring

Players form a circle. One player, the "bull," is in the center. Players hold hands and form a ring around the "bull." The "bull" tries to break through the circle by rushing, lunging, or pulling at it. He or she cannot duck under the circle. If the "bull" escapes, the players chase the "bull." Whoever catches him or her becomes the next "bull."

Alternative: Whoever lets the "bull" escape becomes the next "bull."

I Spy (Hide-and-Seek)

One player, chosen as IT, shuts his or her eyes and counts to 100 at a chosen base, such as a tree. The other players run and hide. After reaching 100, IT shouts, "Here I come, ready or not. All around the base are IT." The player then tries to find the hiders. On spotting one of the other players, he or she shouts, "I see (person's name)," and tries to beat the hider back to base. The person who is IT must call out the name of the person hiding or the hider gets home free. The first player caught is IT the next time.

Streets and Alleys

Materials: Whistle.

Choose 2 players, one to be the runner and the other the chaser. All other players, in rows facing the front, stand in parallel lines with arms outstretched so as to touch hands on either side of them. This makes a series of aisles or "streets."

When the leader blows the whistle or calls "Change," players keep their arms outstretched and make a quarter turn to the right. They now make new aisles or "alleys." Neither runner nor chaser may break through a column nor duck under the players' outstretched arms. Each time the leader blows the whistle, players turn one-quarter turn to the right, making "streets" or "alleys."

The fun of the game consists in sudden changes that the leader calls. When a runner is caught, select new players to take the place of the chaser and runner.

Alternatives: (a) When a runner tires, he or she may stop in front of a player who will then become the new runner; or (b) in large crowds, several chasers and runners may be used.

Kick the Can

Materials: Tin can.

The can is a base. A player who is IT stands by the can, shuts his or her eyes, and counts to 100. The other players hide. IT shouts, "Here I come, ready or not," and then carefully leaves the can to try to find the hiders. When IT sees a hider, he or she returns to base, puts 1 foot on the can and says "I see (*person's name*)."

At the same time, the player who has been spotted runs to the base and tries to kick the can before the player who is IT can touch it and call out the player's name. If unsuccessful, the player is put into "jail." If successful, the player is allowed to free any other players from "jail." The goal is to get all the players in "jail." Suggested time limit for the game: 15 minutes.

Stories

The stories in this section can be used to entertain children in a variety of settings—meetings, camp-outs, outings, or car trips. These stories, however, can be more than entertainment; they can provide learning experiences about Indian culture, values, and beliefs. They often can convey a lesson or provoke questions more effectively than more direct methods. Additional stories can be found in the book *Indian Tales That Teach*, available from the YMCA Program Store. See the Additional Resources section at the end of this manual for ordering information.

Stories are beneficial to tribes in several ways. They create a common focus for the group, giving members a feeling of togetherness. They also raise questions for group discussion or later parent-child talks, especially about values important to child development and the family. In addition, stories give children a chance to exercise their imaginations.

Storytime easily fits into tribal meetings. One natural place for a story is directly after the opening ritual, when the group is already gathered together and focused. A story can also be an opening for an agenda item that needs discussion. Later in the meeting, it can serve as a way to draw the group back together after a break. As an ending, it can bring up questions for discussion by parents and children following the meeting.

Try to actively involve listeners in the story as you tell it. This reinforces the ideas of the story, exercises the listeners' creativity, and makes the listeners feel a part of the group. Use the following methods to get listeners involved:

- Have them make sounds that coordinate with the story.

- Ask them to pantomime as you tell the story.

- Ask them to finish the story.

- Tell an add-a-line story in which each person in the group adds a line to the ongoing story.

TIPS FOR THE STORYTELLER

Good storytellers are made, not born. The guidelines listed below can help you select and tell stories that fit your audience and keep their attention throughout the session. Look the guidelines over carefully, then practice telling your story to others before the tribal meeting. In time, you will be able to bring these tales to life for your listeners and involve them in the experience.

1. The first step in telling a good story is to find the proper story. Know your audience—their age, sex, and interests—and use this knowledge as a guide for choosing story subjects. Avoid morbid, preachy, or overly sentimental tales. Your story can be taken from history, literature, Indian legends and tales, or even a contemporary news item.

2. After finding the proper story, memorize it so that you can tell it without reading from a book. It's difficult to establish close personal contact with your audience when reading aloud to them. Become familiar with the story until you can visualize each

character and each scene in relation to the climax.

3. Tell the tale as dramatically as possible. Use your head, hands, and body to make the story come alive. Change your voice to fit the character or mood; children do not enjoy listening to a monotone narrator. Be sensitive to your listeners' reactions. If they become restless or lose interest, change your voice, speed up the action, ask them if they know what the characters will do next—use any method to liven up the story and recapture the listeners' interest.

4. Open with a dramatic beginning. It's better to say, "'Twas a dark and stormy night; four of us huddled around the campfire. . . " than, "I'm going to tell you a story about . . ." Avoid lengthy, longwinded introductions. Get to the point quickly.

5. After the story is finished, ask a few simple questions to make sure the listeners understood the moral or point of your story. Remember, not all stories must have a moral.

6. Arrange the seating so that you are as close to your audience as possible. The children should sit together—elbow to elbow is the rule. Try to ensure you won't be interrupted by any outside noise or confusion; close the door, take the phone off the hook, do whatever you need to do to guarantee private, quiet time with the children.

If something does interrupt your narrative, treat the incident lightly and proceed with the story. To make sure you have the children's full attention, ask them what was happening in the story when the interruption occurred.

7. End your story with a punch line. Leave the climax for the last paragraph, sentence, or word.

8. Never try to tell a story when the children don't want to hear one. Make storytime one of the treats of the meeting.

9. Never tell a story you don't enjoy telling.

STORIES

The following stories depict various Indian settings and legends. Many are short and can be told in a few minutes. Try out some of the stories on family members or others before telling them to the tribe. Sample discussion questions follow the first story.

Little Flying Cloud

(Reprinted, by permission, from YMCA of Metropolitan Los Angeles, 1978, *Big Brave's Notebook*.)

Little Flying Cloud didn't lead a very happy life. He couldn't run fast, he couldn't shoot well with bow and arrow, and he was a poor hunter. This was because his father had been killed while hunting buffalo many moons ago and couldn't teach him these things.

Other little braves made fun of him. They teased him and never invited him to play games or hunt in the forest with them. But they soon became curious because many times Little Flying Cloud would slip out of the village and be gone most of the morning or afternoon.

One day they followed him to his hidden cave. From a hiding place, they watched him play with several chipmunks and rabbits that he had tamed. After a time, the other braves came out of hiding and asked Little Flying Cloud to teach them how to tame the wild animals and make them friends. This he did willingly. In no time he became popular with the other little braves because they discovered he knew much more about the small animals of the forest than they did.

The little braves, in turn, gave him special lessons in swimming, shooting bow and arrow, and other skills they had learned from their fathers. Now Little Flying Cloud was happy, and soon he was the best-liked young brave in the entire village.

SAMPLE DISCUSSION QUESTIONS

- Can you think of several children in class at school who don't have much fun? Why don't they, do you think? Can you help them? In what ways?

- Is there some boy or girl who lives near you who doesn't have one of his or her parents? Could your mother or father bring him or her along as a "second son/daughter"? If so, how could you help this boy or girl have fun and feel at home in the tribe?

- If your Y-Indian Guide tribe isn't up to full size—nine parent-child teams—do you know someone who might enjoy being invited? How can they be brought to the next meeting? Who will visit them to invite them?

A Friend in Need

"Tell us a story! Please, Wise Father, tell us another of your legends!"

Eagerly the children sat at the feet of Grey Fox, the Chief, to listen and to learn. The Chief smiled at the memory of the story he had chosen to tell and then began:

"Many moons ago two hunters were traveling the trail together. Suddenly they came face to face with a huge bear. One hunter, in great fear and without thought for his companion, climbed a tree as fast as he could and hid himself in the branches.

"The other hunter, seeing that singlehanded he was no match for the bear, threw himself on the ground and pretended to be dead. He had heard from other hunters that a bear will not molest a dead body.

"The gruff old bear lumbered toward him, his huge paws slapping the ground with spinechilling thumps. Soon the shaggy beast stood directly over the man, sniffing at the Indian's nose and ears. With great control, the man held his breath and lay still.

"Soon the bear turned and walked slowly away. As the ponderous animal disappeared from sight, the first hunter came down from his hiding place in the tree and asked his companion what it was the bear had said to him. 'For,' he said, 'I saw that the bear put his mouth very close to your ear and whispered something to you.'

"'Why,' replied the other, 'it's no secret. He advised me not to keep company with those who leave their friends and run away when danger is near.'"

Grey Fox's eyes twinkled with humor as he ended his story. "What lesson do you find in this tale of the hunting trail?" he asked.

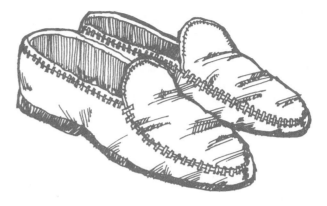

Dead or Alive

(From *Twenty Tepee Tales* by M. Lotz and D. Monahan. New York: Association Press, 1950.)

Many years ago there was an Indian medicine man famous for his wisdom. For many years he had helped the members of his tribe by answering their questions and giving them wise advice. However, because he was so old, many of the young braves of the tribe felt that he ought to give up his position as medicine man and allow a younger brave to have the honor.

Several times the young braves of the tribe had attempted to remove him by asking him questions and posing problems that they hoped he would not be able to answer. If only they could cause him to make a mistake or catch him with a question he would not be able to answer, they were sure they could replace him with a younger man. Each time they attempted to do this, however, they failed. His answers were always right and his advice always trustworthy.

One day, while a group of younger braves was on the hunt, one of the young men turned to the group and said, "Tonight I will ask the old medicine man a question that he will not be able to answer. Gather all our tribesmen before his tepee tonight, and you will see."

The other braves remembered their past failures and wanted to know what he planned to do. The younger brave replied, "I will catch a bird and take it to him, holding it in my hands so that the feathers show through my fingers. I will say to him, 'What have I in my hands?' Seeing the feathers, he will reply, 'A bird.' Then I will say, 'That is correct, but tell me, Wise One, is it dead or alive?' If he says it is dead, I will open my hands and let it fly away. If he says it is alive, I will smother it and drop it, dead, at his feet. So you see, regardless of his answer, he will be wrong, and we will be able to replace him with a younger man."

This pleased the braves; they were certain the plan could not fail. When they returned from the hunt, they spread word around the tribe of the test that the medicine man would face. At sundown the space before the ancient Indian's tepee was crowded with Indians eager for the test.

The young man whose plan it was elbowed his way through the crowd, and, with hands cupped before him, challenged the medicine man to come forth and be tried. The wise man came from his tepee and stood before the throng. "What is it, my son?" he asked.

The young man answered, "It is said that you can answer all questions correctly. If this be so, Father, tell what I have in my hands."

The old man looked and replied, "A bird, my son."

"That is correct," the young brave responded. "But tell me, Father, is it dead or is it alive?"

This was the challenge! All the Indians present held their breath, waiting for the medicine man's answer. The old man paused; then, looking deep into the young man's eyes, he responded, "That, my son, depends on you."

Where the Girl Saved Her Brother

(From *The Sound of Flutes and Other Indian Legends*, by Richard Erdoes. Copyright © 1976 by Richard Erdoes. Reprinted by permission of Pantheon Books, a division of Random House, Inc.)

In the summer of 1876, two of the most famous battles between soldiers and Indians were fought on the plains of Montana. The first fight was called the Battle of the Rosebud. The second battle, fought a week later, was called the Battle of Little Big Horn, where General Custer was defeated. The Cheyennes call the Battle of the Rosebud the fight *Where the Girl Saved Her Brother*. I'll tell you why.

But first let me explain what is meant when an Indian says, "I have counted coup." Counting coup means riding up to an enemy and instead of killing him, touching him with a feathered stick or your hand. This is a test of great courage and can earn you considerable honor in the eyes of the tribe. One of the greatest acts of counting coup is to dash into the midst of your enemies to rescue a friend, take him up on the back of your horse, and gallop out again, saving his life by risking your own. That is counting big coup, indeed!

At the time of these battles, the whites wanted all Indians to live on reservations. Some tribes, however, decided to fight to stay free. White soldiers were sent to force these Indians to surrender and live on reservation land. Many proud tribes and braves joined together to battle the soldiers.

Among them was a brave young woman, Buffalo Calf Road Woman, who rode proudly at the side of her husband, Black Coyote, when the Battle of the Rosebud began. Her brother, Chief Comes-in-Sight, was in the battle, too. When Buffalo Calf Road Woman looked for her brother in the fight, she saw that his horse had been killed under him and that he was surrounded by white soldiers and their Crow scouts. Although hard pressed on every side, he fought off his enemies with bravery and skill.

Buffalo Calf Road Woman uttered a shrill war cry and raced her pony right through the enemies surrounding her brother. Chief Comes-in-Sight saw her coming and jumped up onto her horse behind his sister. Buffalo Calf Road Woman laughed with joy and the excitement of the rescue. The soldiers fired at them and the Crow scouts shot their arrows—but her horse moved too fast for her or Chief Comes-in-Sight to be hit.

Then she turned her horse and raced up the hill from which the old chiefs and medicine men watched the battle. The Sioux and Cheyenne saw what she had done and the white soldiers saw it, too. They all stopped fighting and watched the brave girl saving her brother's life. The warriors raised their arms and set up a mighty shout—a long, trilling war cry that made one's hairs stand on end. Even some of the soldiers threw their caps in the air and shouted "Hurrah!" in honor of Buffalo Calf Road Woman.

The white General Crook thought, "If their women fight like this, what will their warriors be like? Even if I win, I will lose half my men." And so General Crook retreated a hundred miles or so away from the battleground. When Custer needed him a week later, Crook was far away.

Many who saw what Buffalo Calf Road Woman had done thought that she had counted the biggest coup of all—not taking life but saving it. That is why the Indians call the Battle of the Rosebud *Where the Girl Saved Her Brother*. The memory of her deed lives on—and will live on as long as there are storytellers to tell the tale.

Looking for the Good

(Reprinted, by permission, from YMCAs of Greater St. Paul and Metropolitan Minneapolis, *Program Resource Book*.)

Chief Silver Maple called together the members of his tribe. They seated themselves in a circle. In the center of the circle, the medicine man was making an Indian sand painting. Most Indian sand paintings are very colorful. They are made during the day and every trace of them must be destroyed before the sun sets. This time, the picture was different. The braves watched in surprise as the medicine man made a square out of white sand and, in the center of the square, poured a large circle of black sand.

The braves whispered to each other, "I wonder what this is."

The Chief heard them talking and called for silence. He asked, "Braves, what do you see here?"

The first brave said, "I see a black spot." The second brave replied, "That is what I see, too." So said each brave around the circle, each agreeing on what the medicine man had painted.

After they had all spoken, the Chief said, "Braves, why is it that none of you noticed this is a white square with a black spot on it? Many of us, as we think about other tribes and as we think about our fellow braves, look for the most obvious traits and fail to see the rest of the picture. Too often we look for what is bad and do not see what is good. Let us look for the good things in our fellow tribes and in one another from now on."

Stretching the Truth

(Reprinted, by permission, from YMCAs of Greater St. Paul and Metropolitan Minneapolis, *Program Resource Book*.)

One night Little Otter rushed into the tepee and said excitedly, "Mother, I just saw a thousand deer in the meadow!"

Mother said, "Are you sure? Did you count them?"

"It was so dark, I couldn't count them. I think there were a hundred."

Mother said, "Are you sure, my son?"

"Well, I know there were at least ten," said the little brave.

Then his mother patiently said, "Little Otter, you did not count the deer. How do you know?"

Little Otter became impatient and said, "Well, I know there were two deer anyway, a big buck and a small one."

The Chief of the tribe had listened to the conversation. He now said, "Little Otter, let me tell you a story. When I was a young brave, I was in the habit of stretching the truth because I had not learned the importance of being accurate. In my tribe, the Okeewa, I was responsible for keeping track of the food. As animal meats, herbs, roots, berries, and other foods were brought to me, I would store them in the ground and cover them well.

"One day old Chief Kiyi came to me and asked if there was plenty of food for a big tribal feast and ceremony. In haste I took a quick glance at the food that was stored away in the ground. I did not take time to count the number of carcasses of deer or any of the other food supplies. Instead, I became careless and took a chance in reporting what I saw at a quick glance. I reported to the Chief that there was plenty of food.

"When the day of the big feast came, I was very much embarrassed to find there was a shortage of food, and that many of the mothers, little braves, babies, and even warriors would not have enough to eat.

"The Chief was very angry, as were many of the braves. Had it not been for the quick thinking of Watosa, we would all have been disappointed. Watosa got on his pinto horse and galloped away in a cloud of dust. Soon he returned with his arms loaded with food as well as large bags of food thrown over the back of his horse. He had borrowed much food from a nearby tribe, promising to pay back what he had borrowed.

"To teach me a lesson, the Chief required me to hunt for many days for deer as well as other foods to pay back the borrowed food from the other tribe. From that time on I made up my mind to be more accurate and never to exaggerate."

The Indian and the Cricket

(From *Twenty Tepee Tales*, by M. Lotz and D. Monahan. New York: Association Press, 1950.)

One day an Indian left his home to visit a white man with whom he had become friends. Being in a city, with its noises and its crowds, was a new experience for the Indian, and he was fascinated by it.

The Indian and the white man were walking down the street when suddenly the red man touched his friend's shoulder and said quietly, "Stop! Do you hear what I hear?"

His white friend paused, listened, smiled, and said, "All I hear is the tooting of car horns, the noise of the buses, and the voices of people. Just the regular sounds of the city. What is it you hear?"

The Indian replied, "I hear a cricket chirping somewhere nearby."

Again the white man listened, but shook his head. "You must be mistaken," he said, "I hear no cricket. And even if there were a cricket nearby, the chirping would be drowned out by all these other noises."

The Indian would not be persuaded. After a moment he motioned to his friend, and walking a few steps along the sidewalk, they came to a vine growing on the outside of one of the buildings. He pushed the leaves aside, and there, to the amazement of the white man, a tiny cricket was revealed, chirping its loudest. Now that he saw the cricket and was close to it, the white man could hear its call.

As they proceeded on their way, he said to his Indian friend, "Of course, you heard the cricket because your hearing is much better than mine. All Indians can hear better than white people."

The Indian smiled, shook his head, and replied, "No, that is not true. The Indians' hearing is no better than that of the whites. Watch! I'll prove it to you."

He reached into his pocket and found a fifty-cent piece, which he tossed to the sidewalk. As it clinked against the cement, people from several yards around them stopped, turned, and looked. Finally, one of them picked up the piece, pocketed it, and went on his way.

"You see," said the Indian, "the noise made by the fifty-cent piece was no louder than that made by the cricket, yet many white people heard the noise the money made, stopped, and paid attention to it, although they paid no heed to the noise made by the cricket. The reason is not a difference in our hearing. It is a difference in what we have learned to listen for, a difference in the things we turn our attention toward."

Trader Jim

(Reprinted, by permission, from YMCAs of Greater St. Paul and Metropolitan Minneapolis, *Program Resource Book*.)

Did you ever hear of Trader Jim? Trader Jim lived in Boston in the early days. Business was slow in the city. But Jim had heard about the big demand for American furs in Europe, so he decided to close his store and move into Indian country and trade for furs.

After several months of traveling alone, he located an ideal spot of ground in Ohio for a trading post. He built his log cabin on a hill where two big rivers met. After many days and nights of hard work, he completed his store.

He stacked his shelves with hardware, salt, sugar, and seeds. Then he waited.

During all this time he had not seen a single Indian. Then, finally, late one afternoon he saw a fleet of canoes coming around the bend of the river. The Indians beached their canoes far below him, and ignored his presence. Dusk fell and the Indians made camp, built fires, and danced. Trader Jim waited ... and waited. Then he fell asleep.

As the sun rose through the early morning mist, there was a loud rap on the door. A big Indian chief stood alone in the doorway with his arms full of furs. In sign language he counted them to be nine furs. Trader Jim also counted— and recounted—and indicated that there were ten furs with his ten fingers. The chief, however, insisted there were only nine furs and proceeded to select his purchases on this basis. Trader Jim traded for the nine furs and then thrust a large sack of flour into the Chief's arms for the tenth fur and pushed the Chief out the door before he could protest.

It was but a short time later that all the Indians in the camp came to Jim's Trading Post— their arms laden with furs. On his morning trip, the old chief had tested Jim, and Jim's reputation had been established for years to come.

The Unknown Woman

(Reprinted, by permission, from Virginia Pounds Brown and Laurella Owens, 1985, *Southern Indian Myths and Legends*. Leeds, AL: Beechwood Books.)

Two Choctaw hunters camped for the night on a bend in the Alabama River. They were tired and discouraged, having hunted for two days and killed only one black hawk. They had no game to take back to their village.

While they were roasting the hawk on a campfire for their supper, they heard a low, plaintive sound like the call of a dove. The sad notes broke the deep night silence again and again. As the full moon rose across the river, the strange sound became more distinct.

The men looked up and down the river but saw only the sandy shore in the moonlight. Then they looked in the opposite direction and to their astonishment saw a beautiful woman dressed in white, standing on a mound. She beckoned to the hunters.

"I'm very hungry," the woman said.

One of the hunters ran to the campfire and brought the roasted hawk to the woman. After she had eaten some, she gave the rest back to them. "You have saved me from death. I will not forget your kindness. One full moon from now, in midsummer, return to the mound where I am standing."

Suddenly a gentle breeze came up, and the woman disappeared as mysteriously as she had come.

The hunters knew they had seen Unknown Woman, the daughter of the Great Spirit. They returned to their village, but kept secret the strange meeting with the woman.

One month later, when the moon was full, the hunters came back to the place where Unknown Woman had spoken to them. As the moon rose over the opposite bank, they stood at the foot of the mound, waiting. But Unknown Woman was nowhere to be seen.

"She has not come as she promised," they said to each other.

Then one hunter remembered. "She told us to come to the very spot where she stood." So the men climbed the mound. They could not believe what they saw; the mound was covered with a plant they had never seen before. It was a tall plant with leaves like knives and delicate tassels emerging from the spike-like fruit or ears. Inside the ears was a delicious food.

So it was that the Choctaws received the gift of corn. They cultivated corn ever afterward and never again were hungry.

Twigs

(From *The Tales of Running Deer* by D. Monahan. New York: Association Press, 1970.)

"What lesson do you have for us tonight, Running Deer?" Little Bear and Red Fox asked the question at the same moment. Other Indian children gathered around Running Deer's fire waiting for the answer. They came to listen and to learn, as was the custom.

"I would speak this night," responded Running Deer, "of a matter that affects us all—the importance of good habits. We all have habits. We must be sure, then, that our habits are good friends that help us live better lives and not enemies that bring unhappiness and problems."

"What are some good habits, Running Deer?" asked Red Fox.

Running Deer looked into the young faces before him and replied, "It is better for you to answer this question than for me to give the answer. Tell me, what habits do you think are your good companions on the trail of life?"

"Honesty is one, I think," answered a young brave sitting across the campfire circle. Soon a chorus of voices offered other answers.

"We have made for ourselves this night a good list of habits that can be counted on as friends to help us live good lives. You have done very well," Running Deer spoke with appreciation.

"Running Deer, the twigs you have beside you there—what are they for?" asked the ever-curious Red Fox.

"They are part of tonight's lesson. Watch and listen. I hope you will allow them to teach you more about habits—good and bad." Running Deer picked up the first of the twigs. "Each of these twigs we shall give the name of a bad habit. What shall this first one be called?"

"Anger," suggested a young voice.

"Anger it is, then," Running Deer announced. With this he easily snapped the twig in two. "You see how single habits can be broken with only a small effort?" he asked.

Picking up two twigs, and with more effort, he broke them. "You see, two combined are harder to break. Watch closely now," he continued. This time he picked up three twigs. Breaking the three together proved even more difficult. Running Deer added another twig and broke four twigs together. Each time he kept adding another twig until he came to a number that he could not break despite his hardest efforts.

"You see," Running Deer said, "I have now combined so many twigs that I can no longer break them. This is true of habits also. A combination of several bad habits—for instance, anger, dishonesty, impatience, laziness, untruthfulness—can become too strong to break all at once. Be sure that your habits are good ones that need no breaking."

"Running Deer," the voice was that of Little Bear. "By breaking one at a time, the entire bundle can be broken, can it not?"

"True, my friend," answered Running Deer. "This is another lesson we can learn from our twigs. If you have bad habits to break, work on them one at a time until all are conquered. It is also true that good habits can best be achieved one by one."

Wet Feathers

(From *Twenty Tepee Tales* by M. Lotz and D. Monahan. New York: Association Press, 1950.)

Dark clouds rolled out of the west as little Tomahawk walked through the forest near his home. Flashes of yellow lightning danced in the sky, and faraway thunder grew louder. The air was heavy with moisture.

"The clouds will soon be overhead," thought Tomahawk. "I'd better run for the village or I'll get soaked."

He hurried up the path that led to the village. He thought that he would beat the rain, for the wind that comes before a storm was not yet blowing.

A sudden sound made Tomahawk stop. He listened, but all was silent except for the distant roll of thunder. Then, again, he heard the noise; it sounded like a bird in trouble. Searching, he discovered a mallard duck huddled under a bush. The duck did not try to escape from him as he came closer. Looking down, he saw that it had a broken leg. Carefully, he lifted the duck with both hands. In its big brown eyes was a look of fear and pain that would make even a strong man feel sorry for it. Tomahawk quickly tucked the bird under his deerskin jacket and ran for the village. The rain was coming. He would have made the journey faster without the duck, but he remembered how it had looked at him. He held on and ran hard.

Nearly a moon had passed, and the broken leg was completely well. The duck was tame and would run gaily around the wigwam, playing with the Indian children who came each day to see Tomahawk.

The bird had been given a name—"Wet Feathers"—for even though Tomahawk had tried to protect the duck on that rainy day, it had gotten very wet. Tomahawk's father had laughed when he saw the bird and had suggested the name. Actually, he thought it was foolish to have a duck for a pet when it would make such a fine dinner.

Wet Feathers seemed to enjoy its new home, but Tomahawk noticed a longing look in its eye whenever wild ducks, passing overhead, called to it with a loud "honk." So he was not completely surprised when Wet Feathers flew away one day to join its comrades in flight.

Two summers passed. Tomahawk was twelve years old. He had learned to shoot his arrows well and could paddle a canoe with enough skill to please the braves of the tribe.

Each spring the Kickapoo tribe held a canoe race for boys who had not yet reached their eleventh year. Tomahawk stood on the riverbank and watched the race. The young boys of the tribe were straining every muscle, for the winner was to sit at an honored place at the next powwow.

The race was a close one. The river was filled with canoes, and so it was no wonder that many boys were crowded out. Very few people noticed one little fellow who had dropped out right at the start of the race. Not only that, but his paddle was broken.

Later in the day, Tomahawk found this same little boy sitting alone under a big tree, his head in his hands.

"What makes you so unhappy?" asked Tomahawk.

"My father did not expect me to win the race," came the reply, "but he did want me to put up a good fight."

"But you cannot win a race without a paddle," replied Tomahawk.

"I know," said the boy, "but all my father will know is that I did not finish the race. He was not on the riverbank this afternoon."

"But if he wanted you to do well in the race, why did he not come to watch?"

The boy looked up. His eyes were filled with sadness. "Several moons ago, my father was hurt in a fight with a bear. You see, he is blind.

Tomahawk lowered his head. "I am sorry," he said. "I am sorry, too, that you did not do well in the race."

The boy's eyes lighted up. "Perhaps you would come with me and explain to my father about the race. He would understand then how it happened that I did not finish," he pleaded.

"I would be glad to," replied Tomahawk, "but I promised to go fishing with my friend,

Clear Sky, this afternoon. I will help you some other time."

As Tomahawk turned to go, he stopped dead still. There in his path stood No-ha-wiss, the great chief of the Kickapoo tribe. The Chief was looking straight at Tomahawk.

"You are Tomahawk," said the Chief. "I remember the time that you found a duck near the river. You cared for it because it was in trouble. Now you find a fellow brave in trouble, but you refuse to help him? Do you care more for a duck than a fellow brave?"

Tomahawk turned and looked at the boy under the tree. The Chief was right. It was his duty to help. A moment later the boys were walking toward the village. They were going to talk to the boy's father.

Why the Frog Has No Teeth and the Woodchuck Sleeps All Winter

(Reprinted, by permission, from YMCAs of Greater St. Paul and Metropolitan Minneapolis, *Program Resource Book*.)

Once the chief of the squirrel tribe was going through the woods on his regular tour of inspection. When he did this he made himself invisible so that he could find out what was going on. At the foot of a tall pine tree he saw a squirrel, a frog, and a woodchuck engaged in a discussion.

The squirrel was complaining. "Who could have stolen my nuts?" he was saying. "All summer long I have been collecting them; now they are all gone. My nest is empty, swept out clean!"

"What a pity, what a pity!" said the frog, tears rolling down his cheeks.

And the woodchuck made a great bluster and said the culprit ought to be caught.

The chief of the squirrel tribe said to himself, "I'll come around tonight at midnight to investigate further."

That night he came, invisible, and saw the woodchuck digging in his burrow at the foot of the pine tree. After a while the woodchuck stopped and went away; in a few minutes he was back, his cheeks all puffed out. When he came to the hole, he opened his mouth and dropped in the nuts that he was carrying in his cheeks, one by one.

"Where did he get them?" the squirrel chief wondered. "It's a long way from here to a hickory nut tree."

He decided that he would come back at noon the next day to see what else he could discover.

At noon the next day he was back. There was a little spring near the foot of the same pine tree, and from the pool he saw the big green frog come hopping and disappear behind the tree. In a few minutes the frog came back, his cheeks all puffed out. The squirrel chief saw him move aside a tuft of green moss, drop the nuts that he carried in his cheeks into the hole, and then go back for more.

"So that's what happened to poor squirrel's winter store," said the chief of the squirrels, and he sent out a call for all the animals of the forest to come to a great council to decide what punishment the thieves should receive.

When all the animals were seated around in a great circle, they saw that two were missing—the frog and the woodchuck.

"I'll go and get them," said the chief of the squirrels, and, sure enough, in a few minutes he had brought them to the meeting. The frog was all glistening wet; tears were rolling down from his great round eyes. The woodchuck was in a terrible humor with his whiskers bristling.

Now these two were accused of having stolen the squirrel's winter store, and they had no defense. But what should their punishment be? It was the law of the forest that thievery should be punished with death. Some of the animals, however, thought it would be better in this case to have some punishment that would serve as a reminder to future generations.

So they said to the frog, "You, since you have stolen squirrel's nuts, shall never enjoy eating nuts again." Frog, when he heard these words, hopped off in shame and dejection, while from his mouth the teeth dropped out as he went. Frogs have never had teeth from that day to this.

And they said to the woodchuck, "For you who have stolen squirrel's stores, we have another punishment. You shall sleep all through the winter months, and in the summer you shall eat only grasses and vegetables and fruits."

And that's the way it still is.

Indians Discover Fire

After a little brave had attained a certain age, and before he could become a recognized member of the tribe, he had to show that he was worthy of the honor. He had to go out from the tribe, shift for himself, and, on his return, make a contribution that would be a credit to the tribe.

Early one morning a young brave left the Sioux Nation and traveled many miles before nightfall. He had eaten berries and drunk plenty of water from the cool, clear streams. For several days food was plentiful, but as time passed it became more and more scarce. Yet the young brave had found nothing that would prove a benefit to his tribe. He became discouraged and his hunger increased. Finally, finding a cave, he crawled in, hoping the end would be swift, as he could not return to his people a failure.

He lay on the floor of the cave and dozed a minute. Suddenly he opened his eyes in amazement and jumped to his feet as a huge bear stood before him. It said, "Do not be afraid. I am here to tell you that you will make a great discovery this day. You will go back to your tribe and be named 'Great Bear' in my honor." Suddenly the bear disappeared and a strong wind began to blow. The young brave was drawn to the entrance of the cave, where he saw two trees whipped back and forth by strong gusts of wind. The tempo increased as the winds blew furiously, and soon smoke appeared where the trees were rubbing together. In a few moments the dry grass surrounding the trees burst into flame, blazed brightly, and died as the grass burned out.

The young brave waited no more, but hurried back to his tribe and immediately told the Chief of his experience. The Chief was skeptical, but gave the brave a chance to prove himself. After much rubbing of two sticks and moments of great anxiety, a flame was again produced, and Great Bear became a full-fledged member of the Sioux Nation, holding a place of honor beside the Chief at tribal council meetings.

King of the Forest

Long before the forests knew the footsteps of any human, the squirrel was king of all the woods. Among the beasts he was ruler. He was a magnificent animal. Larger than the largest lion, stronger than the strongest buffalo, swifter than the swiftest deer, wiser than the wisest owl. Indeed, he was truly a ruler. Because of his position, he was admired by all the beasts of the forest.

For many years the squirrel ruled well, but the time came when he became so impressed with his authority that he thought of no one but himself. He no longer ruled unselfishly, but grew in selfishness and cruelty. As time passed, his vanity and cruelty became unbearable. Animals who had once loved him now hated and feared him. The fear and hatred for the squirrel grew until the animals felt it necessary to call a meeting of all the beasts of the forest. At this meeting, a prayer was made to the Great Spirit for help.

Hearing the prayer of these worried beasts, the Great Spirit came to earth in the guise of an animal and called upon the squirrel. He found the squirrel mean and ugly, and so, exercising his magic power, he assumed godly form and stood before the squirrel, who cowered at this display of power. The Great Spirit told the huge king he was no longer worthy to rule over the beasts of the forest and that because of his selfishness and cruelty he must be punished.

With this warning, the Great Spirit cast a spell over the squirrel and the once-towering king became so small that the Great Spirit could hold him in one hand. Picking up the now-terrified animal, the Great Spirit threw him high into a tree, saying, "Henceforth you shall spend your days in the trees. Small in stature, you shall fear every living thing. Your food shall be the nuts and herbs of the forest. No longer will you have your kingly roar, but shall chatter in a harmless voice. A new king will be named—one who shall be kind and wise and humble; who will remain unselfish and gentle despite his authority and strength."

With this, the Great Spirit vanished, leaving behind the small, shy animal we know today as the squirrel.

Coyote and the Fox

One day Coyote was going out hunting, so he picked up his bow and quiver. In his quiver he put five arrows; then he started out. The day was hot, and, because Coyote was always lazy,

when he came to a nice, large shade tree, he thought he would lie down awhile. He threw down his bow and quiver and stretched out under the tree. Coyote was lying there looking up through the branches, and what do you think he saw? A great big fox!

"Oh!" said Coyote, "but I am lucky. I did not have to go hunting. I just came out here and lay under a tree, and there is my supper right over my head. Indeed I am lucky. Besides a good supper there is a fine fox skin up there for me.

"Oh, well, I guess I am just about the luckiest one in our tribe—besides being the best marksman, too. When I aim my arrows, I never miss. Just to prove it, I am going to take my five arrows and I will put the best arrow right here in the ground beside me, then I'll shoot one to the north, one to the south, one to the east, and one to the west."

So he did. He shot all his arrows away but one. He picked up the arrow he had put in the ground and said, "Now this is the arrow I am going to kill the fox with. But really, I am so good at shooting I don't even have to shoot with my hands. I am going to shoot this arrow with my toes."

All this time the poor fox was sitting up in the tree listening to Coyote tell how good he was at shooting, and he was nearly frightened to death. In fact, he was trembling so much he nearly fell out of the tree.

Coyote picked up his arrow, placed it between his toes, aimed it very carefully through the branches, and let it fly. But something happened and the arrow did not hit the fox. So, when the fox discovered he had not been shot, he jumped out of the tree and gleefully ran away. When he had reached a safe distance he called back, "Next time, Coyote, don't be so sure of yourself—and don't be so boastful!"

The Quails

(*Storyteller:* Have your listeners make a birdcall every time the word "quail" is used in the story. Teach them the kind of sound you would like them to make so their birdcalls don't disrupt the story.)

Ages ago a flock of more than a thousand quails lived together in a forest. They would have been happy, but they were in great dread of their enemy, the quail-catcher. He used to imitate the call of the quail, and when they gathered together in answer to it, he threw a great net over them, stuffed them into his basket, and carried them away to be sold.

Now one of these quails was very wise, and she said, "My friends, I've thought of a good plan. In the future, as soon as the quail-catcher throws his net over us, each one of you put your head through a mesh in the net and then all lift it up together and fly away with it. When we have flown far enough we can let the net drop on a thorn bush and escape from under it."

All agreed to her plan. The next day when the quail-catcher threw his net, the birds all lifted it together in the very way that the wise quail had told them, threw it on a thorn bush, and escaped. While the quail-catcher tried to free his net from the thorns, it grew dark, and he had to go home. This happened many times, till at last the quail-catcher's wife grew angry and asked her husband, "Why is it that you never catch any more quail?"

Then he said, "The trouble is that all the birds work together and help one another. If only they would quarrel, I could catch them fast enough."

A few days later, one of the quails accidentally stepped on the head of another quail as they landed on the feeding ground.

"Who stepped on my head?" the injured quail demanded.

"Don't be angry," the first quail replied. "I didn't mean to step on you."

But the other quail went on quarreling, and pretty soon blurted out, "I lifted all the weight of the net—you didn't help at all."

That made the first quail angry, and before long all were drawn into the argument. The quail-catcher was watching and saw his chance. He imitated the cry of the quail and cast his net over those who came together. They were still boasting and quarreling, and they did not help one another lift the net. So the hunter lifted the net himself and stuffed them into his basket.

But the wise quail gathered her friends together and flew far away, for she knew that quarrels are the root of misfortune.

Songs

Songs have a definite place in the Y-Indian Guide Programs. There are many songs that will fit into tribal meeting and Longhouse activities. Have fun by joining in an activity that crosses the generations. You can teach new songs at Longhouse workshops for parents, at special YMCA family events, or on camp-outs.

TIPS FOR THE SONG LEADER

A good song leader can make the tribal song-fest a real treat. Children and parents respond to good music and appreciate someone who will help them sing well together. Try these ideas:

- Be enthusiastic; help members enjoy singing as they learn.
- Know the songs you are leading. Begin with one that most of the members know and enjoy.
- Sing along with the group and enjoy yourself.
- Give information about the background of the song.
- Make sure that the group hears the pitch. Don't start too high or too low.
- Give a firm starting signal and set and maintain the tempo of the song.
- Indicate when the group should sing loudly or softly and when to stop together!
- Use action songs when you want to provide movement and energetic involvement. Clapping, stamping feet, standing, and using hand motions all add zest to the occasion.

- Give clear, concise instructions for action songs. Repeat, if necessary, for better understanding.
- Use small, steady, rhythmic beats to guide the group. A broad, clear arm movement works best with large groups. Keeping the rhythm steady is a key to success.

Select songs appropriate for the meeting situation. Rousing choruses and action songs get parents and children off to a good start. Quiet songs have a great impact at campfires and tribal meetings just before the story or devotions.

The following songs are a few suggestions, but try other songs that the tribe enjoys. Take time to prepare, and, if possible, attend a singing skills workshop.

ACTION SONGS

The songs listed here are great fun and can be used in tribal meetings, hikes, camp-outs, and other group activities.

Damper Song

Oh, you push the damper in,
   (Arm forward)
And you pull the damper out,
   (Pull arm back)
And the smoke goes up the chimney just the same.
   (Fingers spiral up)
Just the same, just the same.
   (Full arm sweep right and left)
And the smoke goes up the chimney just the same.
   (Repeat by whistling tune with motions, and on third verse, perform motions without noise.)

Deep and Wide

Deep and wide, deep and wide,
There's a fountain flowing deep and wide.
Deep and wide, deep and wide,
There's a fountain flowing deep and wide.
  (Motions: Use hands in front to describe words:
  Deep—one hand above the other
  Wide—two palms facing each other
  Fountain—both hands move upward
  Flowing—hands move in waving motion)

Do Your Ears Hang Low?

Do your ears hang low?
  (Thumb in each ear)
Do they wobble to and fro?
  (Shake palms together)
Can you tie them in a knot?
  (Tie knot)
Can you tie them in a bow?
  (Tie bow at neck)
Can you throw them over your shoulder
Like a continental soldier?
  (Salute)
Do your ears hang low?
  (Repeat three times, each time faster.)

If You're Happy

(1)
If you're happy and you know it,
Clap your hands.
  (Clap, clap)
If you're happy and you know it,
Clap your hands.
  (Clap, clap)
If you're happy and you know it,
And you really want to show it,
If you're happy and know it,
Clap your hands.
  (Clap, clap)
(2)
If you're happy and you know it,
Stomp your feet
  (Stomp, stomp)
(3)
If you're happy and you know it,
Shout "Hooray."
  (Hooray)

(4)
If you're happy and you know it,
Stand up.
  (Stand up)
(5)
If you're happy and you know it,
Do all four.
  (Clap, stomp, hooray, stand up)

Tommy Tinker

Little Tommy Tinker
Sat on a clinker
And he began to cry:
"Ma-a! Ma-a!"
Poor little innocent guy.
  (Motions: Stand up while singing "Ma-a" and
  then return to sitting position. Sing as a four-part
  round also.)

She'll Be Comin' Round the Mountain

(1)
She'll be comin' round the mountain when she
  comes,
Toot, toot
  (Pull cord)
She'll be comin' round the mountain when she
  comes,
Toot, toot!
  (Pull cord)
She'll be comin' round the mountain, she'll be
  comin' round the mountain, she'll be comin'
  round the mountain when she comes.
(2)
She'll be drivin' six white horses when she comes,
Whoa-back!
  (Pull back reins)
(3)
Oh, we'll all go out to meet her when she comes,
Hi, Babe!
  (Wave hands)
(4)
Oh, we'll kill the old red rooster when she
  comes,
Hack, hack!
  (Chopping motion)

(5)

*Oh, we'll all have chicken and dumplings when
     she comes,*
Yum, yum.
     (Rub tummy)

(6)

*Oh, she'll wear her long red flannels when she
     comes,*
Scratch, scratch.
     (Scratch hip)

(7)

*Oh, she'll have to sleep with Grandma when
     she comes,*
Snore, snore.
     (Snore aloud)

The Cuckoo Song

(1)

Oh, I went to Peter's flowing spring
Where the water's so good,
And I heard there the cuckoo
As she called from the wood.

     (Chorus)

Ho-li-ah, ho-le-rah-hi-hi-rah,
Ho-le-rah ku-kuck,
Ho-le-rah-hi-hi-ah, ho-le-rah-ku-kuck,
Ho-le-rah-hi-hi-ah, ho-le-rah-ku-kuck,
Ho-le-rah-hi-hi-ah, ho!

(2)

After Easter come sunny days
Then will melt all the snow;
Then I'll marry my maiden fair,
Who'll be happy, I know!

     (Chorus)

(3)

When I've married my maiden fair,
What then can I desire?
Oh, a home for her tending
and some wood for the fire.

     (Chorus)

     (Motions: Drum knees on each syllable of "Ho-
     le-rah." Then slap knee on "Ho," clap hands on
     "le-rah," and snap fingers on "hi-hi-rah." Slap
     knee on "Ho," clap hands on "le-rah," and snap
     fingers on "ku-kuck.")

Bingo

*There was a farmer had a dog and Bingo was
     his name-o!*
*B-I-N-G-O, B-I-N-G-O, B-I-N-G-O, and Bingo
     was his name-o!*
*There was a farmer had a dog and Bingo was
     his name-o!*
     (Clap)
-I-N-G-O,
     (clap)
-I-N-G-O,
     (clap)
-I-N-G-O, and Bingo was his name-o!
     (For each succeeding verse, eliminate one letter
     from Bingo and substitute a hand clap.)

Other Action Songs

* Swimming Hole
* My Aunt Came Back

 **FAVORITE MELODIES**

These songs are perennial favorites and are
perfect for intergenerational meetings.

Are You Sleeping

Are you sleeping, are you sleeping,
Brother John, Brother John?
Morning bells are ringing,
Morning bells are ringing,
Ding, ding, dong,
Ding, ding, dong.
     (Repeat as a four-part round.)

Take Me Out to the Ball Game

Take me out to the ball game,
Take me out to the crowd,
Buy me some peanuts and Cracker Jack,
I don't care if we never get back.
We will root-root-root for the home team;
If they don't win it's a shame.
For it's one-two-three strikes you're out
At the old ball game.

I've Been Working on the Railroad

I've been working on the railroad all the live-
long day.
I've been working on the railroad just to pass
the time away.
Don't you hear the whistle blowing? Rise up so
early in the morn.
Can't you hear the captain shouting? Dinah,
blow your horn.
Dinah, won't you blow—
Dinah, won't you blow—
Dinah, won't you blow your horn?
Dinah, won't you blow—
Dinah, won't you blow—
Dinah, won't you blow your horn?
Someone's in the kitchen with Dinah,
Someone's in the kitchen I know-o-o-o,
Someone's in the kitchen with Dinah
Strummin' on the old banjo. And singing—
Fee fi fiddle-i-o,
Fee fi fiddle-i-o-o-o-o,
Fee fi fiddle-i-o,
Strummin' on the old banjo.

Puffer Bellies

Down by the station early in the morning,
See the little puffer bellies all in a row.
See the engine driver turn the little handle.
Chug! Chug! Puff. Puff. Off they go!
    (Melody may be sung in a four-part round.)

There Were Ten in a Bed

There were ten in the bed
And the middle one said,
"Roll over, roll over."
So they all rolled over
And one fell out.
There were nine in the bed
    (etc.)

(End)
There were none on the bed—GOODNIGHT!

The Grand Old Duke of York

The grand old Duke of York,
He had ten thousand men,
He marched them up the hill, and
    (Stand up)
He marched them down again.
    (Sit down)
And when they're up, they're up.
    (Stand up)
And when they're down, they're down.
    (Sit down)
And when they're only halfway up
    (Halfway knees bent)
They're neither up nor down.

The More We Get Together

    (Tune: "Ach Du Lieber Augustine")
The more we get together, together, together,
The more we get together, the happier we'll be.
For your friends are my friends,
    (Point to others)
And my friends are your friends.
    (Point to self)
The more we get together, the happier we'll be.
    (Motions: Stand up when singing "together" or
    sit down if standing. Repeat song a second time
    for all to be seated.)

The Lord Said to Noah

(1)
The Lord said to Noah, "There's going to be a
floody, floody."
The Lord said to Noah, "There's going to be a
floody, floody.
Get your children out of the muddy, muddy,
Children of the Lord."
    (Chorus)
So rise and shine and give God your glory, glory.
Rise and shine and give God your glory, glory.
Rise and shine and give God your glory, glory,
Children of the Lord.
(2)
The Lord said to Noah, "You better build an
arky, arky."

The Lord said to Noah, "You better build an arky, arky.
Build it out of hickory barky, barky.
Children of the Lord."
    (Chorus)
    (3)
The animals, they came on, they came on by twosies, twosies,
The animals, they came on, they came on by twosies, twosies,
Elephants and kangaroosies, -roosies,
Children of the Lord.
    (Chorus)
    (4)
It rained and rained for forty days-y, days-y,
It rained and rained for forty days-y, days-y,
    Almost drove those animals crazy, crazy,
Children of the Lord.
    (Chorus)
    (5)
The Lord said to Noah, "The flood is over, over."
The Lord said to Noah, "The flood is over, over.
Get your children back to the clover, clover,
Children of the Lord."
    (Chorus)

Hey, Ho! Nobody Home

Hey, ho! Nobody home.
Meat nor drink nor money have I none,
Yet I will be me-e-e-erry!
    (Sing as three-part round.)

On Top of Old Smokey

    (1)
On top of old Smokey
All covered with snow,
I learned a great lesson
All people should know.
    (2)
For I met a brave hunter,
He was only a youth,
But he wasn't hunting rabbit,
He was hunting for truth.

    (3)
And he told me he found it
In the red sunset glow,
In the sound of the thunder
And a touch of the snow.
    (4)
And the truth was quite simple,
Just as plain as could be,
And I'll always remember
What the hunter told me.
    (5)
Be fair to your neighbor,
Be honest and true,
Be kind to your neighbor
And he will be kind to you.

Other Favorite Melodies

- The Bear Went Over the Mountain
- The Ants Go Marching

FUN SONGS

The songs in this section can be used on trips and at meetings, and they are especially good for making new members feel welcome.

Animal Fair

I went to the animal fair, the birds and beasts were there;
The big baboon by the light of the moon was combing his long brown hair.
The monkey was a big lunk and sat on the elephant's trunk;
The elephant sneezed, went down on his knees,
And that was the end of the monk, the monk,
And that was the end of the monk.

Elle Ron

Elle Ron, Elle Ron, Elle Ron, Boom, Boom, Boom,
Tum ba, Tum ba, Tum ba, Tum ba la la la lai lai,
Tum ba la la la lai lai, Tum ba la la la LAI!

John Jacob Jingleheimer Schmidt

John Jacob Jingleheimer Schmidt—that's my name, too.
Whenever we go out, the people always shout,
There goes John Jacob Jingleheimer Schmidt,
Tra-la-la-la-la-la-la.
   (Repeat four times, each time more softly except for the "tra-la-la-la-la.")

Little Rabbit Hopping By

In a cabin in the wood
Little man by a window stood.
Saw a rabbit hopping by,
Knocking at his door.
"Help me, help me, sir," he said,
"'fore the hunter shoots me dead."
"Come little rabbit, come inside,
   Safely to abide."

Junior Birdmen

Up in the air, Junior Birdmen,
Up in the air, Birdmen, fly,
And when you hear that grand announcement,
That you have won your wings of tin,
Then you'll know the Junior Birdmen
Have sent their boxtops in.
It takes ten boxtops,
And five bottle bottoms.

Old MacDonald Had a Farm

(1)
Old MacDonald had a farm, ee-i-ee-i-o!
And on this farm he had some chicks, ee-i-ee-i-o!
With a chick, chick here and a chick, chick there,
Here a chick, there a chick,
Everywhere a chick, chick,
Old MacDonald had a farm, ee-i-ee-i-o!
   (2)
Turkey . . . gobble, gobble
   (3)
Cows . . . moo, moo
   (4)
Horses . . . whinney
   (5)
Dogs . . . arf, arf
   (6)
Cats . . . meow, meow
   (7)
Ducks . . . quack, quack
   (8)
Ford . . . rattle, rattle

Row, Row, Row Your Boat

Row, row, row your boat
Gently down the stream.
Merrily, merrily, merrily, merrily,
Life is but a dream.
   (Sing as a four-part round.)

Worms

Nobody loves me, everybody hates me,
Guess I'll eat some w-o-r-m-s.
   (Chorus)
Long, slim, slimy ones,
Short, fat, juicy ones,
Itsy, bitsy, fuzzy, wuzzy w-o-r-m-s.
First you bite their heads off,
Then you chew their tails off,
Then you throw the rest a-w-a-y.
   (Chorus)
Down goes the first one,
Down goes the second one,
Oh, how they wiggle and they s-q-u-i-r-m.
   (Chorus)
Oops, comes the first one,
Oops, comes the second one,
Oh, how they wiggle and they s-q-u-i-r-m.
   (Chorus)

This Old Man

(1)
This old man, he played one,
He played knick knack on my thumb.
    (Chorus)
Knick knack, paddy whack, give a dog a bone,
This old man came rolling home.

(2)
This old man, he played two,
He played knick knack on my shoe.
    (Chorus)

(3)
This old man, he played three,
He played knick knack on my knee.
    (Chorus)

(4)
This old man, he played four,
He played knick knack on my door.
    (Chorus)

(5)
This old man, he played five,
He played knick knack on my hive.
    (Chorus)

(6)
This old man, he played six,
He played knick knack on my sticks.
    (Chorus)

(7)
This old man, he played seven,
He played knick knack up in heaven.
    (Chorus)

(8)
This old man, he played eight,
He played knick knack on my plate.
    (Chorus)

(9)
This old man, he played nine,
He played knick knack on my spine.
    (Chorus)

(10)
This old man, he played ten,
He played knick knack once again,
Knick knack, paddy whack, give a dog a bone,
Now we'll all go running home.

Other Fun Songs

- Camp Smile
- Bubble Gum
- I Know an Old Lady
- The Little Skunk
- Peanut Butter and Jelly
- I'm Being Swallowed by a Boa Constrictor

DEVOTIONAL SONGS

Devotional songs can be sung at the beginning or end of a meeting or around a campfire at the end of the day. They set a mood of reverence and reflection.

Do Lord

(1)
I've got a heavenly Father who hears and answers prayers.
I've got a heavenly Father who hears and answers prayers.
I've got a heavenly Father who hears and answers prayers.
Look away beyond the blue.
    (Chorus, to be repeated after each verse)
Do, Lord, oh, do Lord, oh, do remember me.
Do, Lord, oh, do Lord, oh, do remember me.
Do, Lord, oh, do Lord, oh, do remember me.
Look away beyond the blue.

(2)
You can't wear the crown if you don't bear the cross.

(3)
I took Jesus as my Savior, you take him, too.

(4)
I've got a heavenly Father who hears and answers prayers.

Kum Bi Ya

(1)
Someone's cryin', Lord, Kum bi ya.
Someone's cryin', Lord, Kum bi ya.
Someone's cryin', Lord, Kum bi ya.
O Lord, Kum bi ya.

(Chorus, to be repeated after each verse)
Kum bi ya, my Lord, Kum bi ya.
Kum bi ya, my Lord, Kum bi ya.
Kum bi ya, my Lord, Kum bi ya.
O Lord, Kum bi ya.
    (2)
Someone's prayin', Lord, Kum bi ya.
    (3)
Someone's laughin', Lord, Kum bi ya.
    (4)
Someone's singing, Lord, Kum bi ya.

O Great Spirit

(Tune: "Jesus, Lover of My Soul")
Oh, Great Spirit, now we part;
Enter into each one's heart.
Bless the fellowship we've had;
Follow us, each son and dad.

Taps

Day is done, gone the sun
From the lake, from the hills,
From the sky;
All is well, safely rest,
God is nigh.
Fading light dims the sight,
And a star gems the sky
Gleaming bright;
From afar, drawing nigh,
Falls the night.

Other Devotional Songs

- He's Got the Whole World
- Pass It On

PROGRAM SONGS

These songs are special to the Y-Indian Guide Programs. They can be used to help forge a strong identity among tribal members and reinforce the Y-Indian Guide Programs' aims.

Pals Forever

(Tune: "Clementine")
Pals Forever, Pals Forever,
That's our slogan, that's our song.
Boys are stronger, dads feel younger
When they take the boys along.
Moms are for it, dads adore it,
And the boys all think it's fine.
Pals Forever, Pals Forever,
As Indian Guides we'll have good times.
Through the days and through the years
We will wander side by side.
Pals Forever, Pals Forever,
The Great Spirit is our guide.

Pack the Sleeping Bags

(Tune: "Jingle Bells")
Pack the sleeping bags,
Get out the frying pan,
Shame on he who lags,
Whether boy or man.
We will have some fun,
Out where the coyotes wail;
Oh, dad and son will feel like one
When they're out on the trail.
    (Chorus)
    Indian Guides, Indian Guides
    Happy as can be.
    Indian Guides, Indian Guides
    That's the club for me.
    We'll take a hike
    That's what we like,
    Then home again go we.
    Where dad and son have lots of fun,
    That's where I want to be.

Indian Maiden Song

(Tune: "Clementine")
Friendship Always, Friendship Always,
That's our slogan, that's our code.
And we work and play together
As we travel on life's road.
Dads are for it, Moms adore it,
And the girls all think it's fine.

Friendship Always, Friendship Always,
Indian Maidens have good times.
Through the days and through the years
We will wander side by side.
Friendship Always, Friendship Always,
The Great Spirit as our guide.

Little Brave Chopping

(Tune: "Down at the Station")
Down at the tepees
Early in the morning,
See the Indian camp fires
Burning in a row.
Little brave is chopping

Wood for tepee fires.
Chop! Chop! Crack! Crack!
Watch him go.

Prayer Song

(Tune: "On Top of Old Smokey")
We come to the campfire,
Big braves with their boys.
"Pals Forever" our slogan,
We share many joys.
May the Great Spirit help us
To be clean, brave, and true
To families and neighbors
In all that we do.

Family Activities

$\mathcal{Y}$-Indian Guide Programs help parents and children build a healthy, happy family life. The complex interaction of personalities within a family must be handled wisely if children are to grow into productive, self-confident adults. In many cases, parents enter the task of rearing children with little preparation.

This section of the manual is designed to offer resources in building effective communication and interaction among family members. The techniques provided here address both parents and children, outlining what both can do to help themselves and each other.

The first portion of this section describes an activity that tribe members can use at home to bring the family closer together and clarify personal values. It's called the family circle, and it is a simple way to get family members to talk about themselves and listen to each other. The second part is a collection of communication activities that parent-child teams can try during tribal meetings or on their own. These activities will help them learn more about each other and how they interact.

THE FAMILY CIRCLE

How would you describe the scene at your family dinner table? What is the room like? How does the table look? How many people usually sit at the table? Where do they sit? How fast is the meal eaten and finished? What is the conversation like? How would you describe the atmosphere? Which of the following situations occur too frequently to suit you?

- Everyone talks, no one listens. Stories go uncompleted, and interruptions are frequent.
- No one seems to have much to say. A heavy, sometimes tension-filled silence often hangs in the air.
- One person dominates the conversation. The knowledge that he or she may begin a long lecture or interrupt at any time puts a damper on the conversation.
- Everyone sits down and immediately begins eating. There's no sense of togetherness. Each person is in his or her own private world, except for passing the butter or answering a question.
- The parents' conversation is witty and lively. The children listen obediently but are rarely included in the conversation, except occasionally to answer a question posed by the parents.
- Everyone begins eating so fast that there's no time to appreciate the food—its look, smell, or taste.
- Every discussion turns into an argument. No one seems to want or know how to hear the other person's point of view.
- The children dash away from the table as soon as they are finished eating. They don't feel there is anything worth staying for.

These situations occur so often; not in every home and not all the time in any one home, yet often enough. Parents and children rarely express it, but all want the family mealtime to be more special than it is—more fun, more caring, more interesting.

No one technique can completely change a family's way of relating to each other. Caring, helping, and listening cannot be simulated or learned overnight. They are attitudes and skills that take years to develop. Nevertheless, there is something that families can begin doing today that will help them grow closer together, make the family meal more lively and interesting, and help each member become clearer about his or her own values and sense of identity. It's called the *family circle.*

Family circle is really a very simple procedure. First, after all the food is placed on the table and everyone is seated, everyone holds hands around the table. One member of the family, not necessarily a parent, suggests a topic or question that would be interesting for each person to think about and then to share with the others. For example, the daughter might say, "Everyone think of the nicest thing that happened to you today." (Other family circle topics are suggested later.)

With eyes closed, still holding hands, each person ponders the question or topic suggested. When a person thinks of something—in this case a nice thing that happened—he or she squeezes the hand of the person to the right and left. After a half-minute or so, even if everyone has not thought of something, people drop hands, open their eyes, and proceed to help themselves to dinner. (Families who want to say a formal prayer, in addition to the family circle, can do so either before the topic is suggested or before people begin eating.) Then, one by one, each member of the family volunteers his or her response to the question or topic that was raised.

Everyone should feel free to be silent if they do not care to share thoughts; no one should feel bad about not being able to think of something to say on a given topic. Some people speak up more easily than others, however, and it is often helpful to draw out the quieter members by asking, for example, "Susie, what was the nicest thing that happened to you today?"

Each person gets a turn. If Susie is describing her day, then Mom doesn't come in with a story of her own at this point. She and the others hear Susie out and ask her questions, if they wish. They don't argue or disagree with her, either. For example, if Susie has just finished telling how a particular compliment she re-ceived about her clothes was the nicest thing that happened to her that day, another member should not chime in, "Ugh, that doesn't sound nice at all! That sounds like an insult to me." When a person is the focus of attention, his or her thoughts and feelings are listened to and accepted—that's all. Later on there is time for disagreement or free discussion.

How long each person has the focus of the family depends a great deal on the question posed, the size of the family, the ages of the children, the ability of the children to listen to one another, the general mood of the family on that particular night, and so on. Whether they take two minutes or fifteen minutes for their family circle, each family usually establishes its own norms about time limits, and these are usually quite flexible.

As soon as each member of the family who wants the focus has shared a response, then the family can continue with a free discussion. Members can say, "You know, Susie, the same compliment that made you feel good would have offended me," or "When you told your story, Jerry, it made me think of something that once happened to me." The conversation may even go in an entirely new direction.

Topics for a family circle are infinite. The only requirements are that

- they should be topics about which most members of the family are likely to have something to say;
- they should be questions or issues for which there are no right answers;
- they should clarify values, and should be thought-provoking, interesting, or just plain fun to consider.

To illustrate the variety of family circle topics, a list of topics is provided below. However, you can draw some of the best questions and topics from the lives of your own family members.

SAMPLE FAMILY CIRCLE TOPICS

- What is one thing you'd like to learn how to do?
- Can you recall one of the best meals you've ever had, here or anywhere else?
- What is a funny story you heard or a funny thing that happened to you recently?

- What is something you'd like to do this coming weekend (Christmas, summer, etc.)?
- What was the best thing that happened at school or work today?
- *(Anytime, but definitely at Thanksgiving)* What are you thankful for?
- *(At any holiday)* What does this holiday mean to you?
- What is your earliest memory (or memories)?
- Who is your best friend? What do you like about him or her?
- What is some question you've been wondering about?
- Who is (was) the best teacher you have (had)? What do (did) you like about him or her?
- Where is your favorite spot to be by yourself?
- What is your favorite book (poem, TV show, kind of music, tree, flower, sport)?
- What animal are you most like?
- What is something you wish for that would help someone you know?

How often should the family circle be done? There is really no one answer. In some families it can work almost every night, with many topics repeated frequently and many created by the family members for different occasions. Other families prefer to have a circle once a week, when guests come, or on holidays. There is no correct frequency; each family needs to experiment to discover its own best pattern.

The family meal need not be a battleground, disaster area, or morgue. It can be filled with interesting conversation in which members actually listen to one another. It can be a time when family members get to know one another better and values are clarified and important issues considered.

COMMUNICATION ACTIVITIES

How well do you communicate with your child? Do you listen to each other? Do you

share? Effective communication is one of the most difficult skills to learn, but when we learn it well, the benefits show up in many areas of our lives.

Communication means saying what you mean and hearing what others have to say, listening, and sharing. You have probably found that on some days and with some people you communicate better than on other days and with other people. What makes the difference? Perhaps it's your mood or the weather. Perhaps it's how you are being treated by that other person. Or perhaps it's the topic under discussion. Whatever the reason, awareness of how you're communicating is one giant step toward developing your communication skills.

The following activities are designed to help both parents and children engage in various kinds of communication. Some activities require group participation, but most of the activities are for parent and child to do alone together with minimal group discussion. You may find yourselves talking about topics you've never discussed before. You'll probably learn something about yourself as well as your child. Regardless, you'll both benefit from the shared experience and grow in your communication skills.

Before you begin, read the ground rules listed below and make sure everyone understands them. Then, try doing one activity or perhaps two at a meeting or camp-out. Be sure to allow time for the pairs to have a discussion at the end of each activity. Questions for them to think about might be "What did you learn?" and "How did you feel about the activity?"

Good luck and have fun talking with each other!

GROUND RULES

1. Listen to each other.
2. Speak for yourself.
3. Avoid put-downs.
4. Say what you mean.
5. Be responsible for yourself.

Group Activities

These activities require the participation of the whole tribe, although parts of them may be done by parent-child teams alone.

Name Tags

Purpose: To get acquainted and to share some information about each other.

Materials: 5" × 7" cards; pencils, markers, or crayons; safety pins or tape.

1. Give each person a card and a pencil, marker, or crayon.
2. Ask each person to do the following (one at a time). If the children in your group are nonwriters, have them draw their responses.
   - Write your name somewhere on the card.
   - In one corner write the town where you were born.
   - In another corner write your favorite food.
   - In another corner write the names of two or three friends.
   - In another corner write the name of a place you like.
   - Lightly color the card your favorite color.
3. Have them walk around the room looking at the cards of others and talking with them about their responses.
4. Ask the group to pair off, each with someone he or she didn't know well at the beginning.
5. Have everyone sit in a circle. Have each partner introduce the other person to the entire group using the information on the card.

Respect

Purpose: To understand and discuss the value of respect, to explore reasons why people are respected, and to discuss ways in which respect is earned.

Materials: Paper, pencils.

1. As a group, define the word respect. This is especially important if you have very young children in the group.
2. On your own sheet of paper, list five people for whom you have respect. Then, next to each name, explain why you respect that person.

3. Share your list with others and discuss.
4. On your sheet of paper, list five reasons why you want other people to respect you.
5. Share your list with others when completed.
6. On your sheet of paper, list ten things you can do to be respected by others and by your child or parent.
7. Share and discuss your list when completed.

Getting It All Together

Purpose: To share information in the group about home responsibilities, to discuss the responsibilities without becoming emotional, and to consider change or flexibility in home responsibilities.

Materials: Newsprint, marker, paper, pencils.

1. Begin with a group discussion of the home responsibilities of both parents and children. List these on newsprint so they are easier to recall in the next step.
2. Have the group members pair off into actual parent-child teams. Using the large group list, ask each team to list their individual home responsibilities in two columns, much like the large group list.
3. Next to each item on the list note what happens when that responsibility is not carried out. For example: "Mow lawn: grass goes to seed, neighbors complain, insects breed."
4. Put an "X" by the least favorite responsibilities or the ones that are often forgotten.
5. Discuss the items with an "X."
   a. Are they necessary?
   b. In what way could they be changed?
   c. Who else could do them?
   d. Could the responsibility for them be rotated in the family?
6. Come to some agreement and plan of action for the "X-ed" items.

Surprise!

Purpose: To work together and to share with others.

Materials: This will vary with each parent-child pair. You may want to have handy items such as brown bags, songbooks, glue, magazines, and scissors.

1. Parent and child as partners are to spend five minutes talking about something they could do or make for someone else. Many choices are available for that someone else: family, relatives, neighbors, the other parent, another parent-child pair in the group, and so on.

2. After five minutes, have each pair begin to plan and execute their project. Some may need to go outside for items; others may need the assistance of other parent-child teams in order to carry out their plan.

3. Arrange a time span in which to carry out the projects, perhaps the two weeks until the next meeting.

4. After the projects or plans are completed and delivered, discuss as a group the feelings associated with working out a plan and delivering it. Did you plan well? Did both of you have a part in the plan? What happened when you delivered your project? How did you feel?

Parent-Child Team Activities

The following activities are meant for parent-child teams alone. They can be used both during tribal meetings and at home.

Talking Up and Talking Down

Purpose: To show how physical positions affect communication, to give parents a child's-eye view of the world, and to give children an adult's-eye view of the world.

Materials: A sturdy chair for each pair to stand on.

1. Decide which one of you will be A and which B. A should stand on the chair and B should sit on the floor directly in front of A. Try to maintain eye contact. Talk about how this feels. (Allow two minutes)

   Then change places, with B standing on the chair and A sitting down. Talk with each other about how this feels. (Allow two minutes.)

2. B should reach down and take A's hand and hold it for a few seconds, then reach down and give A a pat on the head. Talk about how this feels. (Allow time.)

   Change positions and try the same things: A and B should make hand contact. A should give B's arm a little yank, then reach down and give B a pat on the head.

3. Now sit at the same level but back to back and carry on a conversation. How does this position feel?

4. Now stand up but stand about ten feet apart and talk. Any change in the conversation?

5. Do what you need to do now to get comfortable and in a good position for talking. Talk about what you felt during the experience. Talk about how your body feels in the position you are in now. What have you learned about the effect of body position on communication? (Allow two minutes.)

Birthday Party

Purpose: To give parents and children an opportunity to talk about friends and what they mean.

Materials: None.

1. Pretend that you and your child are each going to have a birthday party. Begin by asking your child whom he or she thinks should be invited to your party and why. Then share whom you would invite and why.

2. Now reverse the process. Have your child ask you whom you think should be invited to the child's party and why. Your child should then share whom he or she would invite and why.

3. Talk about the following questions:
   a. Why have a party?
   b. Why is it fun to have friends?
   c. What does it mean to be a friend?
   d. When is it hard to be a friend?

If I Could . . .

Purpose: To allow parent and child to daydream and to share dreams and hopes together.

Materials: None.

1. Sit quietly with your eyes closed for 3 minutes and think of dreams and hopes. Think of topics related to the following:

   "If I could, I would like my family to . . ."
   "If I could, I would like to be . . ."
   "If I could, I would like to visit . . ."
   "If I could, I would like my brother/sister/ husband/wife to . . ."
   (Allow 3 minutes.)

2. Share your thoughts with each other. Take enough time to recall as many of your thoughts as possible.

3. Share some insights you had about each other. You may find that this activity will bring up some topics that will be useful for further discussion at home.

Silent Acting

Purpose: To give parent and child an opportunity to act out each other's roles in a make-believe situation while the other person guesses what is being acted out.

Materials: None, or as needed to play the other person.

Each of you takes a turn acting out a situation silently. The idea is to mimic the other person while he or she watches and tries to guess what is being acted out.

ACT I—Child acts out the parent's role.

1. Pick out a situation or an incident between you and your parent that happens a lot.

2. Think of how your parent reacts in that situation.

3. Silently, using facial, hand, or other body expressions, movements, and positions, act out how your parent might react to you in that situation. *Do not use words.*

4. When you're finished, your parent tries to guess what you have acted, including

   • the situation,
   • possible feelings you were trying to show,
   • possible words that might have been said or felt, and
   • why that situation and your reaction to it was chosen.

5. Briefly discuss how that experience was for each of you.

• How did you feel about the play acting, watching, and guessing?
• In real life how do each of you feel in those situations?
• What were the possible feelings your parent was having?
• If needed, what can be done to change the situation?

Act II—Parent acts out the child's role. Follow steps 1 through 5 as described above and silently mimic your child in a situation or recent incident.

Have fun doing this. It might not seem easy at first. However, as you get into it, you'll find it is fun and offers a chance for each of you to express yourself in a different way to one another.

How Will You Know If I Don't Tell You?

Purpose: To give parent and child a chance to share some things they really like about each other that maybe they have wanted to say, but never have said.

Materials: Paper or large blank card, pencils.

1. On your own piece of paper or a large card draw the following tic-tac-toe figure. Draw it quite large.

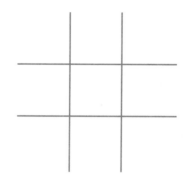

2. On the top-left box write the initials of your best friend.

3. In the top-center box list 4-6 things (behavior, traits, characteristics, etc.) you really like about that best friend.

4. In the middle-left box write the initials of your parent/child.

5. In the middle-center box list 4-6 things (behavior, traits, characteristics, etc.) you really like about your parent/child.

6. In the bottom-left box write your own initials.

7. In the bottom-center box list 4-6 things (behavior, traits, characteristics, etc.) you really like about yourself

8. In the top-right box and middle-right box, next to the list of things you really like, put a check mark if you have told that person in the last 2 weeks that you like that thing about him or her. Put a 0 if you haven't.

9. In the bottom-right box put a check mark in the box if you have been told by someone in the last 2 weeks that he or she really likes that thing about you that is on your list of things you like about yourself. Put a 0 if you haven't been told.

Finally, when both of you have finished your individual charts, share with each other what you have written. The goal is not only to share, but also to discover something new about yourselves and how you feel when you tell or are told something you really like. It may also encourage you to tell and share with another person (e.g., friend, parent, child) the things you really like more often.

My Favorites

Purpose: To allow parent and child to share information about themselves, to learn about each other, and to learn about themselves.

Materials: Paper, pencils.

1. List on the paper all the different kinds of favorite things you can think of; for example, food, drink, sports, TV shows, clothes, shoes, colors, cars, places, kinds of transportation, friends, books, summer activities, or winter activities.

2. Next to each item, put an "X" if it has been a favorite for a long time and an "O" if it is a new favorite.

3. Share your lists with each other. Go through each list slowly and add to each item how you think it got to be your favorite.

4. Briefly discuss the experience.
   a. What did you learn about the favorites on your partner's list?
   b. Were there any surprises?

5. This entire activity may be repeated for least favorites too!

I Want From You—

Purpose: To list "wants," to share and decide what can be done together and individually about wants, and to increase understanding and good feelings in the parent-child relationship.

Materials: Paper, pencils.

1. Each of you should draw on a sheet of paper the illustration shown below and write in the headings.

2. Each of you should then do the following steps separately:
   a. In the "I want from you" column, list 5 things you want from the other person that you don't feel you're getting enough of at present. For example, your child wants you to play backgammon (or another game) more often; you want your child to do agreed-upon household chores on time.

"I Want From You _____"	When? or How Often?	How Important Is It to Me?	What WE Decide to Do About It
1)			
2)			
3)			
4)			
5)			

b. In the next column, "When? or How often?" complete what you would like to happen. For example, your child wants to play backgammon (or another game) once a week; you want chores done on the agreed-upon schedule once a week.

c. In the "How important is it to me?" column, rank items listed in order of their importance to you. Most important is 1, next is 2, and so on down to the least important one on your list.

3. Share your lists and responses. When each of you has shared, use the last column, "What we decided to do about it," to fill in your decision on each issue.

Parent-Child Conversations

Purpose: To help parent and child become aware of the need to listen and share how they feel about certain issues.

Materials: Paper, crayons.

1. One of you should make a short statement about one of the topics listed below. The other partner will then ask several questions, each beginning with "Do you mean?" These questions can only be answered yes or no. When 3 yes answers have been given, switch.

2. The following are some topics you might like to discuss. Be sure to vary these topics so that they are appropriate to your needs.

a. Cooperation
b. Sharing
c. Friends
d. I like to do things with you because . . .
e. Being afraid
f. Love

3. After 2 topics or 10 minutes, stop. Each of you should then draw a picture of something you just talked about. Tell your partner about your picture.

4. Alternative: Instead of drawing a picture, share "I learned" statements with each other:

a. I learned that I . . .
b. I was surprised that I . . .
c. I was pleased that I . . .

Family Life Mural

Purpose: To provide opportunities to share important things about the family.

Materials: Brown mural paper or grocery bags, tape, crayons.

1. Take a piece of large brown paper or cut open several grocery bags and tape them together. Sit down as a team and, working together, draw a picture of the following:

a. What our family looks like
b. Our family's favorite place
c. A way we work together as a family
d. A way we play together as a family

2. Allow time for each of you to share what it is you added to the mural and why.

3. If possible, hang the mural in a visible place at the gathering or display it at home.

Feelings Jar

Purpose: To open up communication between parent and child regarding feelings, to practice talking about feelings, and to label feelings.

Materials: Wide-mouthed jar (or can or bowl), small slips of paper, pencil.

1. Take a jar, can, or bowl (with a mouth wide enough for an adult's hand to get all the way in) and label this the Feelings Jar.

Many feeling words are included on the list below. Write each word on a separate slip of paper and place them all in the jar.

Feeling Words

pleased	impatient
surprised	encouraged
embarrassed	weary
happy	hurt
wonderful	lost
flustered	afraid
comfortable	bugged
glad	cheated
nervous	annoyed
excited	worried
bored	hopeful
put upon	confident
satisfied	eager
fed up	

2. One of you should pick a slip of paper from the jar. The two of you should then discuss the following questions:

   a. Did anyone in our family have that feeling during the week?
   b. When? What were the circumstances at the time?
   c. How does that member of the family feel about the situation now?
   d. When the family member had that feeling, what could have happened that would have made that person feel differently?

3. Repeat the process, with the other partner's removing a slip from the jar.

4. You might take this activity home to do as a family. It's a great way to make it OK to talk about feelings.

Additional family programs and activities can be found in the *YMCA Family Time* handbook and the Character Development Activity Box. Both are available through the YMCA Program Store.

Alternative Parent-Child Programs

WHAT ARE THE Y ALTERNATIVE PARENT-CHILD PROGRAMS?

_A_lthough the Y-Indian Guide Programs are structured to make it easy to establish a program and provide consistency, each YMCA reserves the right to modify the program to meet the needs of the families it serves.

In some YMCAs, this involves slight modifications, such as setting up a coed situation in a new tribe to ensure the participant numbers are high enough to guarantee the program's success. In other YMCAs, this may involve setting up brother-sister tribes so parents with busy schedules can spend time with both children in the program.

Some YMCAs have made an effort to group parents and children in tribes based on their specific needs or interests, such as tribes of second-shift dads or non-custodial parents who can only meet on weekends. If children's disabilities make it difficult for leaders to integrate them into a regular tribe, YMCAs may form a tribe where activities are designed to accommodate the special needs of the children involved. Although integration is always the first choice, sometimes a tribe for children with special needs can really be the support group that parents and children need.

YMCAs in Florida and a few other states are converting some of their tribes into family tribes. Family tribes allow either parent or both to participate with all their children in one tribe.

These tribes are designed to meet the needs of a parent who travels for his or her job or who has a job involving commitments that make it difficult to attend all tribal, Nation, and Federation meetings and events. Under a typical Y-Indian Guide structure, the child would not be allowed to attend when the parent was absent. But in Y-Family Guide Programs, the other parent can fill in as needed.

Some YMCAs have been uncomfortable adopting the American Indian theme due to personal convictions or opposition in their communities. These YMCAs have been able to adapt the Y-Indian Guide Program, using a similar structure but incorporating a different theme. Five examples are included in this section:

- The YMCA of Minneapolis developed a program called "Y-Voyagers."

- The YMCA of St. Paul took a multicultural approach and dropped the Indian name, creating a program called "Y-Guides." In Y-Guides, participants are encouraged to share their own cultures and views or to study and introduce crafts, stories, and games from a variety of cultures.

- Substituting a Wild West theme for the Indian theme, the Mid-Peninsula YMCA in Palo Alto, California, operates a successful program called "Y-Westerners."

- The YMCA of Cincinnati found African American families could relate better to a program highlighting African culture; hence the "Y-African Guide Program."

- The YMCAs of Central Florida in Orlando have changed the Y-Indian Guide Program to include the entire family in a program called "Y-Family Guides."

175

In this section, we'll provide you and your YMCA with the information you'll need to run these alternative programs. As we describe each of these programs, we'll cover the following areas:

- Basic overview or introduction to the program and objectives

- Purpose, slogan, aims, and pledges, where applicable

- The program structure, framework, and organization

- Sample meeting outline

- Property and leadership

As you read through this section, think about how each alternative parent-child program may apply to your situation. Consider how you might adapt ideas from a variety of models to create the best approach for your YMCA population. Moreover, although each of these YMCAs has developed a guidebook for their own YMCA that includes activities and events, arts, crafts, songs, and stories, they are similar to those found in Y-Indian Guide Programs. The program activities as well as the basic instructions in this manual are often appropriate for any parent-child program.

The Crazy Quilt Factory, a longtime YMCA preferred vendor, is willing to help you design patches for your alternative program. You will find their listing in the appendix of this manual.

For additional information on these alternative parent-child programs or other YMCA family programs, contact the YMCA of the USA Program Development Division at 800-872-9622.

Y-Voyager Program

Purpose

The purpose of the Y-Voyager Program is to foster understanding and companionship between father and child.

Slogans

"Pals Forever"—Y-Guides (boys)

"Friends Always"—Y-Pathfinders (girls)

The slogan does not mean that the father and child relate to each other as equals, such as two children who are pals. Rather, it means that father and child have a close, enduring relationship in which there is communication, understanding, and companionship. The Y-Voyager Program encourages such a relationship by providing a means for father and child to share enjoyable experiences, to observe and learn about one another, and to develop mutual respect.

Aims

1. To be clean in body and pure in heart.
2. To be pals forever/friends always with my father/child.
3. To love the sacred circle of my family.
4. To listen while others speak.
5. To love my neighbor as myself.
6. To seek and preserve the beauty of God's creation.

Pledge

"We, father and child, through friendly service to each other, to our family, to this band, to our community, seek a world pleasing to the eye of the Great Spirit."

Program Objectives

1. To strengthen family life.
2. To improve the spiritual, mental, and physical well-being of all people.
3. To develop leadership skills among those in the community.
4. To provide life enhancement opportunities for disadvantaged individuals.
5. To advance international understanding, justice, and peace.
6. To demonstrate and promote equality among all people.

Y-Voyagers is an alternative parent-child program with a structure similar to Y-Indian Guide Programs. Like Y-Indian Guides, the program provides opportunities for a parent and child to spend time together, having fun while learning and sharing values. Unlike Y-Indian Guides, however, the Y-Voyager Program does not use Native American lore or culture as its theme. Instead, as the name implies, parents and children gather to take a voyage, to discover the world together. Instead of tribes, parent-child pairs form "bands." Leaders are called "Navigators."

To introduce the program, you might say the following:

As a Y-Voyager parent, you are beginning a voyage with your child that will be remembered for a lifetime! Probably much more so than most "real" trips that you might take with your family in your child's formative years because this voyage never ends: It is a quest to help foster a meaningful, positive relationship with your child, and in the process, perhaps learn a little about yourself, each other, the world in which we live, and how to make a difference in all of these!

If this sounds like a program purpose that is too lofty to be much fun, don't worry. Fun was the guiding principle in developing the Y-Voyager Program. We believe the path to more meaningful and positive parent-child relationships is not complicated; but it does demand one ingredient for which there is no substitute: time together. Projects and activities require our attention, communication, talents, opinions, and feelings. The kind of time together that leads to real enjoyment and appreciation of life, self, and each other is the basis for a long-lasting, more meaningful relationship.

Why become involved in a "program" to spend time with your child? Can't parents and children do this on their own? Sure they can. But in today's fast-paced world, the truth is that many do not.

Think of this program as your formal commitment to establish a stronger relationship with your child. Use it as the way to have fun with your child and get to know each other better. Invest the time and energy the program requires; take the risks that the program will offer. Encourage your child to do the same, and we can guarantee a voyage of friendship that will last a lifetime.

Starting a Y-Voyager Band

Now that you are joining the Y-Voyager Program, you are probably wondering "How do we get started?" Just follow three steps: form a band, choose a YMCA Council representative, and set up dads' meetings.

Forming a Band

First, you and other new fathers and children will be brought together by a mentor who will pass on to you the tradition and rituals of the Y-Voyager Program. If this is a new program, the mentor may be a YMCA staff member who has researched the program and understands how it works. Once your group understands the purpose of the program, you may form a band.

Each band is made up of fathers and children from local neighborhoods; they meet for monthly band meetings, events, and Y-Voyager Gatherings. Once you have met the other members of your band, you must select a band name (see the list of suggested names at the end of this section) and design a band vest to be worn at all band meetings and Y-Voyager Gatherings.

Choosing a YMCA Council Representative

The next step is to pick your YMCA Council representative. By selecting a representative, each band is connected through the YMCA Council to the other bands in the Y-Voyager Program. In this way, the YMCA Council brings bands together to share ideas for band meetings and outings and to plan the monthly Y-Voyager Gatherings, which are the monthly events sponsored by the YMCA Council.

The YMCA Council is comprised of the Council Navigator, Co-Navigator, Purser, Tallykeeper, YMCA Program Director, and other adult volunteers wishing to assist in the operation and planning of the Y-Voyager Program. Representatives from each band make up the rest of the council members.

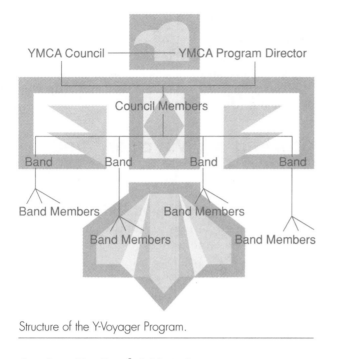

YMCA Council ——— YMCA Program Director

Council Members

Band   Band   Band   Band

Band Members   Band Members

Band Members   Band Members

Structure of the Y-Voyager Program.

Setting Up Dads' Meetings

This final step is probably the most difficult. It involves setting up your first dads' meeting for the fathers in your band. Your mentor will help you, but it takes commitment and organization on the part of each father to make this step successful.

The main purpose of these meetings is to iron out business details. Planning for trips, special events, and so forth, goes much more smoothly when dads meet alone. It is at your first dads' meeting that you should begin planning the dates for your monthly band meetings and band outings. Your mentor can answer any questions you might have as well as offer suggestions to help you plan your first band meeting.

Follow these ideas to run successful dads' meetings:

- *Plan ahead.* Advanced planning can be done for a month or semester at a time at a dads' meeting. Special events or surprises can be discussed without exciting the children too far ahead of time. For example, a weekend camping trip two months away can be planned by the parents without making the children wait too long.

- *Learn and evaluate.* Dads' meetings also offer excellent opportunities for learning. As a group, you can evaluate band meetings, suggest improvements, and discuss weak points objectively without involving the children. This is the most appropriate time for your Y Program Director or your mentor to listen to your problems and help you solve them.

- *Communicate.* Your time in the dads' meeting is best spent trying to understand your own child better, learning how to be closer to your son or daughter, or trying to learn to cope with behavior problems. Although the YMCA is ready to help in this regard, often considerable understanding can be gained by a frank discussion of issues and problems among parents.

- *Improve.* At dads' meetings you will have a chance to review the program manuals or books and magazine articles that will help you to be a better parent and program participant. You can share ideas on improving invitations, games, or stories. Your Y Director and your mentor are always available to help your band develop good dads' and band meetings.

The sample parents' meeting agenda and checklist on pages 21-22 should help you organize your dads' meetings.

Band Leadership Roles

The structure of a band provides several leadership opportunities for both parents and children. So at your first dads' meeting, assign leadership roles to the fathers and children in the band.

The roles for fathers found in many current bands include the Navigator, Co-Navigator, Purser, Tallykeeper, and Band Elder:

- *Navigator.* This father sees that there is continuity in meetings, conducts portions of the meetings, and acts as the leader of the group. He presides at dads' meetings, delegates assignments, and checks to see that tasks are being done. He is the band contact person for the YMCA and represents the band at the monthly or semimonthly YMCA Council meetings. (Some bands change Navigators every six months, but you should recognize the need for continuity and ongoing contact with the YMCA Program Director.)

- *Co-Navigator.* This father assumes the duties of the Navigator when the Navigator is not able to attend meetings. He may accompany the Navigator to YMCA Council meetings and may assume the Navigator's job the following year.

- *Purser.* This father acts as the band's treasurer. Your band may decide to collect dues for its own use, for example, for special treats or other items or events. The Purser is responsible for the collection and safekeeping of the dues.

- *Tallykeeper.* This father acts as the band's recording secretary. He keeps attendance records, conducts all correspondence, maintains historical records, and sends birthday cards and special announcements.

- *Band Elder.* This father is the "wise" parent of the band. Usually a former Navigator assumes this role. He reminds all members of the aims of the program and leads the band in many service projects.

Your band is free to create new or additional offices, and all parents should hold some office, at some time; however, be sure that you assign specific tasks to all offices. Office titles such as Craft Maker, Sign Maker, Council Judge, and the like are acceptable and have been adopted by some groups.

Like parents, you can give children special band responsibilities. Some children's leadership roles we suggest include the following:

- *Young Navigator.* Usually the son or daughter of the Navigator assumes this role. He or she helps keep the children attentive, assists in the ceremonies, and reports on band activities.

- *Runner.* He or she keeps all band property in the property box and runs errands for the Navigator.

- *Scouting Reporters.* The scouting report is an assignment given to the children by the Navigator to be completed between meetings. By making a short report to the band, children develop poise and speaking ability, exercise their inquisitive and thoughtful natures, and practice responsible behavior. Scouting reports could include bringing in magazine pictures of certain scenes, activities, or cultures; making a list of insects found in the backyard; and the like. It is a good idea to recognize the children for their efforts in giving scouting reports.

Band Meetings

So now that you have had your dads' meeting, it is time to host your first band meeting. The other members of your group will arrive at your house ready for some exciting, fun activities. If you follow these simple steps, you are guaranteed a successful meeting:

- *Invitations.* Make invitations to send to your band. You and your child can make beautiful handmade invitations of paper or other materials. Be sure to include the date and time of the meeting, your address, and your telephone number. Mail these at least one week before the meeting. Request that band members who cannot attend notify you.

- *Snack.* Prepare a snack for the people who are coming. It is best to have a snack that can be easily eaten by hand. We also recommend having something to drink (juice, soda pop, milk) available.

- *Agenda.* Set an agenda for the meeting. This will help keep things running smoothly and will help you begin and end your meeting on time.

- *Activity.* Prepare an activity. Songs, crafts, and games can be the most exciting part of any band meeting, but in order to be successful, you must plan in advance. The activity section of this manual provides a variety of activities, a list of supplies needed for each activity, and instructions. Consider the activities carefully so that you can make the best possible choice for your band.

On the following page is a sample meeting agenda you can use. After your band is up and running, involve the children as much as possible in helping to plan the meeting schedule and activities. They will have all kinds of suggestions that you can incorporate into this general outline, and involving them will make for a stronger group.

SAMPLE MEETING AGENDA

6:30   Call to order

Navigator calls the meeting to order. Opening ceremonies can include any or all of the following:

- A thought for the week
- A prayer (if common religious beliefs are shared by group members)
- A song (the kids will know a lot of these)
- A pledge or poem made up by the group for this purpose

6:40   State of the band

Allow children some time to share something that has happened to them or their family. Some type of "talking stick" that is passed around the group is a good device to control talking out of turn.

Scouting reports

6:55   Band plans

What is coming up? Discuss gathering events, band activities, planning, and so on.

7:10   Unit activity

Include any or all of the following: arts and crafts, games, tricks, surprises.

7:45   Cleanup and refreshments

We suggest a story or music during refreshments.

7:55   Closing ritual

Repeat the Y-Voyager slogans, aims, and pledge.

8:00   Head for home.

Band Name

Just about anything connected with the outdoors and exploration will make a fine name for your band. Here are some possible names:

Cedar	Red Rock	Vermillion
Spring	Sturgeon	Basswood
Setting Sun	Great Pine	Portage
Mackenzie	Rose Falls	Algonquin
Big Rock	Lunar	Moose
Summer	Bald Eagle	Bigsby
White Pine	Lac la Croix	Plateau
Namakan	Thunderbay	Taconite
Caribou	Borealis	North Star
Fall	Adventurers	Cascade
Superior	Radisson	Summit
Pemmican	Spruce	Beaver
Fond du Lac	Aurora	Lone Wolf
Iron Wood	Hungry Jacks	Granite

Whitetail	Bearskin	Hudson Bay
Redpine	Mississippi	Meadow
Great Stone	Ottertrack	Winnipeg
Springwater	Dawson	Whitewater
Clearwater	Flambeau	Silver Fox
Jackpine	Brule River	Winter
Mount Rose	Rainy Lake	Timber Wolf
Big Knife	Gunflint	Knife River

Try brainstorming with your group to find a name everyone likes. One that can be easily represented in symbolic form, rhymed, and understood is probably the best.

After you have chosen a name, you might want to do one or more of the following activities (dividing the large group into smaller groups and assigning one group to each of these tasks will help manage the situation):

- Make up a band pledge, rhyme, song, or cheer.
- Have the children design a band insignia that includes symbols that reflect the name of the band or that reflect unique qualities of the people in the group.
- Make a band flag that can be used at gatherings and meetings.
- Make a band poster with your insignia, motto, or pledge.

Band Property

Every band should make its own set of band property, which may include the following items:

- *Talking stick or rock.* During meetings, grant the person holding the talking stick or rock the right to speak. Members can decorate a talking stick or rock with paint, beads, ribbon, felt, buttons, or any other material.
- *Band fire.* Make a "fire" by nailing or screwing six to ten sticks together in the shape of a tepee, log cabin, or combination of both, mounting on a plywood board, and placing a lightbulb in the center to simulate a fire. If possible, set it up so the lightbulb actually lights by using a lamp without a shade or an electric socket.
- *Tallykeeper's book.* Construct a book for the purpose of keeping records of meet-

ings and events. If desired, decorate it with various designs.

- *Purser pouch.* Select a container for holding band funds. Decorate it, if desired.

Band property is made by band members and belongs to the band. So purchase all materials with band funds. Each parent and child should share responsibility for making some of the band property. Keep the band properties in the property box, which is taken by the next host after each meeting. Thus, all property is kept intact and is readily available at the site of each successive meeting.

Y-Guides Program

Purpose

The purpose of the Y-Guides Program is to foster understanding and companionship between parent and child.

Slogan

"Friends Always"

Aims

1. To be clean in body and pure in heart.
2. To be friends always with my parent/child.
3. To love the sacred circle of my family.
4. To love my neighbor as myself.
5. To appreciate the diverse cultures in our community.
6. To seek and preserve the beauty of nature in our world.

Pledge

"We, parent and child, through friendly service to each other, our family, and this club seek a world pleasing to our Creator."

Club Song

"Friends Always" (Tune: "Clementine")

Club meetings follow the same format as a Y-Indian Guide or Y-Voyager meeting. See page 182 for a sample meeting agenda. Modify the agenda to reflect the specifics of your program.

Program Objectives

The YMCA is committed to providing opportunities for family enrichment and personal development. The Y-Guides Program accomplishes this goal in accordance with the following objectives:

1. To foster a friendship between parent and child that will be the basis for a positive, lifelong relationship.
2. To build self-esteem and a sense of self-worth.
3. To develop spirit, mind, and body.
4. To provide a setting for a fun, healthy time together.
5. To enrich family relationships.
6. To offer the parent a chance to be a major part of the child's growth and development.
7. To give the parent and child the opportunity to develop volunteer leadership skills.

Goals to Aid Children's Developmental Learning

The Y-Guides Program strives to provide values-based activities that help children in each of the following ways:

1. To develop a close friendship with and identify with a parent.
2. To gain confidence through acceptance by adults close to them.
3. To feel secure in the parent's love and be able to share that love with others.
4. To develop a sense of self-worth and usefulness through accountability for and completion of assigned tasks.
5. To find satisfaction in sharing and playing with children of the same age.
6. To develop new skills.
7. To understand the need for rules and develop the ability to take direction.
8. To learn to value and accept people for who they are.

Y-GUIDES: ST. PAUL, MINNESOTA

Y-Guides is the Y-Indian Guide Program without the Native American theme. The structure, aims, and purpose in both programs are very similar, however, since Y-Guides offers the opportunity to share the various cultures and backgrounds of all participants instead of focusing on Native American culture. For example, in a diverse club of Euro-Americans, African Americans, Mexican Americans, and Asian Americans, each parent-child pair could assume responsibility for introducing at the club meeting a song, craft, or snack indicative of their culture.

To introduce the program, you might say the following:

Welcome to a fantastic *adventure*! The YMCA has a long history of providing programs to enrich family relationships. The Y-Guides Program is for parents (or a significant adult in a child's life) and five- to eleven-year-old children to help them focus on strengthening the relationship between them. Participation in the program has been described as a fabulous adventure, one that will create lifelong memories and friendships. This is accomplished through fun activities, crafts, club meetings, and special events planned by YMCA staff and volunteer program leaders.

Throughout the program, parents have the opportunity to observe their children interacting with other adults and children and can encourage or discourage behaviors in an informal, comfortable setting. Children have the opportunity to observe parents relating to and having fun with other adults and children outside their own family. Children get very excited about the individual attention they receive from one parent, and this attention helps build self-confidence and self-esteem.

The Y-Indian Guides Program was developed in the mid 1920s by Harold S. Keltner to support the father's role as a friend and guide to his children. In 1926 Keltner, a St. Louis YMCA Director, organized the first group of fathers and sons in Richmond Heights, Missouri. During a hunting and fishing trip in Northern Canada with Joe Friday, an Ojibwa Indian, Keltner was struck by the important role the Native American father played in raising his sons. Inspired by this, Keltner invited Joe Friday to speak to groups of fathers and sons at YMCAs in St. Louis. The audiences were keenly interested, spurring Keltner to form a father-son program based on Native American customs. The Y-Indian Guides Program became a national program in 1935. A few years later, a similar program was started for fathers and daughters.

The program grew and today serves thousands of families each year. Its success can be attributed to its approach: Parents take time away from their busy schedules to focus one-on-one on their relationship with their child. Twice each month, the parent and child meet to play together, learn from and about each other, and participate in activities that are only for them. They share mutually rewarding experiences while growing closer together in love and understanding. No other program facilitates this relationship in this fashion.

As mentioned, originally, the program focused on the Native American culture. Today, our modified Y-Guide Program offers the opportunity to share the cultures and backgrounds of all participants while continuing to strengthen and enrich the parent-child relationship.

Next, we'll look at descriptions of what is involved with the program, specific guidelines for club and parent meetings, tips on getting a club started, and ideas for crafts, songs, stories, games, and field trips.

Starting a Y-Guides Club

Each club is made up of parents and children from the same or nearby neighborhoods. We recommend a club size of seven pairs, made up of children of the same age or grade.

Club meetings offer time away from the rest of the family for each pair to concentrate on their relationship and friendship. Meetings are carefully structured, yet there is room for flexibility and creativity. Clubs that are most active and organized tend to be the most successful and rewarding. Through club meetings, parents have a chance to make a significant impact on their children's religious beliefs and value systems. For children, learning how to participate in a group enhances development and personal growth.

Club and Parents' Planning Meetings

Meet as a club two evenings a month September through May. Hold meetings in members' homes. Plan for each meeting to last about 90 minutes. Structure meetings as described on page 182 of this manual. Substitute references to Indian lore with something more appropriate to your program. Assign parents and children specific responsibilities. One pair serves as "Club Chair" and "Junior Club Chair" for the year, ensuring consistency and leadership at meetings. Hold separate parents' meetings to discuss club business as described on pages 21-22. After each member-pair has held at least one meeting in their home, many clubs opt to go on a field trip. Select the outing or location at a club meeting, but plan for the details at a parents' meeting.

All-Club Events

All-Club Events involving all Y-Guides clubs associated with a YMCA branch are held six times a year. Organized and set up by the YMCA program staff with input and direction from the volunteer Y-Guides leadership, these events include winter and spring camp-outs, the fall Induction Ceremony, and activities such as hayrides, roller-skating, kite flying, a bike trip, a cookout, or a visit to a nature center. You may wish to include the rest of the members' families in these events.

Branch Council

The Branch Council is made up of key volunteers from the Y-Guides clubs. The Branch Council meets once a month with the YMCA program staff to plan and coordinate All-Club Events, discuss concerns, and develop ideas for new Y-Guides Program activities. The Branch Council also helps YMCA program staff put out a periodic Y-Guides Program newsletter distributed to club members, and it maintains the All-Club "shield" (see boxed description). Ideally, at least one representative from every Y-Guides club is represented on the Branch Council. The Branch Council should have at least six members.

The Council Leader works closely with the YMCA program staff, leads council meetings, has the primary role in the All-Club induction and closing ceremonies, and writes the introductory paragraph for the first Y-Guides Program newsletter of the year. This position involves a one-year term; no one should hold it more than two consecutive terms.

Council members help plan, coordinate, and run All-Club Events, have key parts in the All-Club induction and closing ceremonies, serve as the liaisons between the Branch Council and their Y-Guides clubs, and help produce the Y-Guides Program newsletter by writing an introductory paragraph periodically throughout the year. Council member terms are one year long.

Club Organization

The process of getting a club started is itself an important part of the Y-Guides Program. Your group needs to begin learning about the program, organizing your club, and developing friendships. Most of all, you should be creative in setting up your own program to meet the needs of the children and parents involved.

All-Club Shield

Made by the Branch Council and used by the Branch Council Leader at opening and closing campfires, the shield is made once by a newly formed Branch Council and then passed down to subsequent Branch Councils over the years. The newly elected Council Leader receives the shield at the Closing Ceremony. You can make a shield of cardboard or plywood 12 to 16 inches in diameter, using a nature theme. Include a space to write or woodburn the names of parent-child Council Leader pairs and the years they held the leadership position. The Branch Council is responsible for maintaining the shield and bringing it, when needed, to ceremonies and events.

Begin by determining who your club members will be. Remember, an ideal club size is seven pairs with children the same age or grade. Next hold a parents' planning meeting at which you schedule the first club meeting to take place shortly after the parents' planning meeting, using the following checklists.

❏ Select a club meeting night.

❏ Set up meeting dates and choose hosts, inspirational leaders, and storytellers for the first four to nine months of meetings.

❏ Review the section on pages 21-22 that explains the items you need to cover at a parents' planning meeting.

❏ Fill out the Parent-Child Roster and the Program Rotation Sheet found on pages 42 and 43 in the Program Framework section of this manual. The Treasure Keeper is responsible for turning in a copy of the completed roster and meeting schedule to the YMCA program director.

❏ Decide how much club dues will be and collect this amount at the first club meeting.

❏ Choose club leadership and record on the Y-Guides Club Roster and Meeting Schedule sheet. See descriptions of leadership roles under "Club Leadership Roles."

❏ Choose one or two representatives to serve on the Branch Council as described under "Branch Council." Let the YMCA know who your representatives are.

❏ Decide what items need to be made to carry out club activities and set up a time line to make them. See listing of necessary items under "Club Property."

❏ Ask the parents to choose Y-Guides names for themselves before the first club meeting. They should help their children choose names, too. See "Choosing Y-Guides Names and a Club Name" in this section.

❏ Choose values-oriented themes the club will emphasize over the next three to four months.

❏ Assign someone to serve as the inspirational leader and someone to serve as storyteller for the first club meeting. (See "Club Leadership Roles.")

❏ Introduce everyone by his or her Y-Guides name.

❏ Choose a club name. See "Choosing Y-Guides Names and a Club Name" in this section. Register it with the YMCA so it will not be duplicated.

❏ Send your official roster to the YMCA along with completed registration forms and fees.

The Induction Ceremony is the first All-Club Event and will be scheduled by the YMCA in the early fall.

Club Leadership Roles

Have club members elect parent-child pairs to leadership positions. Delegating leadership roles ensures club organization and continuity as well as provides an opportunity to develop leadership skills. Hold the elections for the following positions at the first parents' planning meeting.

- *Club Chair* (parent). This parent makes sure there is continuity in club meetings and leads parts of the meeting. The Club Chair leads parents' planning meetings, delegates responsibilities, makes sure tasks are completed, and ensures that a club meeting schedule is written out and given to all members. This position involves a one-year term.

- *Junior Club Chair* (Club Chair's child). This child helps with club meeting ceremonies, keeps other children focused on activities, and helps report news to the Branch Council.

- *Assistant Club Chair* (parent). This parent fills in when the Club Chair cannot attend a meeting.

- *Property Watcher* (Assistant Club Chair's child). This child assists the Club Chair by keeping track of the club property, making sure it is brought to each meeting, and taking it out and putting it away.

- *Host* (parent). This parent holds the meeting in his or her home, plans the activity, and prepares the snack.
- *Host Child* (Host's child). This child takes charge of the drum for the night, summons everyone to order, and assists with the club ceremonies.
- *Inspirational Leader* (parent). This parent shares a reading or thought about the values-oriented theme of the month. Make sure that the Inspirational Leader is assigned this responsibility before the meeting by the Club Chair.
- *Assistant Inspirational Leader* (Inspirational Leader's child). This child assists the Inspirational Leader in sharing a story or the like about the values-oriented theme of the month.
- *Treasure Keeper* (parent). This parent keeps track of club dues collected at the club meetings. The Treasure Keeper also serves as the club liaison with the YMCA Program Director and collects and sends to the YMCA registration forms and yearly fees, a copy of the Club Roster and Meeting Schedule, the names of the club's Branch Council representatives, program fees for camp-outs, and any other forms or fees that arise during the year.
- *Treasure Collector* (Treasure Keeper's child). This child assists with dues collection and asks the other children how they earned their money.
- *History Keeper* (parent). This parent keeps track of attendance at club meetings and All-Club Events. The History Keeper takes pictures and keeps souvenirs from meetings and events and puts them in the club photo album or scrapbook. The History Keeper keeps the YMCA informed of any special events the club does. This parent may also take minutes at club meetings and send birthday cards to club members. If desired, the Club Chair may spotlight the History Keeper's report periodically at club meetings.
- *Attendance Recorder* (History Keeper's child). This child records attendance at each club meeting and All-Club Event.
- *Storyteller* (parent or child). This person shares a story or song at the club meeting. Make sure that the storyteller is someone assigned this responsibility by the Club Chair before the meeting. Rotate this duty meeting by meeting.
- *Wise Old-Timer* (past Club Chair, or for a new club, a parent). Reminds the club of the aims, themes, and values of the Y-Guides Program and plans the club's service projects.
- *Club Starter* (parent). This parent volunteers to help establish new clubs, getting them off to a strong start. The Club Starter attends new club meetings, offers suggestions, helps organize the new club leadership, and provides guidance in running club meetings.

Club Projects

Time spent together making crafts, participating in events, talking, sharing ideas, going on walks, playing games, and doing community service projects are basic to your experience with the Y-Guides Program. They will create lasting memories for you and your child. Be sure to choose age-appropriate projects for your club as well as projects that encourage parent and child to play together.

Choosing Y-Guides Names and a Club Name

Have each parent and child make up their own special Y-Guides names—the names they will be called during club activities throughout their participation in the program. The Y-Guides name you choose for yourself is one you will remember for many years. Your name should reflect or describe a special part of you. It may be related to nature or animals, or it may come from another language. Parents and children should choose their names together, and the names should be related in some way. For example, a child's name might be "Shooting Star," and the parent's might be "Constant Star."

Here are some ideas to get you started:

Weather

Rain

Wind

Snow

Natural Features

Lakes

Oceans

Stars

Sun

Moon

Mountains

Volcanoes

Plants

Violet

Rose

Daisy

Tulip

Petunia

Iris

Birds

Blackbird

Eagle

Falcon

Owl

Parrot

Hawk

Woodpecker

Animals

Gorilla

Dinosaurs

Ape

Horses

Antelope

Monkey

Deer

Cat

Moose

Lion

Dog

Tiger

Fox

Leopard

Wolf

Cheetah

You can use these suggestions to choose a club name as well. The club name should reflect or describe all club members.

Club Property

When starting a club, have all club members help make certain items in the first two years of the program; these items will become club property. The club parents should develop a time line for completing these projects. Use club funds to purchase the necessary materials.

- *Club drum.* This item symbolizes the club's unity. Decorate the club drum with the club name and other symbols important to the club. Use the club drum at each meeting.

- *Centerpiece.* For use at camp-outs and club meetings, the centerpiece's design and color should reflect the club name.

- *Historian's book.* This item is a club-designed and club-constructed photo album or scrapbook to record club history in.

- *Club flag.* Using pictures, symbols, or words, include the club's name and the Y-Guides names of all members on the flag. Use an old pillow case, scrap material, or any other durable material and make it large enough to add to, as this is another way to document club history.

- *Talking stick or rock.* Use this item during meetings to designate who may speak: Whoever is holding the stick or rock may speak; everyone else should listen. Decorate as desired.

- *Treasure Keeper's bag.* Make this item out of any durable material and decorate with paint, markers, or glitter. The design should distinctly represent the club.

- *Property box.* This should be big enough to hold the club's property and small enough to transport easily. We recommend a plywood box 30 inches long, 18 inches wide, and 12 inches high.

- *Vests or sashes.* All club members should have vests or all club members should have sashes. All vests (or sashes) should be made of the same material so club members can be easily identified.

- *Emblem or Patch.* Have everyone sew this symbol of your club on their vests (or sashes).

- *Name tags.* Include your Y-Guides name and, if desired, a symbol that reflects your name.

Y-Westerners Program

Purpose

The purpose of the Y-Westerners Program is to help members become closer together as father and son and to be strong in body, mind, and spirit.

Aims

1. To respect and help my family and others.
2. To strive to be healthy.
3. To show good sportsmanship at all times.
4. To always do my best in every task.
5. To show reverence and be faithful to my religion.
6. To enjoy and preserve the beauty of nature.
7. To be both a good leader and a good follower.
8. _____

   (Have each father and child fill in what is important to them.)

Program Objectives

1. To help boys increase their self-confidence and feelings of self-worth.
2. To help boys learn to be effective members of and carry out personal responsibilities in groups.
3. To strengthen the family by focusing on the following:
   - Improving each family member's ability to communicate with and understand one another at a crucial time in their lives
   - Increasing each family member's ability to express concern and appreciation for one another
   - Increasing each family's ability to work and play together

Code

- To respect and help my family and others strive to be healthy
- To show good sportsmanship at all times
- To always do my best in every task
- To enjoy and preserve the beauty of nature
- To be a good leader and a good follower
- What is important to you?

  _____

[to be filled in by each father and child]

Y-WESTERNERS: PALO ALTO, CALIFORNIA

Y-Westerners is another version of the Y-Indian Guides Program. The purpose, to strengthen parent-child relationships, remains the same. A western theme, however, replaces the traditional Native American theme. Bandannas, shirts, patches, and buttons replace vests, feathers, and beads. Parent-child pairs form ranches instead of tribes. Y-Westerners is designed for fathers and sons.

To introduce this program, you might say the following:

In Y-Westerners, fathers and their sons are bound together by common interests. Fathers guide boys in grades kindergarten through third grade as they learn to accept responsibility. With recommendations and guidance from their fathers, boys take on responsibility for running the ranch and planning activities. To this end, the Y-Westerners Program uses activity and program ideas that reinforce the concept that fathers and sons can enjoy and learn from each other.

Ranches meet to plan activities, service opportunities, and outings. Y-Westerner activities and events are limited only by the imagination and resourcefulness of each ranch.

Starting a Y-Westerners Ranch

Each ranch is made up of fathers and sons from local neighborhoods. They meet for regular ranch meetings twice a month.

To build ranch spirit, try some of these suggestions. Keep in mind that they have value beyond that of building spirit—that of meeting the needs of boys for adventure, new experiences, and a sense of "belonging."

- Choose a ranch name they can all be proud of.
- Develop a yell, hoot, or special whistle by which members can recognize each other at a distance. Include it in ranch rituals.

- Design ranch apparel, such as a cowboy hat, jacket, pin, or emblem with name, brand, or the like on it.
- Make a ranch flag or branding iron as a craft project.
- Make sure ranch events get a plug in local newspapers and, especially, in the Range newsletter.
- Unite the members of your ranch by participating in overnight activities, a winter camp, fishing trip, mountain hike, or the like.
- Encourage discussions at every point, making a real effort to involve each child.

Y-Westerner Range Council

The Y-Westerner Range Council consists of representatives from each ranch, the Range Foreman, and the Y-Westerner YMCA director. The Range Council meetings are open to all Y-Westerner members who have paid their YMCA dues. Members openly discuss and vote on all program policies, activities, and general business at Range Council meetings.

Ranch Leadership Roles

Parents can hold various leadership roles within their ranch, such as the following:

- *Ranch Foreman.* This parent presides over meetings.
- *Shotgun.* This parent safeguards the ranch "gold" and collects and records all financial business.
- *Wagon Master.* This parent keeps records of dates set and assignments made. He also attends Range Council meetings monthly.
- *Top Hand.* This parent takes care of ranch properties, brings them to meetings, and leads the flag salute and reciting of the code.
- *Deputies.* Deputies can have several duties. They can coordinate and lead range activity sponsored by the ranch; they can coordinate ranch food and equipment for the spring roundup (rough-out, camp-out); they can send articles to the Y-Westerners

Gazette, the program newsletter; and they can coordinate a booth for the All-Clubs Carnival in June.

Y-Westerners Dads' Meetings

The basic purpose of Y-Westerners is to increase the things that a dad and son can enjoy doing together at a time when a boy thinks his dad is the greatest man on Earth. Ranch meetings are a means to this end. It is important, then, that your ranch meetings are interesting to your little Y-Westerners and that they have ample opportunity to participate in these meetings. The program should be geared to the interests and abilities of the children. All business should be saved for the dads' (parents only) meetings.

Nothing is as important to ranch success as the monthly dads' meetings. Most of the common shortcomings of ranches can be eliminated by meeting without the boys once each month.

The big value of dads' meetings is that you can iron out tiresome business details without boring the boys. Any business that takes more than five minutes in a ranch meeting ought to be referred to the dads' meeting instead. Plans for trips, outings, and so on go much smoother with the dads alone.

Making assignments never inspires the boys, so do this for a month or a semester at a time in a dads' meeting. In addition, the dads with logical excuses may be more comfortable explaining their reasons for not caring to do a certain task when their children are not present.

The biggest advantage of dads' meetings, however, is that you can discuss the big things to come without getting the boys excited too early. For example, you can plan a weekend camp-out two months away, then delay telling the boys about it so that the wait is not too long for them.

Another great feature of dads' meetings is the learning possibilities. Evaluations, ways to improve, discussions of weak features of ranch meetings, or complaints about absentee dads can be mulled over objectively by the dads, keeping the boys oblivious of any shortcomings. This is a place where the Y Program Director or your organizer can listen to your problems and then help you to solve them.

The best use of a dads' meeting time is spent in trying to better understand your own boys, learning how to be closer pals to your sons, trying to cope with behavior problems, and so on. Again, the Y is anxious to help in this area, but you can often gain much understanding through a frank discussion among the dads themselves.

Dads' meetings also give you and the other dads a chance to review the Y manuals or the latest books and magazine articles that will help you be better parents or Y-Westerners. You can share ideas on improving invitations, games, or stories. You can muster group courage to learn to dance or take that overnight camping trip.

Best of all, at dads' meetings, you can get to know each other as true friends, without the usual clamor and confusion of regular meeting nights.

If you have trouble finding a time for dads' meetings, try having them after your regular meeting. Have one or two of the mothers come by to pick up the little Y-Westerners and take them home, while you stay for the dads' meeting.

Remember, the Y staff stands ready to help your ranch develop good dads' meetings.

Ranch Name

You can use any western-related word as a ranch name. Here are some suggestions:

Frontiersman	Frontier	Red River Riders
Bronco	Critters	Prairie
Vaquero	Prospectors	Palomino
Butterfield	Carson City	Wind River
Buckaroo	Dudes	Puncher
Vigilante	Coyote	Bandito
Laramie	Sante Fe	Rocky Mountain
Bulldog	Herd	Quirt
Wrangler	Prairie Dogs	Plateau
Pecos River	Snake River	Pathfinder
Burro	Leather	Ranger
Raiders	Jackrabbit	Pioneers
Dakota	Green River	Pony Express
Calico	Maverick	Rawhide
Diggers	Gold (Miner)	Canyon
Wyoming	Alamo	Colorado
Chuck Wagon	Mustang	Road Runner
Desert	Cheyenne	Trailblazers
Bighorn	Cimarron	Lone Star
Cowhand	Pinto	Rope
Cactus	Six-Shooters	Desert Rats

Red River Rustlers	Spurs	Badlands
Rustler	Roadrunners	Stirrup
Bunkhouse	Faro Kids	Center City
Santa Fe Slingers	Stage Coach	James Boys
Saddle	Wells Fargo	Tenderfoot
Saddleback Kids	Keno Kids	Rough Riders
Abilene	Stampede	Thoroughbred
Sagebrush	Longhorns	Adobe
Bronco Busters	Steer	Thong
Wichita Wranglers	Durango	Alfalfa
Sidewinder	Dakota Dandies	Top Hand
Straightshooters	Stetson	Boot Hill
Frisco	Dune	Tumbleweed

Y-Westerners Ranch Meetings

The first two ranch meetings will differ from other meetings. You will need to make some decisions and to set up the ranch and meeting structure. The following are examples of the agenda items for the first and second ranch meetings.

Y-Westerners First Ranch Meeting

In the first meeting, dues are collected, announcements of the upcoming induction ceremony and camp-out are made, and the ranch name is chosen. In selecting a name, the leaders of the group should come prepared with some suggestions. After listing the possibilities, participants should discuss them and choose a name and a design they can be proud of based on the traits, schools, interests, and geographical location of the particular ranch.

Next on the agenda is an activity in which the ranch invents a story of "How the _____ Ranch Got Its Name." Try starting with one dad and going around the circle. After writing the story, have members participate in a game, a sing-along ("Home on the Range" would be appropriate), and a craft (making a "brand" nameplate, for example).

Brand Nameplate

Using various shades of brown construction paper, draw the ranch's brand, cut it out, glue it onto colored paper, and write the ranch name under the brand. Punch holes in the top and tie a piece of brown yarn through the holes so that participants can hang the nameplates around their necks.

Conclude the meeting with refreshments. Close with everyone sharing their favorite part of the meeting.

Y-Westerners Second Ranch Meeting

Follow a format similar to the first meeting. Encourage participants to wear the Y-Westerners T-shirt (either provided by the YMCA or designed by each ranch). The craft project for the second meeting is to make a ranch banner.

Ranch Banner

Materials: Muslin or other white cotton; dye, acrylic paint, tempera paint, or all; liquid embroidery paint; crayons; pole (1" dowel long enough to span banner and then some).

Using any of the suggested materials, make a banner with your ranch's name and brand. When dry, mount it on the pole for use at the induction ceremony, the camp-out, and other range events.

Conclude the ranch meeting with refreshments and an appropriate closing.

TYPICAL Y-WESTERNERS MEETING

7:00	The Ranch Foreman calls the meeting to order. The Top Hand leads the ranch in the flag salute and the Y-Westerners Code.
7:10	Foreman makes important announcements. Wagon Master shares and hears information for the Range Council.
7:15	Shotgun collects dues, asking each little Y-Westerner to share how it was earned. Then each big Y-Westerner shares what special thing he did with his son since the last meeting.
7:25	Make any quick decisions regarding next meeting or outings (save lengthy discussions for dads' meetings).
7:30	Make program assignments and give reminders for next meeting: Who? Where? When?
7:35	Run the program: story, game, craft, trick, song, special project. A program may involve just one activity or several, depending on time available.
8:00	Serve refreshments (limit to two items).
8:05	Closing: Recite Code or share new learning or just say good-bye for now.
8:10	Head for home.

Test your ranch meetings against the following list of procedures:

GOOD Y-WESTERNERS MEETING PROCEDURES

- Start and close meetings on time.
- Stay carefully within the time allowed for the ritual. Do not drag it over into program time.
- The ritual part of your meetings should be geared toward the children. They should do most of the talking during meetings. It should be fun for them.
- All phases of your meetings should be planned carefully: the reports, the stories to be told, the games, and so on. It is the Ranch Foreman's job to see that this preparation has been done before the meeting.
- Thought and preparation must precede each program period of your ranch meetings. Good programs do not just happen. They are carefully planned and prepared!
- Ranch business matters should be taken up at dads' meetings, not at ranch meetings. Too much "adult talk" causes your sons to lose interest in the meeting. Dads' meetings are normally held monthly.

If you have problems with your ranch meetings, try using some of the actions suggested in the chart on page 32.

Y-African Guide Program

Purpose

The purpose of the Y-African Guide Program is to foster understanding and companionship between parents and children.

Slogan

"United Always"

Aims

1. To be clean in body and pure in heart.
2. To be united always with my parents/children.
3. To love the sacred circle of my family.
4. To be attentive when others speak.
5. To love my neighbor as myself.
6. To seek and preserve the beauty of the Great Spirit's work in forest, field, and stream.
7. To take pride in myself.
8. To take pride in my heritage.

Pledge

"We, parents and children, united in service and the support given to each other, to our family, to this family compound, and to our community, under the four winds of heaven, seek a world pleasing to God."

Elder Oaths

I will not abuse my children.

I will not neglect my children.

I will not ignore my children.

I will not discourage my children.

I will not curse my children.

I will provide for my children.

I will share with my children.

I will encourage my children.

I will inspire my children.

I will express my love for my children.

Youth Oaths

I will not talk back to my parents.

I will not bring shame to my parents.

I will not be dishonest with my parents.

I will not disobey my parents.

I will not talk about the personal affairs of my parents.

I will respect my parents.

I will support my parents.

I will honor my parents.

I will appreciate my parents.

I will express my love for my parents.

Program Values

The Y-African Guide Program has significant values for children, parents, and the entire family. Amidst the many social changes impinging upon the modern urban family, the YMCA parent-child programs provide many opportunities for families to fulfill their growth needs in:

1. Finding adventure and recreation together and separately.
2. Improving health, fitness, and physical skills.
3. Relating to others in the community.
4. Fulfilling parental and marital roles.
5. Sharing responsibility for family living.
6. Developing and maintaining communication.
7. Deepening feelings of acceptance, mutual respect, and love for one another.
8. Internalizing lasting values with a growing sense of identity.

Y-AFRICAN GUIDES: CINCINNATI, OHIO

The Y-African Guides Program was designed to strengthen the family to meet the multiple pressures of urban living in our technological age. African lore replaces American Indian lore in this modified version of the Y-Indian Guide Program. YMCAs that adopt this program are encouraged to work with participants to research African lore and design a program that reflects the diverse culture and heritage of the participants. See the resources on pages 210-211 that can help your group get started on research.

You might introduce the program by saying the following:

Welcome to the Y-African Guide Program! Y-African Guides is based on the Y-Indian Guide Program, which is part of the YMCA's work with families. The Y-Indian Guide Program has long been recognized as a significant experience for parents and children by the National Board of YMCAs.

The Y-African Guide Program enables parents and their children ages seven to twelve to participate together in a wide range of wholesome activities that nurture mutual understanding, love, and respect. The theme of the program is African lore, which offers a common interest for both parent and child and opportunities for exciting, innovative activities, projects, and special events. Possible program activities include African arts and crafts, folklore, music and dance, games, cooking, farming techniques, herbology, and nature lore. Outings, service projects, and camping are other options. The dignity, loyalty, and deep concern of African parents for their families and all of their children are used as a vibrant example of parent and teacher in just relations with others, in knowledge of all living creatures in nature, and in respect and awe of spiritual things.

The parent-child pair is the basic unit of the program, and groups of up to ten parents and children form a family compound. Compound members meet in members' homes on a rotating basis once a month and at the YMCA center once a month as well as meeting for occasional special events. The families of compound members support members' experiences together and share in some of the program experiences and special events.

Organization of Y-African Guides

A Y-African Guides family compound is a group of parents and their seven- to twelve-year-old children who live in the same neighborhood. The family compound is the smallest organizational unit, and all organizational work is planned to help the family compound succeed locally.

Family compounds are organized within the framework and program of the local YMCA. Both parents and children in the Y-African Guide Program are members of their local YMCA, and through this membership they are part of the nationwide and worldwide YMCA movement. Local YMCAs determine the basis of YMCA membership for Y-African Guide parents and children, including to what extent Y-African Guide members participate in the financial support of the association to which their family compound is related.

A cluster of family compounds connected with a particular Y are also part of a larger group called an Extended Family Compound and an even larger group called a Village Compound, which is a cluster of Extended Family Compounds. The family compounds elect representatives to take part in the Elder Council. The Elder Council supports the program planning of the family compounds, coordinates special events, and establishes policies and standards. The Elder Council also serves on a Village Council, which relates directly to the YMCA Program Committee responsible for working with families.

You can organize your own family compound under the auspices of the YMCA once your group has agreed to six basic requirements:

1. Neither a parent nor a child may join a family compound or attend meetings without the other.
2. Meetings of the family compound will be held in the homes of members on a rotating basis.
3. Membership of a family compound will not exceed ten parents and their children.

4. Meetings of the Extended Family Compound (a group of family compounds) will be held for special activities at the YMCA.

5. The Elder Council (leadership) meetings of the Village Compound will be held at the YMCA center once a month or as needed.

6. Membership in a Village Compound will be open to an unlimited number of family compounds as long as those family compounds are all connected to a single YMCA center.

Finally, the YMCA works with Y-African Guide members in a layman-staff partnership to give them guidance and support. Much of the work of the YMCA is carried out by volunteers; parents may volunteer to serve as Y-African Guide family compound organizers and supervisors.

Family Compound Leadership Roles

Parents should take on various leadership roles within the family compound. Some of the possible roles include the following:

- *Baale or Iyale of the Family Compound.* This is the eldest person in the compound. As the head of the family compound, he or she is its foremost representative and serves as ceremonial officer for the family compound, giving spiritual depth and meaning to the meetings. He or she presides at all meetings of the family compound and at all compound programs. If he or she is unable to preside, he or she is represented by the second eldest person in the compound who is under those circumstances temporarily referred to as the Baale or Iyale.

- *Musicians.* The Musicians are a male and female who are elected by each family compound. The Extended Family Compound has its own musical instruments, and the family compound has its own musical instruments. The Musicians are responsible for their family compound's musical instruments and have the job of calling the meeting to order. Youth may

also hold these positions in the family compound.

- *Baale or Iyale of the Village Compound.* This appointed official provides leadership to the Village Compound. As the head of the Village Compound, the Baale or Iyale is its foremost representative and serves as ceremonial officer for the Village Compound.

- *Griot.* This is a male who is elected by his family compound. He acts as the recording secretary for all happenings in the family compound and special meetings. He keeps a permanent record of attendance at meetings and is responsible for most of the family compound correspondence. He should have a sense of humor and the creative ability to put an African atmosphere into his tally and the reading of the minutes. In these ways, he can provide an added cultural dimension to the family compound. He keeps the historical record of the family compound's activities. He also provides news items of interest for the Village Compound or Extended Family Compound newsletters.

- *Advisor.* The Advisor is always of the opposite sex from the family compound head. The advisor may be nominated or may volunteer as a candidate. He or she is responsible for developing program resource materials for compound projects and activities. He or she may assist the Baale or Iyale in membership maintenance and recruitment. If he or she is the second eldest member of their family compound and should be required to stand in for the Baale or Iyale, the compound must appoint someone as a temporary advisor.

- *Basket Carrier.* This person is elected by the compound. Candidates may be nominated or be volunteers. The Basket Carrier is in charge of family compound property between meetings and collects supplies at the end of each meeting. A Youth may hold this office.

- *Iyalode.* This is a female who serves as treasurer of the family compound and is elected by her compound. She encourages each Youth to report how he or she was able to earn his or her dues through service to parents or the community. She is also in charge of fund-raising projects.

- *Emissary.* The emissary is elected by the Extended Family Compound. He or she represents the YMCA center at Village Compound meetings. He or she may take other members of the family compound along as assistants. He or she is responsible for reporting back to the family compound. He or she may also hold office on the Village Compound level.

The assigning of some offices to the eldest members on a permanent basis is consistent with the African tradition of not only honoring elders but also placing expectations on them as those who have had more life experiences. Even for those offices that are elective, it is important that those who prove themselves competent are able to be reelected to those offices rather than for all the members to have an opportunity to hold offices for which they are not well-suited.

It is important that the leadership for the family compound be effective and capable. The children identify with the leadership role carried out by their own parents and by other parents in the family compound. They learn through observation of their parents and through their own leadership experiences within the program.

Responsibilities of the Host Parent and Child

For the family compound meetings, the Host Parent and Child have four primary responsibilities:

- To prepare and deliver the invitation to each family member
- To plan for the recreation at the meeting, such as a game
- To provide the feast (refreshments)
- To check with the Baale or Iyale about any special needs or arrangements that may be required

Planning by Host Parent and Child can also involve the other members of the family who may be especially helpful by offering suggestions.

Planning for Family Compound Meetings

The family compound meeting calls for careful preparation. To help you prepare, follow the orderly pattern modeled. If you cannot easily fit the program demands into the time allotted for the meeting, shorten reports or recreation programs.

Parent-child teams meet together for family compound meetings. Your family compound must work out a schedule in advance so that each family will know when it is scheduled to be Host as well as its duties at other meetings and activities.

Initial Family Compound Meetings

The first and second family compound meetings will require compound members to make decisions and set up the structure for future meetings. Here are some ideas for how to best run your first few meetings.

First Family Compound Meeting

The first meeting with parents and children will require explanation of certain business points. The first meeting is conducted by a parent organizer who is an officer of the Village Compound or by the director of the sponsoring YMCA. To be as helpful as possible, the first meeting should include all the elements of a regular family compound meeting to serve as a demonstration of agenda and program for future meetings of the new family compound. A parents' meeting scheduled prior to the first family compound meeting could provide an opportunity to plan and take care of business items. These details are best handled without children, who might get restless while adults discuss items the children can't comprehend.

At the first meeting, include the following:

- Read through the opening ceremonial script to start the meeting (see the script on page 204)
- Briefly describe the Y-African Guide Program for the special benefit of the new children, emphasizing unity with their

parents and the fun that they will have with the theme in compound meetings, camp-outs, and Extended Family Compound or Extended Village Compound activities and festivals.

- Take care of business items, such as the following:
  —Collecting dues to pay for materials
  —Discussing a family compound name
  —Setting the amount for regular compound dues
  —Deciding about the time and place of the next meeting
  —Announcing that at the third meeting compound officers will be elected
  —Selecting compound and individual African names
- Include an African folktale.
- Play a good game; plan this carefully so as to involve all members in a happy experience.
- Have a feast (refreshments).
- Hold the closing ceremony (see the script on page 204) and adjournment.

It is wise to delay the election of officers until after the compound has had the opportunity to become better acquainted. The personalities and leadership abilities of these first officers is extremely important to the success of your new family compound.

Recognize and accept that this first meeting is out of necessity loaded with "business." Therefore, be careful to keep the meeting moving so that the children will not be required to sit quietly for too long.

SCRIPT FOR OPENING AND CLOSING CEREMONIES

Begin and end meetings promptly with the Baale or Iyale calling the Elders and Youth to order. Have parents and children form a double circle with children standing in front of their respective parents. Conduct the opening and closing ceremonies when all are quietly focusing on the dignity and meaning of the ceremonies. For the first two meetings, choose volunteers to read the script as you have not had a chance to elect compound officers. Do not ac-

tually collect dues or expect to hear scout reports. Substitute words in brackets as appropriate.

Opening

Begin by lighting the lamp.

The Musicians play call to order music.

The Musicians play African music.

[Baale]: *(Singing)* Who are the Y-African Elders and Youth?

Everyone: *(Singing)* We are the Y-African Elders and Youth.

[Baale]: *(Singing)* What is the slogan?

Everyone: *(Singing)* United Forever.

[Baale]: Musicians, what are the duties and meaning of your office?

Musicians: The musical instruments call the compound together, tell its members to come to order, and provide the music for songs.

[Baale]: Basket Carrier, what are the duties and meaning of your office?

Basket Carrier: I stand guard over the compound property.

Acknowledge all officers, each reciting their duties and responsibilities.

[Baale]: What is the daily pledge of all Y-African Guides?

Everyone: Our daily pledge is "We, parent and child, united in service and the support given to each other, to our family, to our family compound, to our community, under the four winds of heaven, seek a world pleasing to the eye of God."

[Baale]: Griot, read the scroll. *(Griot reads the minutes of the last meeting.)* [Disregard for the first meeting.]

[Baale]: Griot, will you take the roll while the Iyalode collects the dues and calls for the scout reports and (or) how money was earned.

Griot: [Baale], the roll has been called.

Iyalode: [Baale], the dues are collected, the scout reports received, and the money well-earned.

[Baale]: Griot, what is the old and new business? *(Keep this brief.)*

Closing

Extinguish the lamp.

Sing a song with verses and a chorus. The [Baale] can sing the verses, and everyone can sing the chorus.

Say a prayer of thanksgiving.

Second Family Compound Meeting

Since compound officers have not yet been named, the organizer who led the first meeting also presides at the second session. This, too, is a "demonstration" meeting. Again, the program should follow the pattern of a regular meeting:

- Have parents and children read through the opening ceremony.
- In the business of this meeting, include a ceremony of taking African names for the family compound and individuals, make plans for the appointment or election of officers at the next meeting, collect compound dues for the first time, explain scout report idea and tell parents to help the children look for subjects to report at the following meeting, and seek assistance with a totem.
- Include a short African folktale.
- Play a game led by the Host Parent and Child.
- Have a feast (refreshments).
- Hold the closing ceremony and adjourn.

At the third meeting of the family compound, appoint or elect leaders so that future meetings can be carried out by those chosen.

Attendance at Meetings

Your compound must enforce the rule that parents must attend with their children. Always keep in mind that the Y-African Guide Program is not a children's program: it is a parent *and* child program. Indeed, its central purpose is to foster unity between parents and children.

Remember, too, that you can hold a successful meeting with only a few parents and their children. So avoid canceling meetings simply because some parents and children are unable to attend. Compounds that have the most success at fostering good attendance set up a schedule and stick to it.

Procedures for the Y-African Guide Family Compound Meetings

In order that solemnity and dignity be maintained at meetings, each officer must know his or her part. Youth should sit on the floor in front of the parents, with everyone seated in a circle around the altar (see "Family Compound Property").

Consider family programs on the Village Compound level for summer activities, such as a kite flying contest, a family picnic, a day at the beach, a visit to the zoo, a camp-out, or a nature outing. As often as weather permits, plan outdoor meetings.

The following are suggested activities for Y-African Guide meetings:

- *Opening ceremony.* Execute this ceremony with solemnity and sensitivity. Note in the sample (page 204) it includes opening prayer, lighting of the lamp, and singing of an appropriate African song.
- *Discussion periods.* Encourage the group to talk to help members think about the meaning of the slogan, purpose, aims, pledge, and oaths as well as how these apply in their lives.
- *Snacks.* Stress eating together. Serve at an eating mat in the traditional African manner. Observe African eating customs. (Your compound may need to research this topic. See the resources listed at the end of this section, on pages 210-211.) Serve African food as snacks whenever possible.
- *Quiz contests.* Hold contests on Y-African Guide aims, slogan, African history, or other subjects interesting to the children that are consistent with the focus of your Y-African Guide Program.
- *Storytelling.* Rotate the responsibility for storytelling.
- *Games.* Make Hosts responsible for the selection of one or two games. These should be planned ahead of time. These games should be fun and teach aspects of developing healthy human relationships.
- *African scouting reports.* Have children present reports to increase the observation

skills of each parent and child in regard to nature (e.g., animals, birds, insects, trees, flowers) and to foster confidence in speaking to a group. Ask each child to report at the meeting when she or he has observed something that might be interesting to the compound.

- *Handicraft exhibits, nature study, hobbies, brief educational talks by parents.* All of these can open new horizons of information for both children and parents.
- *Talks given by a guest speaker.* Especially good are stories of African life of special interest to your family compound.
- *Songs.* Keep in mind that singing promotes fellowship and the sharing of talent.
- *Closing ceremony.* The ceremony might include the singing of "Ise Oluwa," or another African song, extinguishing the lamp, and saying a closing prayer.

Religious Emphasis

The Baale or Iyale should make sure that religious emphasis related to the YMCA purpose is provided in each compound meeting. If he or she is not willing to accept leadership of this part of the program, he or she should seek the help of one of the other parents or an advisor so that the religious purposes of the Y-African Guide Program and the YMCA find expression in every meeting. Any religious activity should be related to compound aims, including stressing spiritual values, such as a belief in God, the Golden Rule, prayer, etc. Moreover, when planning a religious activity, leaders should keep in mind the ecumenical stance of the YMCA, which enables families of various backgrounds to share in meaningful experiences of prayer, praise, thanksgiving, and worship.

Good Practices to Consider

The Baale or Iyale and compound officers should give attention to effective group practices in their planning and appraisal of compound development. The following suggestions may be helpful:

- Be concerned about all group members, the shy as well as the outgoing.
- Start meetings on time; close them on time.

- Focus program activities on the interests and capabilities of the children. Be alert and sensitive to their needs.
- Plan carefully; contact families with special responsibilities in advance.
- Be wary of the parents talking too much in compound meetings; regularly use Elder Council meetings to handle most business.
- Facilitate team discussion and decision making on matters of behavior, program development, and policy for the compound.
- Be warm, supportive, understanding, and flexible. Be more concerned about the feelings and attitudes of compound members than protocol.

Family Compound Property

It is most important that each family compound have a complete set of family compound property. This property serves several purposes. Primarily, it adds authenticity to compound meetings. In addition, making the property is fun, and friendships may develop through such activities. Some possible property items include the following:

- Musical instruments
- Compound basket
- Totem banner
- Charter frame
- Compound lamp
- Water bowl
- Griot's scroll
- Money pouch
- Staff of authority
- Staff holder
- Y-African Guide shield
- Serving bowls
- Eating bowls and eating utensils
- Altar

Every family compound, Extended Family Compound, and Village Compound should make as many of these items as possible or at least decorate ready-made items. Purchase supplies to make the items with funds your compound has raised, so that the items truly belong to the compound. Between meetings, the Basket Carrier should store compound property in the compound basket.

While everyone should share in the responsibility of making the compound property, it is nevertheless important to have all these items available as soon as possible. Remember, this achievement knits the compound members more closely together. Moreover, the compound property adds color and meaning to meetings, increasing the satisfaction of all members.

- *Musical instruments.* An authentic African ceremony always begins and ends with the sound of musical instruments. Thus, musical instruments are indispensable pieces of equipment for a Y-African Guide family compound. Every compound should try to make or at least decorate its own musical instruments. This can be an outstanding early family compound project, leading to a strong feeling of ownership. Indeed, the compound musical instruments become a symbol of the unity of the compound. Examples include a thumb harp, rhythm sticks, or drums.

  Your compound should elect Musicians based on their ability to play the musical instruments skillfully. Finally, everyone should consider the compound musical instruments to be ceremonial pieces, not toys.

- *Staff of authority.* The staff of authority is a straight stick approximately 1" in diameter and approximately 4' long; choose one that is not brittle or cracked. Make it by shaving, sanding, and then painting it with African designs. Lastly, adorn the staff of authority with strips of cloth and bells. The Baale or Iyale strikes the stick on the floor to open and close all compound meetings.

- *Staff holder.* Make the staff holder from a long cardboard tube such as those that hold carpet or linoleum. Decorate the staff holder with African designs. Keep it with the compound basket when the Baale or Iyale is using the staff of authority.

- *Y-African Guide shield.* Make the Y-African Guide shield by stretching canvas on one side of a homemade shield frame. Use a piece of cloth on which the Y-African Guide emblem has been printed, aligning it so that the emblem will be in the center of the shield. The YMCA will provide the design but each compound is responsible for imprinting the design on the canvas.

- *Totem.* Each Y-African Guide family compound has a totem, as do family compounds in Africa. This is a symbol, usually in the form of an animal, bird, or fish, that distinguishes or designates a particular family compound based on the parents' spiritual affiliation, occupation, place of birth, or some other aspect of the family's history or culture.

  Each family totem is sewn onto a cloth appliqué panel one foot square. These panels, when put together, are known as a "totem banner."

- *Totem banners.* These are some of the most important pieces of compound property. After each family has developed a totem banner, they place it on the family compound panel. The family compound panel is a larger piece of fabric hung from a dowel or rod to which each family attaches their totem panel. This occurs at the beginning of each meeting to signify that the family is present at the meeting. At an Extended Family Compound meeting, have the Basket Carrier bring the family compound panel and place it around the Extended Family Compound panel. This same process occurs in the case of Village Compound meetings.

- *Charter frame.* Make a charter frame by lashing sticks together with leather thongs and stretching rawhide between the sticks. After your family compound receives its official charter from the YMCA, paste it onto rawhide and place it in the charter frame.

- *Compound lamp.* Purchase a traditional African fitilu lamp, which has a palm oil wick to light. Have the Basket Carrier place the compound lamp in the center of the altar at the beginning of meetings.

- *Talking bowl.* Decorate a wooden bowl that is able to hold water with the Nigerian Nsibidi hieroglyph for "word" on the inside and the Nigerian Nsibidi hieroglyph for "compound consensus" on the outside. Place water in the bowl before the Baale or Iyale places each topic of discussion before the compound. To use the talking bowl, have each person come forward before speaking. Some of the water is poured by the Baale or Iyale into the right palm of the person who wishes to address the compound. This water must be tasted before speaking in compound meetings. When a consensus has been reached on a topic of discussion, the Baale or Iyale pours any remaining water out and turns the bowl upside down, hiding the symbol for word and exposing the symbol for compound consensus.

- *Griot's scrolls and holders.* The Griot writes the minutes of each meeting on a scroll. Make a scroll holder by painting African designs on an empty paper towel spool. Use a new scroll holder each week to hold that week's minutes. After each meeting, the Griot carefully rolls the minutes and stores them in the scroll holder for future reference. Have the Griot bring all previous scroll holders to each compound meeting.

- *Altar.* Make an altar from a large metal serving tray onto which you paint the Adinkira hieroglyph "Nyame Dua," which means "The Altar of God."

    (Safety precaution: The tray should always be metal because of the burning wick in the compound lamp.)

- *Money pouch.* Make or obtain a leather pouch with a drawstring for holding the family compound dues. Decorate it with African designs. This pouch is called "apowo."

- *Eating bowls and eating utensils.* Paint the outsides of wooden cups and bowls that can hold liquids with African designs to use for compound feasts.

- *Serving bowls.* Paint the outsides of large wooden bowls that can hold liquids with African designs to use for compound feasts.

Family Compound Name

When you organize a new group of parents and children, have the members decide on a family compound name, based on your group's common goal or something else that is important to all of you. If possible, these should be represented by the appropriate symbols from the hieroglyphic scripts of West Africa.

The Family Compound Induction Ceremony

Once you have formed your new family compound, have family compound members go through an induction ceremony. Qualifications for induction and a sample induction ceremony follow.

Qualifications for Induction

Each parent-child team, as well as your whole Y-African Guide family compound, needs to take the following important steps to qualify for the official induction ceremony:

- Parents and children should be members of the local YMCA, having paid membership dues.

- Parents and children must take part in the induction together.

- Your family compound must have completed registration of your group with your local YMCA.

- Each parent must accept the time requirement for effective participation in meetings and special events.

- Each child must understand that respect, participation, and obedience are essential to the fun of all members in the family compound.

- Each parent and child team must have already completed a project together for members of their family, family compound, or community.

- Each team must know and recite the Y-African Guide slogan and aims and must be prepared to take the pledge and appropriate oath at the induction ceremony.

These principles can guide local YMCA policy and practice. YMCA staff and Y-African Guides Elder Council officers must likewise seek to assist each parent and child to have meaningful program experiences and relationships during their membership affiliation.

Y-African Guide Induction Ceremony

Conduct your Y-African Guide induction ceremony as an open public gathering for the families of participants. The ceremony should be dignified and in keeping with the spirit of dedication for a lasting union between parents and children. Hold the ceremony in the YMCA center or at the YMCA camp within the first two months of a new membership year. Y-African Guides officers, along with the YMCA director and chairman of the YMCA program committee, should guide the official program. Careful advance planning should ensure that seating arrangements, the compound fire, the totem banner, the musical instrument, the charters, and the Baale's or Iyale's clothing (if they choose to dress in traditional African clothing) are in good order.

Substitute "Baale" for "Iyale" if appropriate in the following script:

[Iyale] of the compound that the new parent-child team want to join: Hear me, Olori O.

Village [or Compound] Head: Who speaks?

[Iyale]: [Iyale] _____ of the _____ Family Compound.

Village Head: [Iyale] _____ of the _____ Family Compound, proceed.

[Iyale]: Olori, I speak for these Elders and their children who have heard the call of God, the Master of life. They have been drawn by the warmth and light of the compound lamp and want the peace of the water bowl and wish to become a part of our _____ Village.

Village Head: It is well; prepare your friends for induction.

[Iyale]: Olori, our compound is now ready.

Village Head: Do they know the purpose, slogan, pledge, and aims of Y-African Guides?

[Iyale]: They do.

Village Head: Are they ready and willing to accept the duties that come with membership?

[Iyale]: They are.

Village Head: Elders of the new Ile (families) what brings you to this compound?

New Elders: We seek to be united with our children, Olori.

Village Head: And you, Youth of the new Ile what brings you to this compound?

New Youth: We seek to be united with our parents, Olori.

Village Head: This union, is it something to be plucked from a tree like a piece of fruit? Is it something to be bought from another with money? Is it something to be remembered only when time allows and forgotten otherwise?

[Iyale]: It is none of these, Olori.

Village Head: Then what is this union you Elders and Youth seek?

[Iyale]: (Speaking directly to the Elders and Youth) Parent and child, united, may better understand one another, help one another, work, play, and worship side by side. Have I spoken for you, Elders and Youth?

Inductees: (In unison) Yes! Yes! Yes!

Village Head: My brothers and sisters you have heard the [Iyale] _____ of the _____ Family Compound, on behalf of the new Elders and new Youth. Shall we accept them?

All Other Elders and Youth: Yes! Yes! Yes!

Village Head: It is well. [Iyale], you will now instruct our friends for the first step of their induction. (Inductees enter and form a semicircle in front of the fire or altar with the parents and children holding hands, children standing in front of their parents.)

Village Head: (Holding the water bowl forward, above his or her head) God, accept this bowl of cool water, the symbol of our compound and brotherhood. We ask blessings for our compound. O Great Elder of the East, what words of wisdom have you for us tonight?

Elder of the East: In the East, we think of the dawn, which brings a new day and with each new day a new opportunity to learn to fulfill your oath and for parent and child to grow closer together. May you start each day with renewed strength to become better Y-African Guides.

All Elders and Youth: So be it.

Elder of the East: This is the word of wisdom from the East: 'renewal.'

Village Head: We are grateful for your words of wisdom, Great Elder of the East. O Great Elder of the North, what words of wisdom have you for us tonight?

Elder of the North: All great travelers knew that to keep in mind the North Star is to keep them on the true course. Even as the compass points always to the North to remind us of our goals, so the purpose of Y-African Guides is always before us to remind us of our goal as parents and children—to develop a closer relationship between parent and child. May you never lose your way.

All Elders and Youth: So be it.

Elder of the North: This is the word of wisdom from the North: 'stick to your goals.'

Village Head: We are grateful for your words of wisdom, Great Elder of the North. O Great Elder of the South, what words of wisdom have you for us tonight?

Elder of the South: From the South, we feel warm gentle breezes and the friendliness that they give, and so the message I bring from the South is one of friendship. Friendship between parent and child and friendship among all Elders and all Youth. May the strength of friendship ever be with you as you work together as Y-African Elders and Youth.

All Elders and Youth: So be it.

Elder of the South: This is the word of wisdom from the South: 'United Always.'

Village Head: We are grateful for your words of wisdom, Great Elder of the South. O Great Elder of the West, what words of wisdom have you for us tonight?

Elder of the West: The West signifies the setting sun, the close of the day. And so the message I bring is live in such a way that at the close of each day you can know you have made others happier for knowing you. May you look back upon a work well done.

All Elders and Youth: So be it.

Elder of the West: This is the word of wisdom from the West: 'reflection.'

Village Head: We hear your words of wisdom, O Great Elder of the West. *(Have the parents face their children, each parent clasping the child's right hand. Then have each parent place his or her left hand on the right shoulder of the parent on his or her left and each child place his or her hand on the shoulder of the child on his or her left to complete the circle.)*

Village Head: Elders and Youth, the position you have now assumed denotes, first, by the right-hand clasp, the close relationship of parent and child. The hands on shoulders denote the unity of compound. The hand clasp of the parents shows the connecting bonds of the compound with the executive committee, guiding the hand of the Y-African Guide Program. All Elders and Youth repeat the pledge and the oath.

All Elders and All Youth: We, parents and children, united in service and in the support we give to each other, to our family, to our family com-

pound, and to our community, under the four winds of heaven, seek a world pleasing to God.

All Elders: I will not abuse my children.

I will not neglect my children.

I will not ignore my children.

I will not discourage my children.

I will not curse my children.

I will provide for my children.

I will share with my children.

I will encourage my children.

I will inspire my children.

I will express my love for my children.

All Youth: I will not talk back to my parents.

I will not bring shame to my parents.

I will not be dishonest with my parents.

I will not disobey my parents.

I will not talk about the personal affairs of my parents.

I will respect my parents.

I will support my parents.

I will honor my parents.

I will appreciate my parents.

I will express my love for my parents.

Village Head: New Elders and Youth, you have now been inducted into the Federation of Y-African Guides.

African Resources

Again, Y-African Guides participants are encouraged to research African lore to make sure their programs are authentic and accurate. The following resources are a good place to start.

Books

Akbar, Na'im. *Light from Ancient Africa.* 1994. Tallahassee, FL: Mind Productions & Associates, Inc.

Asante, Molefi. 1994. *Classical Africa.* Maywood, NJ: Peoples Publishing Group.

Asante, Molefi. 1990. *Kemet, Afrocentricity, and Knowledge.* Trenton, NJ: Africa World Press.

Asante, Molefi, and Mark Mattson. 1991. *The Historical and Cultural Atlas of African Americans.* New York: Macmillan.

Diop, Cheikh Anta. *African Origins of Civilization: Myth or Reality.* Chicago: Chicago Rev. Press.

Karenga, Maulana. 1984. *The Husia: Sacred Wisdom of Ancient Egypt.* Los Angeles: University of Sankore Press.

Karenga, Maulana, and Jacob Carruthers. 1986. *Kemet and the African World View.* Los Angeles: University of Sankore Press.

Kunjufu, Jawanza. *African-American History I & II.*

Latif, Sultan A., and Naimah Latif, 1994. *Slavery: The African-American Psychic Trauma.* Chicago: Latif Communications Group, Inc./Tankeo Communication Group.

Organizations

Chicago Rev. Press/Lawrence Hill Books
814 North Franklin
Chicago, IL 60610

Latif Communication Group, Inc./
Tankeo Communication Group
6 North Michigan Avenue, Suite #909
Chicago, IL 60602

Mind Productions & Associates, Inc.
324 North Copeland
Tallahassee, FL 32304

Y-Family Guides Program

Purpose

The purpose of the Y-Family Guides Program is to foster understanding and companionship among all members of the family.

Slogan

"Friends Forever"

This slogan stands for lasting positive relationships within the family circle.

Aims

1. To be clean in body and pure in heart.
2. To be friends forever with my family.
3. To love the sacred circle of my family.
4. To listen while others speak.
5. To love my neighbor as myself.
6. To seek and preserve the beauty of the Great Spirit's work in forest, field, and stream.

Pledge

"We, this circle we call a family, through friendly service to each other, to this tribe, to our community, seek a world pleasing to the eye of the Great Spirit."

Program Objectives

The YMCA, locally, nationally, and internationally, is dedicated to providing opportunities for people to achieve their greatest and most satisfying potential as caring, responsible human beings. All YMCA programs help individuals and families to do the following:

Grow personally. We encourage people to set personal goals and work toward them through programs structured to help develop healthy self-images and self-reliance.

Clarify values. Programs provide opportunities for reflection on personal values and the relationship between stated values and actual behavior. There is an emphasis on the match of individual values with Christian traditions and beliefs.

Improve personal and family relationships. YMCAs help people develop cooperative attitudes and communication skills through programs for individuals and families.

Appreciate diversity. Programs encourage diversity of thought, cultures, and religious and ethnic traditions, leading to communication, respect, and understanding among all people.

Become better leaders and supporters. In YMCA programs, shared leadership and support are basic organizational principles that are taught, practiced, and encouraged.

Develop specific skills. The development of individual skills and knowledge is essential in accomplishing personal goals and in improving confidence and self-esteem.

Have fun. Fun, enjoyment, and laughter are essential qualities of all programs and contribute to people's feeling good about themselves and the YMCA!

Developmental Tasks

Although children in these important developmental years are not all the same, they do share some general characteristics. By considering these characteristics you can better understand your child and, along with other parents in your tribe, plan activities that are appropriate to the ages of your children.

The Y-Family Guides Program goals are based on the developmental tasks of helping children to do each of the following:

1. To develop a growing self-confidence that they are liked and accepted by adults close to them.
2. To feel secure in their parents' love and be able to share some of this love with others.
3. To develop a sense of personal worth within the family, feeling responsible for tasks and for others.
4. To find increasing satisfaction in playing with others their own age and in sharing their possessions.
5. To develop identification with their fathers and mothers and a growing pride in being male or female.
6. To derive increasing satisfaction from physical skill development and active play.
7. To become useful in their homes and share in household tasks.
8. To find something they can do well and on their own.
9. To develop a growing appreciation of the need for rules and the ability to take direction.
10. To accept and value each person for himself or herself.

Y-FAMILY GUIDES: ORLANDO, FLORIDA

To better meet the needs of families in the 90s, some YMCAs have adapted their Y-Indian Guide Program to include the entire family. Single parents, parents that travel for their jobs, or parents who are otherwise overcommitted have an opportunity to participate in a loosely structured parent-child program. In addition, so that busy parents may be able to enjoy participating with all their children, all siblings are able to be a part of the same tribe.

To introduce the program, you might say the following:

Welcome to the Y-Family Guides Program! In this program, you and your child will meet with other parent-child teams in a small group, called a "tribe." You will participate in tribal meetings with other families to share fun and educational activities to help build a healthy, happy family life. The complex interaction of personalities within a family must be handled wisely if children are to grow into productive, self-confident adults. This program is designed to build and strengthen the bonds of love, understanding, and respect between you and your child.

Y-Family Guides is an outgrowth of the Y-Indian Guides Program. Y-Indian Guides, originated in 1926 by Harold Keltner, a St. Louis YMCA director, and Joe Friday, an Ojibwa Indian, was at first a father-and-son program. The rise of the family YMCA after World War II and the continued success of the program led to the development of the YMCA parent-daughter groups. The mother-daughter program was established in South Bend, Indiana, in 1951, and was followed three years later by a father-daughter program founded in Fresno, California. For its first forty-three years all branches of the Y-Indian Guides Program had been designed for children ages five to eight, but in 1969 Y-Trail Blazers, a father-son program for boys nine to eleven, was recognized. In 1980, a mother-son program was founded, and in 1992, a Y-Papoose program was founded and approved on the national level. The Y-Papoose program is an extension of the Y-Indian Guides Program, and it was sparked by a real-life need. A YMCA staff member in Orlando, Florida, had an older daughter in a Y-Indian Princess tribe. Each week, when he and his older daughter went to tribal meetings, the younger daughter, a preschooler, began to cry. She could not understand why there was not a special time for her. In asking around, the YMCA staff member found that other families had the same problem. It was easy for them to find enough parents to put together the first Y-Papoose tribe.

The original program and its offshoots are still evolving today to meet families' needs. As our life-styles change to keep pace with the ever-changing world around us, the time that we spend together with our children becomes more and more valuable. It is for this reason that the Y-Family Guides Program was created. Regardless of the age or sex of the children, the Y- Family Guides Program offers parents and children the opportunity to spend quality time together.

Program Structure

In this section we will tell you something about tribal activities, meetings, outings, and Multitribal Events, as well as what you and your child are expected to do as program participants.

Organization

Every participant in a Y-Family Guides Program is also part of the YMCA movement, which is active throughout the United States and in 130 countries around the world. Each Y-Family Guides Program is organized through a local YMCA, and a YMCA staff member remains in contact with each tribe, usually through the tribe's Chief.

All Y-Family Guides members participate in groups called tribes. A tribe usually consists of five to seven family units. Tribe members meet at each other's homes regularly, either during the school year or throughout the entire year, for program activities. The size of the tribe may dictate the need to meet outside members' homes.

Tribes elect a Chief and other officers, plan their own events, and conduct projects. Each member of the tribe chooses an Indian name by which he or she is addressed during tribal meetings.

Tribal Activities

Each tribe has two or more tribal activities a month, at least one of which is a tribal meeting. The others may be either meetings or outside activities. Several times a year, large Intertribal Events are also held.

Tribal Meetings

Hold your tribe's meetings in the homes of members on a rotating basis. The size of your tribe, however, may dictate the need to meet outside members' homes, such as in local schools, churches, or parks. A typical tribal meeting includes the following:

- Ceremonies such as opening and closing rituals (see pages 26-28)
- A sharing time, usually called scouting reports, in which each parent-child pair (or family) talks about something that happened to them recently or something they brought in to share with the group
- Activities such as crafts, stories, Indian lore, games, songs, and service projects (see pages 19-21 for ideas)
- Refreshments provided by the host family

Start and end tribal meetings on time, and in general do not allow the meeting to last longer than 90 minutes. Keep business and planning activities to a minimum; take care of business during refreshments or separate parents' meetings.

Outside Activities

A key to the success of a tribe is the planning of varied outside activities. Some examples might include the following:

A tribal camp-out

Ice-skating or roller-skating

A visit to a museum or historic park

A tribal picnic

A trip to an aquarium or zoo

A visit to an Indian reservation

A trip to a movie or play

A boat or train ride

Multitribal Activities

Several times a year events may be held in which all Y-Family Guides tribes or all Y-Indian Guides tribes participate. Such activities might include the following:

Induction ceremony	Pinewood derby
Christmas party	Statewide camp-out
Weekend camp-out	Kite flying and show
Beach party	Participation in a parade

Parents' Responsibilities

Your foremost responsibility in the Y-Family Guides Program is attending meetings with your children. Y-Family Guides Programs are not children's programs, but rather parent-child programs. Their purpose is to foster the companionship between parents and their children.

You are also expected to attend parents' meetings for long-range planning of tribal activities, to hold offices in the tribe, and to help with the crafting of tribal property.

Parents' Meetings

Hold parents' meetings several times during the year to do advance planning and to iron out details without the children present. Refer any business that takes more than five minutes in a tribal meeting to a parents' meeting. Such a meeting allows parents to talk freely, make suggestions, and plan special events without getting the children too excited too far ahead of time. (Material for running parents' meetings efficiently can be found on pages 21-22.)

Parents' Leadership Roles

Tribal offices provide shared leadership opportunities for personal development. The roles found in many tribes include Chief, Assistant Chief, Wampum Bearer, Tallykeeper, and Sachem. See page 22 of this manual for descriptions of each office. The Y-Family Guides Program is identical to the Y-Guides Programs in the following areas: tribal property, dues, children's responsibilities, scouting reports, and meeting format. Please refer to pages 19 through 31 of this manual for detailed descriptions of these aspects of the program.

Appendix

$\mathcal{T}$his Appendix contains additional resources for Y-Indian Guide and alternative parent-child programs.

American Indian Culture

The following addresses and phone numbers are resources for information concerning American Indian culture, issues, and concerns.

Bureau of Indian Affairs Area Offices

Aberdeen Area Office
115 Fourth Avenue, SE
Aberdeen, SD 57401
605-226-7943

Albuquerque Area Office
P.O. Box 26567
Albuquerque, NM 87125
505-766-3754

Anadarko Area Office
W.C.D. Office Complex
P.O. Box 368
Anadarko, OK 73005
405-247-6673

Billings Area Office
316 North 26th Street
Billings, MT 59101
406-247-7943

Eastern Area Office
3701 North Fairfax Drive
MS: 260-VASQ
Arlington, VA 22203
703-235-3006

Juneau Area Office
P.O. Box 25520
Juneau, AK 99802
907-586-7177

Minneapolis Area Office
331 South Second Avenue
Minneapolis, MN 55401
612-373-1000

Muskogee Area Office
101 North Fifth Street
Muskogee, OK 74401
918-687-2296

Navajo Area Office
P.O. Box 1060
Gallup, NM 87305
505-863-8314

Phoenix Area Office
Box 10
Phoenix, AZ 85001
602-379-6600

Portland Area Office
The Federal Building
911 NE 11th Avenue
Portland, OR 97232
503-231-6702

Sacramento Area Office
2800 Cottage Way
Sacramento, CA 95825
916-979-2600

American Indian Organizations

American Indian Historical Society
1493 Masonic Avenue
San Francisco, CA 94117

American Indian Movement (AIM)
1209 Fourth Street SE
Minneapolis, MN 55414

Honor Our Neighbors' Origins and Rights, Inc.
    (H.O.N.O.R.)
2647 North Stowell Avenue
Milwaukee, WI 53211

National Congress of American Indians
804 D Street NE
Washington, DC 20002

National Indian Youth Council
318 Elm Street SE
Albuquerque, NM 87102

National Tribal Chairman's Association
818 18th Street NW Suite 840
Washington, DC 20006

Sources for Y-Indian Guide Craft Materials

* Denotes preferred vendor status.

*Beckley Cardy
1 East First Street
Duluth, MN 55802
800-227-1178

Early childhood care, after-school programs, thousands of arts and crafts items, games, sports, and recreational equipment. Call for a catalog.

Berman Leather Craft
25 Melcher Street
Boston, MA 02210-1599
617-426-0870

Leathercraft supplies. Write for a catalog.

Bob Siemon Design
11609 Martens River Circle
Fountain Valley, CA 92708
714-549-7136

Jewelry-making kits and charms.

Boin Arts & Crafts Company
91 Morris Street
Morristown, NJ 07960
201-539-0600

Various craft materials. Write for a catalog.

Craft Kits
P.O. Box 11195
Champaign, IL 61826
217-352-2552

Simple Indian kits for tribal meetings, including peace pipes, tomahawks, necklaces, drums, arm and ankle bands, tepees, and other projects (including some assembled projects). Write for a catalog.

Crazy Crow
P.O. Box 847
Pottsboro, TX 75076
903-786-2287

Indian crafts and bead jewelry.

*Crazy Quilt Patch Factory
477 West Fullerton Avenue
Elmhurst, IL 60126
800-537-2824
630-530-0177

Embroidered patches for Y-Indian Guide Program officers, events, awards, year bars, etc. Unique patch designs for Nation Chiefs, tribal Chiefs, and honor tribes.

*Eagle's View Publishing
6756 North Fork Road
Liberty, UT 84310
810-393-4555

Quality books, videos, and patterns for third-year participants. An example is Plains Indians and Mountain Man Arts and Crafts, *Volumes I and II.*

Great North American
  Companies, Inc.
2828 Forest Lane, Suite 2000
Dallas, TX 75234
214-243-3232

Arts and crafts supplies.

Grey Owl
P.O. Box 340468
Jamaica, NY 11434
718-341-4000

Great pre-assembled Indian theme kits and literature. Write for a catalog.

Indy Products
1225 North Indianapolis Road
Mooresville, IN 46158
317-831-1114

Pine car derby racers.

*Pine Car & Woodland Scenics
101 East Valley Drive
P.O. Box 98
Linn Creek, MO 65052
573-346-5555

Pine car derby racers, kits, and accessories. Y-Indian Guide crafts and accessories.

*Printworks, Inc.
5695 West Franklin Drive
Franklin, WI 53132
800-421-5401

T-shirts and promotional items.

*S&S Worldwide Games
75 Mill Street
Colchester, CT 06415
800-243-9232

Arts and crafts, feathers, games and activities, group packs, Lego building sets, jewelry, beads, leather and belt kits, wood projects and kits for all ages, and much more. Call for catalogs.

S&W Crafts Manufacturing
P.O. Box 5501
Pasadena, CA 91117
818-793-2443

Indian crafts, wood projects, pinewood derby, games, and derby decals.

Saliz Corporation
60 East 600 South
Salt Lake City, UT 84111
801-531-8600

Rock art boards and stencils.

*SMB Creations, Inc.
P.O. Box 4065
Missoula, MT 59806
800-735-6380

T-shirts, promotional banners, flags, and posters.

*Sports Awards Company
4351 North Milwaukee Avenue
Chicago, IL 60641
800-621-5803

Awards, plaques, trophies, balloons, pins, pens, custom promotional programs, Y-Indian Guide medallions and emblems.

Tandy Leather Company
1400 Everman Parkway
Fort Worth, TX 76140
800-433-5546

Y-Indian Guide leather logos and leathercraft kits.

Triarco Arts & Crafts
14650 28th Avenue North
Plymouth, MN 55447
612-559-5590

Group projects available at low prices. Used by many day camps. Write for a catalog.

True to Nature, Inc.
14 Village Row
Logan Square
New Hope, PA 18938
215-862-3610

Wooden snap-together birdhouses, feeders, key racks, and more.

Woodkrafter Kits, Inc.
P.O. Box 808
42 North Elm Street
Yarmouth, ME 04096
207-846-3746

Wood projects.

National Y-Indian Guide Center

The Frank Phillips Foundation, Inc., owns and operates the National Y-Indian Guide Center as part of WOOLAROC Museum and Wildlife Preserve, located 14 miles southwest of Bartlesville, Oklahoma, on Highway 123. It is open to the public. Y-Indian Guide Program parents and children will find it well worth visiting. The Museum has a large collection of Western art. The American Indian Heritage Center includes authentic Indian exhibits; Enchanted Walkway, with trailside displays of native Oklahoma trees, flowers, fossils, and minerals; and Thunderbird Canyon Nature Trails. For further information contact Blue Hill Townsend, WOOLAROC, Route 3, Box 2100, Bartlesville, Oklahoma 74003, 918-336-0307.

Additional Resources for Your Y-Indian Guide Programs

See the YMCA Program Store catalog for details about these additional items for your Y-Indian Guide Programs, or contact the Program Store, P.O. Box 5076, Champaign, IL 61825-5076, phone (800) 747-0089. To save time, order by fax: (217) 351-1549.

Prices shown are subject to change.

5332	Friends Always: The Y-Indian Guide Programs Participants Manual (Second Edition) (Approx 240 pp)	$14.00
5340	Y-Indian Guide Programs Leaders Manual (Second Edition) (Approx 120 pp)	$20.00
5163	Y-Papoose Tribal Kit (5 parents' manuals, 10 headbands, 10 emblems)	$52.00
4919	Indian Tales That Teach (80 pp)	$10.00

Y-Indian Guide Programs Tribal Kits

(10 copies of *Friends Always: The Y-Indian Guide Programs Participants Manual* (Second Edition), 20 emblems, 20 cloth headbands, and one Y-Indian Guide Programs Charter)

4940	Y-Indian Guides Tribal Kit	$149.00
4941	Y-Indian Braves Tribal Kit	$149.00
4942	Y-Indian Princesses Tribal Kit	$149.00
4943	Y-Indian Maidens Tribal Kit	$149.00

Y-Indian Guides

4485	Y-Indian Guide Programs Charter	$1.40
436	Y-Indian Guide Programs Emblem	$2.75
4076	Y-Indian Guide Chevron	$2.40
1281	Cloth Headband	10/$18.00
1282	Paper Headband	100/$6.50
687	Embroidered Emblem	10/$18.00

Y-Indian Braves

4077	Y-Indian Braves Chevron	$2.40
1287	Cloth Headband	10/$18.00
820	Embroidered Emblem	10/$18.00

Y-Indian Princesses

4079	Y-Indian Princesses Chevron	$2.40
1285	Cloth Headband	10/$18.00
745	Embroidered Emblem	10/$18.00

Y-Indian Maidens

1283	Cloth Headband	10/$18.00
744	Embroidered Emblem	10/$18.00

Y-Trail Programs

4971	Y-Seniors Trail Blazers (36 pp)	$4.25
4894	Y-Trail Programs Manual (56 pp)	$8.75
5044	Y-Trail Programs Charter	$1.40
752	Y-Trail Blazers Emblem	$2.40
817	Y-Trail Maidens Emblem	$2.40
818	Y-Trail Mates Emblem	$2.40
819	Y-Coed Trail Blazers Emblem	$2.40
440	Y-Trail Mates Chevron	$2.25

Character Development Resources

5293	YMCA Character Development (76 pp)	$8.00
5335	Next Steps for Implementing Character Development (50 pp)	$8.00
5326	Character Development Activity Box	$40.00
5345	Character Development Cards	40/$5.00
5383	Character Development Stickers	50/$5.00
5297	Character Development Posters	5/$22.00
5318	Kids for Character Video & Activity Booklet	$14.95